P9-CNC-187

P9-CNC-187

Taste of Home's
CONTEST WINNING
ANNUAL RECIPES 2004

Taste of Home Books

Taste of Home's
CONTEST WINNING
ANNUAL RECIPES 2004

Editor: Heidi Reuter Lloyd
Art Director: Lori Arndt
Food Editor: Janaan Cunningham
Associate Editors: Jean Steiner, Beth Wittlinger
Associate Food Editors: Coleen Martin, Diane Werner
Senior Recipe Editor: Sue A. Jurack
Recipe Editor: Janet Briggs
Test Kitchen Director: Karen Johnson
Senior Home Economists: Mark Morgan, Pat Schmeling, Amy Welk, Karen Wright
Home Economists: Sue Draheim, Tamra Duncan, Peggy Fleming, Wendy Stenman
Test Kitchen Assistants: Suzanne Kern, Rita Krajir, Kris Lehman, Megan Taylor
Food Stylists: Kristen Koepnick, Joylyn Trickel
Food Photography: Rob Hagen, Dan Roberts
Senior Food Photography Artist: Stephanie Marchese
Food Photography Artist: Julie Ferron
Photo Studio Manager: Anne Schimmel
Graphic Art Associates: Ellen Lloyd, Catherine Fletcher
Chairman and Founder: Roy Reiman
President: Russell Denson

Taste of Home Books
© 2004 Reiman Media Group, Inc.
5400 S. 60th St., Greendale, WI 53129
International Standard Book Number:
0-89821-407-6
International Standard Serial Number:
1548-4157
All rights reserved.
Printed in U.S.A.
Third Printing, August 2004

PICTURED ON FRONT COVER AND PAGE 1:
Deep-Dish Sausage Pizza (p. 93)
PICTURED ON BACK COVER:
Pronto Taco Soup (p. 63), Halibut Chowder (p. 43), Hearty
Hamburger Soup (p. 45), and Creamy Swiss Onion Soup (p. 52).

To order additional copies of this book, write to: *Taste of Home* Books, P.O. Box 908, Greendale, WI 53129.
To order with a credit card, call toll-free 1-800/344-2560 or visit our Web site at **www.reimanpub.com**.

🎗🎗🎗
Table of Contents

Introduction 4

Appetizers & Snacks 6

Salads 22

Soups & Sandwiches..................................40

Breakfast & Brunch 64

Main Dishes 80

Side Dishes & Condiments 130

Breads 152

Brownies, Bars & Cookies.......................168

Cakes & Cheesecakes.............................184

Just Desserts..202

Index..228

Mozzarella Sticks, p. 14

Baked Potato Soup, p. 46

Skillet Bow Tie Lasagna, p. 85

Sesame Wheat Braids, p. 155

Chocolate Chip Cookie Dough Cheesecake, p. 188

✿✿✿
It's All in One Big, Must-Have Book–360 National Recipe Contest Winners

IT SEEMS some of our readers were asking "what if" just about the same time we were. What if we put all of the winners of our national recipe contests into one big cookbook?

Well, we loved the idea but we soon discovered that *all* of the winners wouldn't fit into one book. Or even two or three, for that matter. So we decided to make an *annual* cookbook filled with the contest winners from *Taste of Home* and its sister publications.

Welcome to the very first one—*Taste of Home's Contest Winning Annual Recipes 2004.* We think of this cookbook as the cream of the crop, the best of the best, because it contains only prize-winning recipes; 360, in fact.

But the real winner is you, because you get *all* of the winners from a full year of contests from four of our national magazines, all under one durable cover. That's *Taste of Home*—the largest cooking magazine in North America—plus *Quick Cooking, Country Woman* and *Country.*

First, let's explain how a recipe becomes a prize winner. It starts when great cooks across the country hear our call for contest entries and send in their favorites. For example, *Taste of Home* asked for the tastiest recipes that put those garden-fresh tomatoes to good use.

Grilled Fare Contest Winners: Garden Turkey Burgers (p. 47), Cool-Kitchen Meat Loaf (p. 97), Summertime Chicken Tacos (p. 85) and Gingered Honey Salmon (p. 88).

Ground Beef Roundup Contest Winners: Western-Style Beef 'n' Beans (p. 117) and Meatballs with Cream Sauce (p. 107).

More than 1,000 folks from across North America responded, and our Test Kitchen staff got busy. Our professional home economists sifted through the loads of mail, sorted recipes into groups, tested a number of the most promising entries and prepared the top contenders for our taste-test panel. The panel consists of experienced food editors, home economists and cooking magazine editors.

✿✿✿
Winners from Dozens of Contests

The contests featured in this book cover a wide range of recipes but they're all unbelievably delicious. Here are just a few examples:

Memorable Muffins: If you start your day with the Breakfast & Brunch chapter, you might not make it to any of the other chapters. Our muffin contest generated these finger-licking wonders: Chocolate Cookie Muffins (p. 66), Cappuccino Muffins (p. 76), Sweet Raspberry Muffins (p. 66), Cherry Almond Muffins (p. 69) and more.

Ground Beef Roundup: Our ground beef recipe contest produced a bounty of main dishes, soups and sandwiches that have big flavor but won't take a big bite out of your grocery budget. Check out Baked Chili (p. 50), Garlic Beef Enchiladas (p. 102) or Li'l Cheddar Meat Loaves (p. 129).

Comforting Casseroles: Your family will eat up the winners of our casserole contest, where the top finishers included the incomparable Meatball Sub Casserole (p. 129), Creamy Chicken and Rice (p. 104) and Tasty Meat Pie (p. 118).

Pizza Party: You can add pizzazz to your next pizza party with these tempting, out-of-the-ordinary choices: Pleasing Potato Pizza (p. 90), Chicken Fajita Pizza (p. 96) and Roasted Veggie Pizza (p. 82).

Celebrate Corn: At its simplest, late-summer corn tastes great grilled or boiled, then coated with butter. This contest takes it to the next level. How about Corn and Bacon Dip (p. 11), Chili Corn Bread Salad (p. 32), Corny Tomato Dumpling Soup (p. 57) or Egg and Corn Quesadilla (p. 68)? We've conveniently covered every category except dessert!

Brownie Bonanza: Chocolate lovers, we had you in mind when we sponsored our national brownie contest. The tantalizing choices, beginning on p. 168, include Raspberry Truffle Brownies (p. 171), German Chocolate Brownies (p. 175) and Chocolate Cream Cheese Brownies (p. 171).

Say Cheesecake: Your clan will be smiling when you say cheesecake. The winners in this national contest range from decadent Chocolate Truffle Cheesecake (p. 192) to refreshing Tangy Lemon Cheesecake (p. 196) and festive Cranberry Cheesecake (p. 186).

How to Find a Recipe

We grouped the recipes in chapters based on how you'd use the book. Categories include Appetizers & Snacks; Salads; Soups & Sandwiches; Breakfast & Brunch; Main Dishes; Side Dishes & Condiments; Breads; Brownies, Bars & Cookies; Cakes & Cheesecakes; and Just Desserts. See the Table of Contents on p. 3 to find the chapter you'd like to check out first.

When you're trying to decide what to make for dinner, you can look at the index by major ingredient or cooking method. For example, you'll find the delectable Broccoli Ham Stroganoff under the headings "Microwave Recipes", "Casseroles", "Pasta & Noodles", "Broccoli" and "Ham." The general index begins on p. 228, and the alphabetical listing of all 360 recipes starts on p. 238.

So, now it's time to turn the pages, choose a recipe (or two) and start cooking. We hope you'll enjoy this one-of-a-kind collection.

Top Two Cheesecake Contest Finishers: Chocolate Chip Cookie Dough Cheesecake (p. 188) and Cranberry Cheesecake (p. 186).

Taco Meatball Ring, p. 10

Hot Kielbasa Dip, p. 13

Sweet-Hot Sausage Meatballs, p. 9

Mexican Deviled Eggs, p. 16

Appetizers & Snacks

Whether you want to serve an appealing appetizer to start a family meal or you're entertaining guests with an array of hearty snacks, you'll find what you need in this chapter.

Mozzarella Sticks, p. 14

Bacon Cheeseburger Balls......................8

Colorful Crab Appetizer Pizza 8

Sweet-Hot Sausage Meatballs.................9

Toasted Zucchini Snacks.......................9

Taco Meatball Ring...........................10

Asparagus Appetizer Spread 10

Corn and Bacon Dip 11

Mushroom Bacon Bites 12

Ground Beef Snack Quiches 12

Taco Tater Skins.............................13

Hot Kielbasa Dip 13

Mozzarella Sticks.............................14

White Bean Dip 15

Four-Cheese Pate 15

Mexican Deviled Eggs 16

Orange-Pecan Hot Wings 16

Bacon-Broccoli Cheese Ball...................17

Breaded Cauliflower...........................17

Fried Onion Rings 18

Three-in-One Cheese Ball.....................18

Beefy Taco Dip.................................19

Apple Salsa with Cinnamon Chips........19

Sweet-Sour Chicken Dippers...............20

Fiesta Appetizer...............................21

Creamy Crab Cheesecake 21

Fried Onion Rings, p. 18

Bacon Cheeseburger Balls

(Pictured at right)

Cathy Lendvoy, Boharm, Saskatchewan

When I serve these, my husband and two sons are often fooled into thinking we're having plain meatballs until they cut into the flavorful filling inside.

- **1 egg**
- **1 envelope onion soup mix**
- **1 pound ground beef**
- **2 tablespoons all-purpose flour**
- **2 tablespoons milk**
- **1 cup (4 ounces) finely shredded cheddar cheese**
- **4 bacon strips, cooked and crumbled**

COATING:

- **2 eggs**
- **1 cup crushed saltines (about 30 crackers)**
- **5 tablespoons vegetable oil**

1. In a bowl, combine egg and soup mix. Crumble beef over mixture and mix well. Divide into 36 portions; set aside.

2. In a bowl, combine the flour and milk until smooth. Add cheese and bacon; mix well. Shape cheese mixture into 36 balls. Shape one beef portion around each cheese ball.

3. In a shallow bowl, beat the eggs. Place cracker crumbs in another bowl. Dip meatballs into egg, then coat with crumbs.

4. In a large skillet over medium heat, cook meatballs in oil for 10-12 minutes or until the meat is no longer pink and coating is golden brown. **Yield:** 3 dozen.

Colorful Crab Appetizer Pizza

(Pictured above)

Diane Caron, Des Moines, Iowa

If you're looking for a really easy and special appetizer, this one stands out. It's a fresh-tasting and lovely variation on a cold vegetable pizza. I make it as a snack for parties all the time and even for a light main dish with a soup or salad.

- **1 tube (8 ounces) refrigerated crescent rolls**
- **1 package (8 ounces) cream cheese, softened**
- **1-1/2 cups coarsely chopped fresh spinach,** *divided*
- **1 green onion, thinly sliced**
- **1-1/2 teaspoons minced fresh dill *or* 1/2 teaspoon dill weed**
- **1 teaspoon grated lemon peel,** *divided*
- **1/2 teaspoon lemon juice**
- **1/8 teaspoon pepper**
- **1-1/4 cups chopped imitation crabmeat**
- **1/4 cup chopped ripe olives**

1. Unroll crescent roll dough and place on an ungreased 12-in. pizza pan. Flatten dough, sealing seams and perforations. Bake at 350° for 8-10 minutes or until lightly browned; cool.

2. In a small mixing bowl, beat cream cheese until smooth. Stir in 1 cup spinach, onion, dill, 1/2 teaspoon lemon peel, lemon juice and pepper. Spread over the crust. Top with crab, olives and remaining spinach and lemon peel. Cut into bite-size squares. **Yield:** 8-10 servings.

✿✿✿
Sweet-Hot Sausage Meatballs
(Pictured on page 6)
Claire Stryker, Delta, Utah

These good-tasting sausage meatballs seem to disappear before anything else on the table or buffet. They have a delightful tang with a bit of crunch from the water chestnuts. I've used the recipe when entertaining for over 20 years because it's so easy to do and comes out perfect every time.

2 cans (8 ounces *each*) water chestnuts, drained
1 pound bulk pork sausage
1 pound bulk hot pork sausage

1/4 cup cornstarch
1 cup maple syrup
2/3 cup red wine vinegar
1/4 cup soy sauce

1. In a blender or food processor, process water chestnuts until minced. Transfer to a bowl; add sausage. Mix well. Shape into 1-in. balls. Place in ungreased 15-in. x 10-in. x 1-in. baking pans. Bake, uncovered, at 350° for 20-25 minutes or until meat is no longer pink.

2. Meanwhile, in a saucepan, combine cornstarch, syrup, vinegar and soy sauce; stir until smooth. Bring to a boil; cook and stir for 2 minutes or until thickened and bubbly. Drain meatballs; add to sauce and heat through. **Yield:** 12-14 servings.

✿✿✿
Toasted Zucchini Snacks
(Pictured above)
Jane Bone, Cape Coral, Florida

I added green pepper to this recipe I got years ago from a friend. I prepare this rich snack for company when zucchini is plentiful. Everyone seems to enjoy it—even those who say they don't care for zucchini.

2 cups shredded zucchini
1 teaspoon salt
1/2 cup mayonnaise *or* salad dressing

1/2 cup plain yogurt
1/4 cup grated Parmesan cheese
1/4 cup finely chopped green pepper
4 green onions, thinly sliced
1 garlic clove, minced
1 teaspoon Worcestershire sauce
1/4 teaspoon hot pepper sauce
36 slices snack rye bread

1. In a bowl, toss the zucchini and salt; let stand for 1 hour. Rinse and drain, pressing out excess liquid. Add the next eight ingredients; stir until combined.

2. Spread a rounded teaspoonful on each slice of bread; place on a baking sheet. Bake at 375° for 10-12 minutes or until bubbly. Serve hot. **Yield:** 3 dozen.

Taco Meatball Ring

(Pictured on page 6)

Brenda Johnson, Davison, Michigan

While it looks complicated, this attractive meatball-filled ring is really very easy to assemble. My family loves tacos, and we find that the crescent roll dough is a nice change from the usual tortilla shells or chips. There are never any leftovers when I serve this as a party appetizer or even as a meal!

- **2 cups (8 ounces) shredded cheddar cheese,** *divided*
- **2 tablespoons water**
- **2 to 4 tablespoons taco seasoning**
- **1/2 pound ground beef**
- **2 tubes (8 ounces** *each***) refrigerated crescent rolls**
- **1/2 head iceberg lettuce, shredded**
- **1 medium tomato, chopped**
- **4 green onions, sliced**
- **1/2 cup sliced ripe olives**

Sour cream
   2 small jalapeno peppers, seeded and sliced*
Salsa, optional

1. In a bowl, combine 1 cup cheese, water and taco seasoning. Add beef and mix well. Shape into 16 balls. Place 1 in. apart in an ungreased 15-in. x 10-in. x 1-in. baking pan. Bake, uncovered, at 400° for 12 minutes or until meat is no longer pink.

2. Drain meatballs on paper towels. Reduce heat to 375°. Arrange crescent rolls on a greased 15-in. pizza pan, forming a ring with pointed ends facing the outer edge of the pan and wide ends overlapping. Place a meatball on each roll; fold point over meatball and tuck under wide end of roll (meatballs will be visible). Bake for 15-20 minutes or until rolls are golden brown.

3. Fill the center of ring with lettuce, tomato, onions, olives, remaining cheese, sour cream, jalapenos and salsa if desired. **Yield:** 8 servings.

   ***Editor's Note:** When cutting or seeding hot peppers, use rubber or plastic gloves to protect your hands. Avoid touching your face.

Asparagus Appetizer Spread

(Pictured at left)

Linda Stotts, Lowell, Ohio

The first time I made this spread for a potluck it brought such great comments, I've been making it ever since.

- **1 pound fresh asparagus, trimmed**
- **1-1/2 cups (12 ounces) sour cream,** *divided*
- **1 package (8 ounces) cream cheese, softened**
- **1 envelope unflavored gelatin**
- **1 cup finely chopped cooked ham**
- **1 tablespoon chopped chives**
- **1/2 teaspoon seasoned salt**
- **1/8 teaspoon black pepper**

Assorted crackers

1. Cook asparagus in a small amount of water until tender. Drain, reserving 1/4 cup liquid. Cool. Puree asparagus until smooth. Add 1 cup sour cream and the cream cheese; blend well.

2. In a saucepan, combine gelatin and reserved liquid; heat slowly until the gelatin is dissolved. Remove from the heat; stir in the asparagus mixture, ham, chives, salt and pepper. Pour into a greased 1-qt. round-bottom bowl. Cover and chill until set, about 6 hours.

3. Unmold onto a plate and spread with reserved sour cream. Garnish with additional chopped ham and cooked asparagus if desired. Serve with crackers. **Yield:** 6-8 servings.

🎗️🎗️🎗️

Corn and Bacon Dip

(Pictured above)

Carolyn Zaschak, Corning, New York

The recipe for this creamy appetizer or snack dip was given to me about 20 years ago by a friend. It becomes a favorite wherever I share it. People are constantly asking me for the recipe. Sometimes, I simply serve it with corn chips.

  1 package (8 ounces) cream cheese, softened
  1 cup (8 ounces) sour cream
1/4 cup mayonnaise
  2 garlic cloves, minced
1/4 teaspoon hot pepper sauce
  1 can (15-1/4 ounces) whole kernel corn, drained
  8 bacon strips, cooked and crumbled
Assorted raw vegetables *and/or* crackers

In a mixing bowl, combine the first five ingredients. Stir in corn and bacon. Cover and refrigerate for several hours. Serve with vegetables and/or crackers. **Yield:** 3 cups.

Mushroom Bacon Bites

(Pictured at left)

Gina Roesner, Ashland, Missouri

This is the perfect appetizer for most any occasion. The tasty bites are easy to assemble and brush with prepared barbecue sauce. When we have a big cookout, they're always a hit ...but they make a nice little "extra" for a family dinner, too.

  24 medium fresh mushrooms
  12 bacon strips, halved
    1 cup barbecue sauce

1. Wrap each mushroom with a piece of bacon; secure with a toothpick. Thread onto metal or soaked bamboo skewers; brush with barbecue sauce.

2. Grill, uncovered, over indirect medium heat for 10-15 minutes or until the bacon is crisp and the mushrooms are tender, turning and basting occasionally with remaining barbecue sauce. **Yield:** 2 dozen.

Ground Beef Snack Quiches

(Pictured at right)

Stacey Atkinson, Rugby, North Dakota

My husband, Cory, farms, so supper can sometimes be quite late. A hearty appetizer like these meaty mini quiches is a perfect way to start the meal. They taste super made with ground beef, but I sometimes substitute bacon, ham, ground pork or sausage.

  1/4 pound ground beef
  1/8 to 1/4 teaspoon garlic powder
  1/8 teaspoon pepper
    1 cup biscuit/baking mix
  1/4 cup cornmeal
  1/4 cup cold butter
    2 to 3 tablespoons boiling water
    1 egg
  1/2 cup half-and-half cream
    1 tablespoon chopped green onion
    1 tablespoon chopped sweet red pepper
  1/8 to 1/4 teaspoon salt
  1/8 to 1/4 teaspoon cayenne pepper
  1/2 cup finely shredded cheddar cheese

1. In a saucepan over medium heat, cook beef, garlic powder and pepper until meat is no longer pink; drain

and set aside. In a bowl, combine the biscuit mix and cornmeal; cut in butter. Add enough water to form a soft dough. Press onto the bottom and up the sides of greased miniature muffin cups. Place teaspoonfuls of beef mixture into each shell.

2. In a bowl, combine the egg, cream, onion, red pepper, salt and cayenne; pour over beef mixture. Sprinkle with cheese. Bake at 375° for 20 minutes or until a knife inserted near the center comes out clean. **Yield:** 1-1/2 dozen.

✿✿✿ Taco Tater Skins

(Pictured at right)

Phyllis Douglas, Fairview, Michigan

The idea for this recipe started with a food demonstration I didn't like. That version used things most people don't have on hand. So I decided to experiment, and out came Taco Tater Skins. My family often makes a meal out of these skins, but they're also great for parties as appetizers. (Have the recipe handy…you'll be asked for a copy!)

- 6 large russet potatoes
- 1/2 cup butter, melted
- 2 tablespoons taco seasoning
- 1 cup (4 ounces) shredded cheddar cheese
- 15 bacon strips, cooked and crumbled
- 3 green onions, chopped

Salsa *and/or* sour cream, optional

1. Bake potatoes at 375° for 1 hour or until tender. Remove potatoes and reduce heat to 350°. When cool enough to handle, cut the potatoes lengthwise into quarters. Scoop out pulp, leaving a 1/4-in. shell (save pulp for another use).

2. Combine the butter and taco seasoning; brush over both sides of potato skins. Place skin side down on a greased baking sheet. Sprinkle with cheese, bacon and onions.

3. Bake for 5-10 minutes or until the cheese is melted. Serve with salsa and/or sour cream if desired. **Yield:** 2 dozen.

✿✿✿ Hot Kielbasa Dip

(Pictured on page 6)

Mary Bondegard, Brooksville, Florida

My husband and I are retired, and I like to look for simple, speedy ways to cook. This thick cheesy dip, with the unusual addition of sausage, goes together in a jiffy. Accompanied by crackers or fresh veggies, it's a hearty appetizer for a football party or family gathering.

- 1 package (8 ounces) cream cheese
- 1/2 cup sour cream
- 1/3 cup milk
- 1 tablespoon mayonnaise
- 1/2 teaspoon Worcestershire sauce
- 8 ounces fully cooked kielbasa *or* Polish sausage, finely chopped
- 1/2 cup sliced green onions, *divided*
- 1/4 cup grated Parmesan cheese

Assorted crackers *or* raw vegetables

1. In a 1-1/2-qt. microwave-safe bowl, heat cream cheese, uncovered, on high for 1 minute. Stir in the sour cream, milk, mayonnaise and Worcestershire sauce. Add the kielbasa, 1/4 cup of onions and cheese; mix well.

2. Microwave, uncovered, on high for 3-4 minutes or until heated through, stirring once. Sprinkle with remaining onions. Serve with crackers or vegetables. Store in the refrigerator. **Yield:** about 3 cups.

Editor's Note: This recipe was tested in an 850-watt microwave.

What's Kielbasa?

Kielbasa is a garlic-flavored smoked sausage that is most commonly made of pork or a combination of pork and beef. It is traditionally sold in precooked rings.

Heating enhances the flavor of kielbasa, whether it's served in simple slices or as part of a recipe for a hearty appetizer, main dish or soup.

The word kielbasa is also sometimes used as a generic synonym for Polish sausage.

Say 'Cheese' When It Comes to Appetizers

It's no surprise that cheese is among the favorite foods to serve at an appetizers-only party. Numerous variations can be found even in small neighborhood grocery stores, plus cheese can be served in many ways.

If you're in a hurry or want to serve simple dishes, your guests will welcome a cheese platter featuring three to five cheeses or a combination of cheese and fruit or sausage.

Here are a few pointers on identifying, choosing and serving cheese:

- Natural cheese fits into two broad categories—fresh and ripened. Fresh includes cream cheese, cottage cheese and ricotta. Ripened cheeses are divided into four categories based on texture: firm (or hard), semi-firm, semi-soft and soft-ripened.
- Firm cheeses, such as Parmesan and Romano, should be inspected for cracks, which are signs that the cheese is drying out. Also make sure the color is even from edge to center before buying hard cheese.
- Semi-firm cheeses include Cheddar, Swiss and Edam. Before placing wrapped semi-firm cheese in your grocery cart, check that the wrapping is not torn, the edges aren't starting to crack and there's no mold. Always check the "sell-by" date to make sure you have plenty of time to use the cheese.
- Gouda and Monterey Jack are examples of semi-soft cheese. They're creamy yet easy to slice. They, too, should be checked for torn packaging, cracked edges, mold and an expired sell-by date.
- Soft-ripened cheeses such as Brie and Camembert are sold in rounds. When fully ripe, they have a soft, creamy texture from the center to the edges. If you buy rounds that are thicker than 1 inch, you run a risk of getting cheese that's overripe on the edges but not yet ripe in the center.
- The white round of soft-ripened cheese is natural and can be eaten, although some people prefer to remove it. To do so, chill the cheese; use a sharp knife to cut off the rind.
- Cheese tastes best served at room temperature.
- If you have a variety of cheeses out for guests, it would be helpful to label the kinds.

Mozzarella Sticks

(Pictured on page 7)

Mary Merchant, Barre, Vermont

I'm fond of these tasty snacks because they're baked, not fried. Cheese is one of my family's favorite foods. Being of Italian descent, I often use ricotta and mozzarella cheeses.

    2 eggs
    1 tablespoon water
    1 cup dry bread crumbs
2-1/2 teaspoons Italian seasoning
  1/2 teaspoon garlic powder
  1/8 teaspoon pepper
   12 sticks string cheese*
    3 tablespoons all-purpose flour
    1 tablespoon butter, melted
    1 cup marinara *or* spaghetti sauce, heated

1. In a small bowl, beat eggs and water. In a plastic bag, combine bread crumbs, Italian seasoning, garlic powder and pepper. Coat cheese sticks in flour, then dip in egg mixture and bread crumb mixture. Repeat egg and bread crumb coatings. Cover and chill for at least 4 hours or overnight.

2. Place cheese sticks on an ungreased baking sheet; drizzle with butter. Bake, uncovered, at 400° for 6-8 minutes or until heated through. Allow to stand for 3-5 minutes before serving. Use marinara or spaghetti sauce for dipping. **Yield:** 4-6 servings.

*Editor's Note: Regular mozzarella cheese, cut into 4-in. x 1/2-in. sticks, can be substituted for the string cheese.

White Bean Dip

(Pictured at right)

Linn Landry, Honeydew, California

My family and I enjoy eating this with tortilla chips, crackers and just about anything else we can find to dip into it—including our fingers!

✓ Uses less fat, sugar or salt. Includes Nutritional Analysis and Diabetic Exchanges.

- 1 can (15 to 16 ounces) cannellini beans *or* great northern beans, rinsed and drained
- 1 tablespoon lemon juice
- 2 tablespoons plain yogurt
- 2 tablespoons chopped fresh parsley
- 1/2 teaspoon freshly ground black pepper
- 1/4 teaspoon hot pepper sauce
- 2 to 3 garlic cloves

Salt to taste
Pita bread, corn chips *or* vegetable dippers

1. In a food processor or blender, combine the beans, lemon juice, yogurt, parsley, pepper, hot sauce, garlic and salt. Cover and process until smooth. Chill.

2. Serve with toasted pita bread triangles, corn chips or fresh vegetables. **Yield:** 1-1/4 cups.

Nutritional Analysis: One tablespoon serving (prepared with fat-free yogurt and no added salt) equals 29 calories, 78 mg sodium, trace cholesterol, 6 gm carbohydrate, 2 gm protein, trace fat. **Diabetic Exchange:** 1/2 starch.

Four-Cheese Pate

(Pictured at right)

Jeanne Messina, Darien, Connecticut

This impressive and festive-looking cheese spread is simple to put together and never fails to get raves at parties. Before I retired, I looked for recipes like this that can be prepared way ahead.

- 3 packages (8 ounces *each*) cream cheese, softened, *divided*
- 2 tablespoons milk
- 2 tablespoons sour cream
- 3/4 cup chopped pecans
- 4 ounces Brie *or* Camembert, rind removed, softened
- 1 cup (4 ounces) shredded Swiss cheese
- 4 ounces crumbled blue cheese
- 1/2 cup pecan halves

Red and green apple slices *or* crackers

1. In a mixing bowl, beat one package of cream cheese with milk and sour cream until smooth. Spread into a 9-in. pie plate lined with plastic wrap. Sprinkle with chopped pecans.

2. In a mixing bowl, beat Brie, Swiss, blue cheese and remaining cream cheese until thoroughly combined. Gently spread mixture over chopped pecans, smoothing the top to form a flat surface. Cover and chill overnight or up to 3-4 days.

3. Before serving, invert onto a plate and remove plastic wrap. Arrange pecan halves on top. Serve pate with apples or crackers. **Yield:** 16-20 servings.

🎗🎗🎗

Mexican Deviled Eggs

(Pictured on page 6)

Susan Klemm, Rhinelander, Wisconsin

With our two children, my husband and I live on a beautiful lake and host lots of summer picnics and cookouts. I adapted this recipe to suit our tastes. Folks who are expecting the same old deviled eggs are surprised when they try this delightful tangy variation.

    8 hard-cooked eggs
  1/2 cup shredded cheddar cheese
  1/4 cup mayonnaise
  1/4 cup salsa
    2 tablespoons sliced green onions
    1 tablespoon sour cream
  Salt to taste

1. Slice the eggs in half lengthwise; remove yolks and set whites aside.

2. In a small bowl, mash yolks with cheese, mayonnaise, salsa, onions, sour cream and salt. Evenly fill the egg whites. Serve immediately or chill until serving. **Yield:** 16 servings.

🎗🎗🎗

Orange-Pecan Hot Wings

(Pictured above)

June Jones, Hudson, Florida

We like to use oranges and orange juice in different ways—we even have an orange tree in our yard. These chicken wings are a fun appetizer that our friends are very fond of.

    3 pounds whole chicken wings*
    3 eggs
    1 can (6 ounces) frozen orange juice
       concentrate, thawed
    2 tablespoons water
    1 cup all-purpose flour
  1/2 cup finely chopped pecans
  1/2 cup butter, melted
  RED HOT SAUCE:
    2 cups ketchup
  3/4 cup packed brown sugar
    2 to 3 tablespoons hot pepper sauce

1. Cut chicken wings into three pieces; discard wing tips. In a bowl, whisk eggs, orange juice concentrate and water. In another bowl or a resealable plastic bag, combine flour and pecans. Dip wings in egg mixture, then roll or toss in flour mixture.

2. Pour butter into a 15-in. x 10-in. x 1-in. baking pan. Arrange wings in a single layer in pan. Bake, uncovered, at 375° for 25 minutes.

3. Meanwhile, combine sauce ingredients. Spoon half over the wings; turn. Top with remaining sauce. Bake 30 minutes longer or until meat juices run clear. **Yield:** 8-10 servings.

*Editor's Note: 3 pounds of uncooked chicken wing sections can be substituted for the whole chicken wings. Omit the first step of the recipe.

Bacon-Broccoli Cheese Ball

(Pictured at left)

Tamara Rickard, Bartlett, Tennessee

Needing a quick appetizer one night when dinner was running late, I combined a few leftovers into this easy cheese ball. For variety, you can shape it into a log or substitute your family's favorite herbs for the pepper.

> 1 package (8 ounces) cream cheese, softened
> 1 cup (4 ounces) finely shredded cheddar cheese
> 1/2 teaspoon pepper
> 1 cup finely chopped broccoli florets
> 6 bacon strips, cooked and crumbled

Assorted crackers

1. In a mixing bowl, beat cream cheese, cheddar cheese and pepper until blended. Stir in broccoli. Shape into a ball and roll in bacon. Cover and refrigerate.

2. Remove from the refrigerator 15 minutes before serving. Serve with crackers. **Yield:** 2-1/2 cups.

Breaded Cauliflower

(Pictured at right)

Sandra Furman-Krajewski, Amsterdam, New York

My mother gets the credit for this delicious dish, which is a mainstay at our house. It can be a hearty appetizer or side dish. It's wonderful served with turkey, roast beef and ham. I always receive compliments when I serve it.

> 1 small head cauliflower, broken into florets (about 5 cups)
> 4 egg yolks
> 1 teaspoon garlic powder
> 1 teaspoon onion powder
> 1 teaspoon minced fresh parsley
> 1/2 teaspoon sugar
> 1/2 teaspoon salt
> 1/4 teaspoon pepper
> 1 cup seasoned bread crumbs
> 3 tablespoons grated Parmesan cheese
> 3/4 cup butter

Minced fresh parsley, optional

1. Place cauliflower and a small amount of water in a skillet. Bring to a boil. Reduce heat; cover and simmer until crisp-tender, about 8 minutes. Drain and set aside.

2. In a bowl, whisk egg yolks and seasonings. Place bread crumbs and Parmesan cheese in a large resealable plastic bag. Add a few florets at a time to the egg mixture; toss to coat. Using a slotted spoon, transfer cauliflower to crumb mixture; toss to coat.

3. In a skillet, melt the butter over medium-high heat. Cook cauliflower in batches until golden brown, about 4 minutes. Sprinkle with parsley if desired. **Yield:** 4-6 servings.

🎗🎗🎗

Fried Onion Rings

(Pictured on page 7)

Marsha Moore, Poplar Bluff, Missouri

Here's a yummy snack that's also a great side dish. Try it as an accompaniment to hamburgers or fried fish, or with steaks on the grill. The recipe's from my mom, and it's one of her most popular. (As a newlywed years ago, I often found myself on the kitchen "hotline" to her!)

        2   large sweet onions
        1   egg, lightly beaten
      2/3   cup water
        1   tablespoon vegetable oil
        1   teaspoon lemon juice
        1   cup all-purpose flour
    1-1/2   teaspoons baking powder
        1   to 1-1/4 teaspoons salt
      1/8   to 1/4 teaspoon cayenne pepper
    Oil for deep-fat frying

1. Cut onions into 1/2-in. slices; separate into rings. Place in a bowl; cover with ice water and soak for 30 minutes.

2. Meanwhile, combine egg, water, oil and lemon juice in a bowl; mix well. Combine flour, baking powder, salt and cayenne; stir into egg mixture until smooth.

3. Drain onion rings; dip into batter. In an electric skillet or deep-fat fryer, heat 1 in. of oil to 375°. Fry onion rings, a few at a time, for 1 to 1-1/2 minutes per side or until golden brown. Drain on paper towels. **Yield:** 4-6 servings.

   Editor's Note: Onion rings may be kept warm in a 300° oven while frying remainder of batch.

🎗🎗🎗

Three-in-One Cheese Ball

(Pictured below)

Mary Anne Marston, Almonte, Ontario

Every Christmas, I make these cheese balls for an annual get-together. They aren't only for the holidays, however. You'll find they freeze well and will last for a week in the refrigerator. I have even re-formed leftovers into smaller balls for snacks. I do my cooking in an 1892 home we've renovated.

        1   package (8 ounces) cream cheese, softened
        4   cups (16 ounces) shredded cheddar cheese, at
            room temperature
        2   tablespoons milk
        2   tablespoons minced onion
        2   tablespoons Worcestershire sauce
    Coarsely ground pepper
      1/2   cup (2 ounces) crumbled blue cheese
    Minced fresh parsley
      1/4   teaspoon garlic powder
    Finely chopped pecans
    Assorted crackers

1. In a mixing bowl, beat cream cheese, cheddar cheese, milk, onion and Worcestershire sauce until mix is fluffy. If a smoother spread is desired, process in a food processor until creamy.

2. Divide mixture into thirds (about 1 cup each). Shape first portion into a ball; roll in pepper. Add the blue cheese to the second portion; mix well. Shape into a ball; roll in parsley. Add garlic powder to the remaining portion; mix well. Shape into a ball; roll in nuts.

3. Cover and refrigerate cheese balls. Let stand at room temperature 1 hour before serving time. Serve with crackers. **Yield:** 3 cheese balls.

Beefy Taco Dip

(Pictured below)

Faye Parker, Bedford, Nova Scotia

This taco dip is a combination of several different recipes I received from friends. I experimented till I came up with my favorite! It's always a hit wherever I bring it.

- 1 package (8 ounces) cream cheese, softened
- 1 cup (8 ounces) sour cream
- 3/4 cup mayonnaise
- 1 pound ground beef
- 1 envelope taco seasoning
- 1 can (8 ounces) tomato sauce
- 4 cups shredded lettuce
- 2 medium tomatoes, diced
- 1 small onion, diced
- 1 medium green pepper, diced
- 2 cups (8 ounces) shredded cheddar *or* taco cheese

Tortilla chips

1. In a mixing bowl, beat cream cheese, sour cream and mayonnaise until smooth. Spread on a 12- to 14-in. pizza pan or serving dish. Refrigerate for 1 hour.

2. In a saucepan over medium heat, cook beef until no longer pink; drain. Add taco seasoning and tomato sauce; cook and stir for 5 minutes. Cool completely. Spread over cream cheese layer. Refrigerate.

3. Just before serving, sprinkle with lettuce, tomatoes, onion, green pepper and cheese. Serve with chips. **Yield:** 16-20 servings.

Apple Salsa with Cinnamon Chips

(Pictured at right)

Carolyn Brinkmeyer, Aurora, Colorado

I serve this treat as an appetizer and a snack. Plus, it's sweet enough to be a dessert and easy to transport besides.

SALSA:
- 2 medium tart apples, chopped
- 1 cup chopped strawberries
- 2 medium kiwifruit, peeled and chopped
- 1 small orange
- 2 tablespoons brown sugar
- 2 tablespoons apple jelly, melted

CHIPS:
- 8 flour tortillas (7 *or* 8 inches)
- 1 tablespoon water
- 1/4 cup sugar
- 2 teaspoons ground cinnamon

1. In a bowl, combine apples, strawberries and kiwi. Grate orange peel to measure 1-1/2 teaspoons; squeeze juice from orange. Add peel and juice to apple mixture. Stir in brown sugar and jelly.

2. For chips, brush tortillas lightly with water. Combine sugar and cinnamon; sprinkle over tortillas. Cut each tortilla into 8 wedges. Place in a single layer on ungreased baking sheets. Bake at 400° for 6-8 minutes or until lightly browned. Cool. Serve with salsa. **Yield:** 4 cups.

⚜⚜⚜
Sweet-Sour Chicken Dippers

(Pictured at right)

Kari Caven, Post Falls, Idaho

Since you can chop up all the ingredients the night before, this can be ready in about 30 minutes. You can serve it as a snack, an appetizer or a great after-work dinner.

- 1 can (8 ounces) crushed pineapple
- 1-1/2 cups sugar
- 1 can (14-1/2 ounces) diced tomatoes, undrained
- 1/2 cup vinegar
- 1/2 cup chopped onion
- 1/2 cup chopped green pepper
- 1 tablespoon soy sauce
- 1/4 teaspoon ground ginger
- 1 tablespoon cornstarch

BATTER:
- 1 cup all-purpose flour
- 1 cup cornstarch
- 2 teaspoons baking powder
- 2 teaspoons baking soda
- 2 teaspoons sugar
- 1-1/3 cups cold water
- Oil for deep-fat frying
- 1-1/2 pounds boneless skinless chicken breasts, cut into chunks

1. Drain pineapple, reserving the juice. In a saucepan, combine the pineapple and next seven ingredients. Simmer for 20 minutes.

2. In a bowl, combine cornstarch and the reserved pineapple juice until smooth; add to tomato mixture. Bring to a boil; boil and stir for 2 minutes or until slightly thickened. Remove from the heat; set aside.

3. In a bowl, combine the flour, cornstarch, baking powder, baking soda, sugar and water until smooth.

4. In a deep-fat fryer, heat oil to 375°. Dip chicken pieces in batter; drop into oil and fry until golden brown and juices run clear, about 5 minutes. Serve immediately with sweet-sour sauce. **Yield:** 4 dozen.

Appetizer Buffet Pointers

Every host wants guests to ooh and aah over the food, but why not the serving dishes, too? If you're hosting a party with a buffet of appetizers and snacks, consider these party pointers:

- Feel free to break out your favorite serving pieces. They don't have to match but they should look like you planned to use them together. For example, a sunny yellow tray, a bright orange bowl and a cobalt blue dish will work together if you have something with similar colors to pull the look together. A brightly striped pitcher full of ice water, a multicolor tablecloth or a few patterned napkins would do the trick quite nicely.

- Think of unusual containers that go with the foods you're serving. Hollow out red, yellow or green peppers (or one of each) to use as bowls for a zippy dip.

- Use serving pieces of varying heights to add interest. That gorgeous cake platter that seldom comes out of the cupboard will hold a variety of hors d'oeuvres. Place it next to a flat serving dish or low bowl.

- Place a colorful one-of-a-kind bowl on a solid-color square or oval serving platter to match up chips and salsa or other food pairs.

- Layer linens to add visual interest. For example, one or two lace doilies placed under serving pieces can add elegance to a plain tablecloth. A solid-color table runner will help "quiet down" a busy patterned tablecloth.

Fiesta Appetizer

(Pictured at right)

Clarice Schweitzer, Sun City, Arizona

This dip is always a big hit with men—maybe because of the hearty blend of flavors. It stands up great as a leftover besides…if there's any left over.

- 1 can (16 ounces) refried beans
- 1 envelope taco seasoning
- 3 ripe avocados
- 1 tablespoon lemon juice
- 1/4 cup sour cream
- 1 can (2-1/4 ounces) sliced ripe olives, drained
- 1 can (4 ounces) chopped green chilies, drained
- 2 medium tomatoes, chopped
- 6 green onions, sliced
- 1 cup (4 ounces) shredded cheddar cheese

Tortilla chips

1. Combine beans and taco seasoning. Spread mixture on a round 12-in. serving platter.

2. Mash avocados with lemon juice. Spread over beans. Spread sour cream over avocado. Sprinkle olives, chilies,

tomatoes, onions and cheese over sour cream. Serve with tortilla chips. **Yield:** 8-10 servings.

Creamy Crab Cheesecake

(Pictured below)

Cathy Sarrels, Tucson, Arizona

A savory appetizer cheesecake such as this one is sure to grab the attention and tempt the taste buds of party guests. It's an elegant spread that you make ahead, so there's no last-minute fuss.

- 1 cup crushed butter-flavored crackers (about 25 crackers)
- 3 tablespoons butter, melted
- 3/4 cup sour cream, *divided*

- 2 packages (8 ounces *each*) cream cheese, softened
- 3 eggs
- 2 teaspoons grated onion
- 1 teaspoon lemon juice
- 1/4 teaspoon seafood seasoning
- 2 drops hot pepper sauce
- 1/8 teaspoon pepper
- 1 cup crabmeat, drained, flaked and cartilage removed

Additional seafood seasoning, optional

1. In a small bowl, combine cracker crumbs and butter. Press onto the bottom of a greased 9-in. springform pan. Bake at 350° for 10 minutes. Cool on a wire rack. Reduce heat to 325°.

2. In a mixing bowl, beat 1/4 cup of sour cream and cream cheese until smooth. Add eggs; beat on low just until combined. Add onion, lemon juice, seafood seasoning, hot pepper sauce and pepper; beat just until blended. Fold in crab. Pour over crust. Bake for 35-40 minutes or until center is almost set.

3. Cool on a wire rack for 10 minutes. Carefully run a knife around edge of pan to loosen. Cool 1 hour longer. Spread remaining sour cream over top. Refrigerate overnight.

4. Remove sides of pan. Let stand at room temperature for 30 minutes before serving. Sprinkle with seafood seasoning if desired. **Yield:** 20-24 servings.

Spicy Ravioli Salad, p. 31

Grilled Chicken Pasta Salad, p. 34

Idaho Potato Salad, p. 29

Salads

Whether you want a cool and creamy salad to serve as a summer side dish or a hearty salad that your family will enjoy as an entree any time of the year, you'll find it right here.

Lemony Chicken Fruit Salad, p. 27

Deluxe German Potato Salad.................24

Zippy Radish Salad............................25

Colorful Corn Salad...........................25

Warm Bean and Chard Salad................26

Artichoke Heart Salad.........................26

Lemony Chicken Fruit Salad.................27

Sesame Beef and Asparagus Salad...........27

Picante Broccoli Chicken Salad.............28

Idaho Potato Salad.............................29

Broccoli Orange Salad.........................29

Eastern Shore Seafood Salad.................30

Crunchy Chicken Salad........................30

Spicy Ravioli Salad.............................31

Green Bean Potato Salad......................31

Chili Corn Bread Salad........................32

Southern Sweet Potato Salad.................33

Creamy Summer Vegetable Salad............33

Grilled Chicken Pasta Salad..................34

Grape and Cabbage Salad.....................34

Lettuce with Hot Bacon Dressing..........35

Creamy Cranberry Salad......................35

Summertime Strawberry Gelatin Salad....36

Baked German Potato Salad..................37

Broccoli Cauliflower Salad....................37

Creamy Sliced Tomatoes......................38

Hot Chicken Salad.............................38

Layered Fresh Fruit Salad.....................39

Warm Mustard Potato Salad.................39

Creamy Sliced Tomatoes, p. 38

Deluxe German Potato Salad

(Pictured above)

Betty Perkins, Hot Springs, Arkansas

I make this salad for all occasions—it goes well with any kind of meat. I often take the salad to potlucks, and there's never any left over. The celery, carrots and mustard are a special touch not usually found in traditional German potato salad.

1/2 **pound sliced bacon**
  1 **cup thinly sliced celery**
  1 **cup chopped onion**
  1 **cup sugar**
  2 **tablespoons all-purpose flour**
  1 **cup vinegar**
1/2 **cup water**
  1 **teaspoon salt**
3/4 **teaspoon ground mustard**
  5 **pounds unpeeled red new potatoes, cooked and sliced**
  2 **medium carrots, shredded**

  2 **tablespoons chopped fresh parsley**
Additional salt to taste

1. In a skillet, cook bacon until crisp. Drain, reserving 1/4 cup drippings. Crumble bacon and set aside. Saute the celery and onion in drippings until tender.

2. Combine sugar and flour; add to skillet with vinegar, water, salt and mustard. Cook, stirring constantly, until mixture thickens and bubbles.

3. In a large bowl, combine potatoes, carrots and parsley; pour the sauce over and stir gently to coat. Season to taste with additional salt. Spoon into a serving dish; garnish with crumbled bacon. Serve warm. **Yield:** 14-16 servings.

Zippy Radish Salad

(Pictured at right)

Carol Stevens, Basye, Virginia

The first time I prepared this salad for my husband, he was skeptical! He loved it, though. Served with a rich entree or hot barbecue, it makes a light and refreshing side dish. Growing up during World War II, when food and money were scarce, I learned from my mother how to make a little go a long way.

- 2 cups thinly sliced radishes
- 1/2 cup cubed Swiss cheese
- 2 green onions, thinly sliced
- 1 garlic clove, minced
- 1 tablespoon tarragon vinegar
- 1/2 teaspoon Dijon mustard
- 1/4 teaspoon salt
- 1/8 teaspoon pepper
- 3 tablespoons olive oil

Leaf lettuce

1. In a bowl, combine radishes, cheese and onions. In a small bowl, combine garlic, vinegar, mustard, salt and pepper; whisk in oil until smooth.

2. Pour over radish mixture; toss to coat. Chill for 2 hours. Serve on a bed of lettuce. **Yield:** 4 servings.

Colorful Corn Salad

(Pictured below)

Helen Koedel, Hamilton, Ohio

This colorful, tasty corn salad is an excellent way to perk up a summer picnic. The seasonings add a bold, refreshing Southwestern flavor that brings people back for seconds. It's nice to have a different kind of salad to share.

- 2 packages (10 ounces *each*) frozen corn, thawed
- 2 cups diced green pepper
- 2 cups diced sweet red pepper
- 2 cups diced celery
- 1 cup minced fresh parsley
- 1 cup chopped green onions
- 1/2 cup shredded Parmesan cheese
- 2 teaspoons ground cumin
- 1-1/2 teaspoons salt
- 3/4 teaspoon pepper
- 1/2 teaspoon hot pepper sauce
- 1/8 teaspoon cayenne pepper
- 3 tablespoons olive oil
- 2 garlic cloves, minced
- 6 tablespoons lime juice

1. In a large bowl, combine the first 12 ingredients. In a microwave-safe dish, combine oil and garlic. Microwave, uncovered, on high for 1 minute.

2. Cool. Whisk in lime juice. Pour over the corn mixture and toss to coat. Cover and refrigerate until serving. **Yield:** 16-18 servings.

✦✦✦
Warm Bean and Chard Salad
(Pictured at right)

Sandra Louth, Burlingame, California

This is one of those dishes I make when I'm bored with the usual fare. Chard is grown here, and it's delicious in this salad.

> 1 small red onion, chopped
> 1 tablespoon olive oil
> 1/4 cup tomato paste
> 1 teaspoon honey
> 2 cans (15 ounces *each*) garbanzo beans *or* chickpeas, rinsed and drained
> 1 cup water
> 12 to 13 cups loosely packed julienned chard *or* spinach leaves (about 1-1/2 pounds)
> 1/2 teaspoon salt
> 1/4 teaspoon pepper

1. In a Dutch oven or a large saucepan, saute onion in oil until tender. Add tomato paste and honey; cook for 1 minute. Add the beans and water; bring to a boil. Add chard, salt and pepper; return to a boil.

2. Reduce heat; cover and simmer for 15-25 minutes or until the greens are wilted. Serve immediately. **Yield:** 4-6 servings.

✦✦✦
Artichoke Heart Salad
(Pictured at left)

Elizabeth Birkenmaier, Gladstone, Missouri

I put together this fast five-ingredient salad after sampling a similar mixture from a salad bar. Bottled Italian dressing gives robust flavor to this simple treatment for canned artichoke hearts. It is a snap to make as a last-minute side dish.

> 1 can (14 ounces) water-pack artichoke hearts, drained and quartered
> 1 can (2-1/4 ounces) sliced ripe olives, drained, optional
> 1/3 cup chopped green pepper
> 1/3 cup thinly sliced green onions
> 3/4 cup Italian salad dressing

1. In a bowl, combine artichokes, olives if desired, green pepper and onions. Add dressing and toss to coat.

2. Cover and refrigerate for at least 30 minutes. Serve with a slotted spoon. **Yield:** 3-4 servings.

Lemony Chicken Fruit Salad

(Pictured on page 23)

Johnece Stuard, Mansfield, Texas

Back in the 1950s, I was a home economist for the electric company, which is how I came across this recipe. During spring and summer, when it is hot here, my family especially likes it. I've also found this chicken salad is good for women's luncheons and covered-plate meals since it's so different.

 2 cans (8 ounces *each*) pineapple chunks
 1 medium apple, diced
 3 cups cubed cooked chicken
 1 cup seedless grapes, halved
 3 tablespoons butter
 3 tablespoons all-purpose flour
 1/4 cup sugar
 1 teaspoon salt
 1/2 cup lemon juice
 2 egg yolks, lightly beaten
 1/2 cup heavy whipping cream
Lettuce leaves
 1/2 cup slivered almonds, toasted

1. Drain pineapple, reserving the juice. Set aside pineapple and 1/2 cup juice. Toss remaining juice with apple; drain. In a large bowl, combine chicken, grapes, pineapple and apple. Cover and refrigerate.

2. In a saucepan, melt butter. Stir in flour, sugar and salt until smooth; gradually add lemon juice and the reserved pineapple juice. Bring to a boil; boil and stir for 2 minutes. Reduce heat. Add a small amount to egg yolks; return all to pan. Bring to a gentle boil; cook and stir for 2 minutes.

3. Remove from the heat; chill for 10-15 minutes. Beat cream until stiff peaks form; fold into cooled dressing. Pour over chicken mixture; gently stir to coat. Chill for 1 hour. Serve in a lettuce-lined bowl. Sprinkle with almonds. **Yield:** 6-8 servings.

Sesame Beef and Asparagus Salad

(Pictured at right)

Tamara Steeb, Issaquah, Washington

Especially during the summertime, this makes a nice light meal. When I prepare it for guests, I also serve rice and bread—it's quick and easy!

✓ Uses less fat, sugar or salt. Includes Nutritional Analysis and Diabetic Exchanges.

 1 pound top round steak
 4 cups sliced fresh asparagus (cut in 2-inch pieces)
 3 tablespoons soy sauce
 2 tablespoons sesame oil
 1 tablespoon rice wine vinegar *or* white wine vinegar
 1/2 teaspoon minced fresh gingerroot
Sesame seeds
Lettuce leaves, optional

1. Broil steak to desired doneness. Cool and cut into thin diagonal strips. Cook asparagus in a small amount of water 30-60 seconds. Drain and cool.

2. Combine beef and asparagus. Blend the next four ingredients; pour over beef and asparagus. Sprinkle with sesame seeds and toss lightly. Serve warm or at room temperature on lettuce leaves if desired. **Yield:** 6 servings.

Nutritional Analysis: One serving equals 179 calories, 696 mg sodium, 48 mg cholesterol, 6 gm carbohydrate, 21 gm protein, 8 gm fat. **Diabetic Exchanges:** 2 lean meat, 1-1/2 vegetable, 1/2 fat.

Picante Broccoli Chicken Salad

(Pictured above)

Krista Shumway, Billings, Montana

Since our family likes things spicy, I often add a fresh jalapeno pepper to this salad. It's a simple, savory way to use up leftover chicken. Plus, it's so eye-catching, it could double as the main dish and the table centerpiece!

- 1/2 cup mayonnaise
- 1/4 cup picante sauce
- 1 garlic clove, minced
- 1/2 to 1 teaspoon chili powder
- 2 cups cubed cooked chicken
- 2 cups broccoli florets
- 1 cup diced fresh tomato
- 1/2 cup shredded cheddar cheese
- 1/2 cup chopped onion
- 1/4 cup julienned green pepper
- 1/4 cup julienned sweet red pepper

Flour tortillas, warmed

1. In a large bowl, combine the first four ingredients; mix well. Add chicken, broccoli, tomato, cheese, onion and peppers; toss to coat.

2. Refrigerate for at least 30 minutes before serving. Serve with tortillas. **Yield:** 6-8 servings.

Idaho Potato Salad

(Pictured on page 22)

Rhonda Munk, Boise, Idaho

Mom used to make this potato salad without a recipe. When I got married, she and I made it one afternoon and wrote down the ingredients so I could make it at home. Of course, we use our famous Idaho potatoes.

4 pounds potatoes, cooked and peeled
3/4 cup sliced peeled cucumber
2 hard-cooked eggs, chopped
2 green onions, sliced
4-1/2 teaspoons chopped dill pickle
1 cup mayonnaise *or* salad dressing
1-1/2 teaspoons dill pickle juice
1-1/2 teaspoons prepared mustard
3/4 cup sliced radishes

1. Cut the potatoes into 1/4-in.-thick slices; place in a large bowl. Add cucumber, eggs, onions and pickle. In a small bowl, combine the mayonnaise, pickle juice and mustard; pour over the potato mixture and toss gently to coat.

2. Cover and refrigerate. Fold in radishes just before serving. **Yield:** 10-12 servings.

Broccoli Orange Salad

(Pictured at right)

Cathy Lavers, Scotsburn, Nova Scotia

Every time I take this sweet orangy salad to a potluck, I pass around the recipe, too. There's something special about the tasty combination of ingredients.

1 egg
1/4 cup sugar
1-1/2 teaspoons honey
1 teaspoon ground mustard
1/2 teaspoon cornstarch
2 tablespoons water
2 tablespoons white wine vinegar
2 tablespoons mayonnaise
2 tablespoons sour cream
4-1/2 teaspoons butter
4 cups broccoli florets (about 1 medium bunch)
1 cup salted cashews
1 cup cubed Swiss cheese
1 can (11 ounces) mandarin oranges, well drained
1/2 cup raisins
6 bacon strips, cooked and crumbled
1/2 cup chopped red onion, optional

1. In a heavy saucepan, combine egg, sugar, honey, mustard and cornstarch with a whisk until smooth. Gradually whisk in water and vinegar. Cook and stir over

medium heat until a thermometer reads 160° and mixture is thickened.

2. Remove from heat; stir in mayonnaise, sour cream and butter until blended. Cool. Meanwhile, in a large bowl, combine broccoli, cashews, cheese, oranges, raisins, bacon and onion if desired. Just before serving, add dressing and toss to coat. **Yield:** 8-10 servings.

❧❧❧
Eastern Shore Seafood Salad
(Pictured below)
Kimberly Brennan, Clear Spring, Maryland

We live just a short distance from the Chesapeake Bay area, so crabmeat dishes are very popular here. This is a recipe I came across that I think is extra special.

- 1 pound cooked medium shrimp
- 3 cups cooked *or* canned crabmeat, drained, flaked and cartilage removed
- 1 small onion, chopped
- 1 celery rib, thinly sliced
- 1/2 cup mayonnaise
- 2 teaspoons seafood seasoning
- 1 teaspoon lemon juice
- 1/2 teaspoon salt
- 1/8 teaspoon pepper

Leaf lettuce, optional
- 1 hard-cooked egg, sliced, optional

1. In a large bowl, combine shrimp, crab, onion and celery. In a small bowl, combine mayonnaise, seafood seasoning, lemon juice, salt and pepper; add to the shrimp mixture and mix gently.

2. Cover and refrigerate for at least 1 hour. If desired, serve in a lettuce-lined bowl and garnish with egg. **Yield:** 6 servings.

❧❧❧
Crunchy Chicken Salad
(Pictured at right)
Lisa Buese, Olathe, Kansas

When I was first married, I experimented with a lot of recipes. I guess I got carried away. My husband told me that although he enjoyed trying new recipes, sometimes he'd like to have something familiar. I've arrived at a happy medium since then. This is one "test" that's become a favorite!

- 1/3 cup vegetable oil
- 1/4 cup white wine vinegar
- 2 tablespoons honey
- 2 tablespoons sesame seeds, toasted
- 2 tablespoons soy sauce
- 1 teaspoon dried parsley flakes
- 1/2 teaspoon ground ginger
- 1/2 teaspoon ground mustard
- 3 cups coarsely chopped cooked chicken
- 2 cups shredded green *or* Chinese cabbage
- 1 cup fresh snow peas, halved
- 1 cup sliced carrots
- 1/2 cup sliced green onions
- 1/2 cup sliced radishes

Salted peanuts, optional

1. In a large bowl, combine the first eight ingredients; mix well. Stir in the chicken. Cover and refrigerate for at least 1 hour.

2. Just before serving, toss vegetables in a serving bowl; top with the chicken mixture. Sprinkle with peanuts if desired. **Yield:** 6-8 servings.

Spicy Ravioli Salad

(Pictured on page 22)

Paula Marchesi, Lenhartsville, Pennsylvania

You'll be sitting down to dinner in no time when you prepare this main-dish salad. A convenient combination of frozen ravioli and pantry staples (including canned tomatoes, corn and olives) is dressed with easy taco sauce for tangy, fresh-tasting results.

- 1 package (25 ounces) frozen beef, sausage *or* cheese ravioli
- 1 can (10 ounces) diced tomatoes and green chilies, undrained
- 1 can (8-3/4 ounces) whole kernel corn, drained
- 1 bottle (8 ounces) taco sauce
- 1 can (2-1/4 ounces) sliced ripe olives, drained
- 1 small cucumber, peeled, seeded and chopped
- 1 small red onion, sliced
- 2 garlic cloves, minced
- 1/4 teaspoon ground cumin
- 1/4 teaspoon salt
- 1/4 teaspoon pepper

1. Cook ravioli according to package directions. Meanwhile, combine remaining ingredients in a large bowl.

2. Drain ravioli; stir into tomato mixture. Cover and refrigerate for at least 2 hours. **Yield:** 8-10 servings.

Green Bean Potato Salad

(Pictured at right)

Bea Vrsaljko, Belle Chasse, Louisiana

I have a taste for beans and find them a great companion to potatoes. Just add ham to make this versatile side salad a meal in itself—this one's among the recipes that I've invented myself.

- 1-1/2 pounds small red potatoes, quartered
- 1 garlic clove, peeled and halved
- 2 cups cut fresh green beans (1-1/2-inch pieces)
- 1 can (14-1/2 ounces) chicken broth

TARRAGON DRESSING:
- 3 tablespoons olive oil
- 3 tablespoons cider vinegar
- 1 garlic clove, minced
- 1 tablespoon minced fresh parsley
- 1 to 1-1/2 teaspoons minced fresh tarragon *or* 1/4 to 1/2 teaspoon dried tarragon
- 1/2 teaspoon ground mustard
- 1/2 teaspoon salt
- 1/4 teaspoon pepper
- 1/4 teaspoon Creole *or* Cajun seasoning

Lettuce leaves, optional

1. In a saucepan, cook potatoes and garlic in boiling salted water for 5 minutes. Add beans; cook 10-14 minutes longer or until vegetables are tender. Drain; discard garlic. Place vegetables in a bowl.

2. Warm broth; pour over vegetables. Cover and refrigerate for at least 2 hours, stirring several times. In a small bowl, combine oil, vinegar and seasonings; mix well. Drain vegetables; add dressing and toss to coat. Serve in a lettuce-lined bowl if desired. **Yield:** 6-8 servings.

Chili Corn Bread Salad

(Pictured above)

Kelly Newsom, Jenks, Oklahoma

A co-worker brought this wonderful dish to a potluck several years ago. She had copies of the recipe next to the pan. Now I make it for get-togethers and also supply copies of the recipe. I never have any leftover salad or recipes.

> 1 package (8-1/2 ounces) corn bread/muffin mix
> 1 can (4 ounces) chopped green chilies, undrained
> 1/8 teaspoon ground cumin
> 1/8 teaspoon dried oregano

Pinch rubbed sage

> 1 cup mayonnaise
> 1 cup (8 ounces) sour cream
> 1 envelope ranch salad dressing mix
> 2 cans (15 ounces *each*) pinto beans, rinsed and drained

> 2 cans (15-1/4 ounces *each*) whole kernel corn, drained
> 3 medium tomatoes, chopped
> 1 cup chopped green pepper
> 1 cup chopped green onions
> 10 bacon strips, cooked and crumbled
> 2 cups (8 ounces) shredded cheddar cheese

1. Prepare corn bread batter according to package directions. Stir in the chilies, cumin, oregano and sage. Spread in a greased 8-in. square baking pan. Bake at 400° for 20-25 minutes or until a toothpick inserted near the center comes out clean. Cool.

2. In a small bowl, combine the mayonnaise, sour cream and dressing mix; set aside.

3. Crumble half of the corn bread into a 13-in. x 9-in. x 2-in. dish. Layer with half of the beans, mayonnaise mixture, corn, tomatoes, green pepper, onions, bacon and cheese. Repeat layers (dish will be very full). Cover and refrigerate for 2 hours. **Yield:** 12 servings.

🎀🎀🎀
Southern Sweet Potato Salad
(Pictured at right)

Marlyn Woods, Lakeland, Florida

I do some catering, so I'm always looking for good new recipes. I love to take this deliciously different potato salad to potlucks and cookouts. Even folks who are reluctant to try it at first come back for more!

- 2 pounds sweet potatoes, peeled and cut into 1/2-inch cubes
- 2 tablespoons lemon juice
- 1 cup mayonnaise
- 2 tablespoons orange juice
- 1 tablespoon honey
- 1 teaspoon grated orange peel
- 1/2 teaspoon ground ginger
- 1/4 teaspoon salt
- 1/8 teaspoon ground nutmeg
- 1 cup sliced celery
- 1/3 cup chopped dates
- 1/2 cup chopped pecans
- Lettuce leaves
- 1 can (11 ounces) mandarin oranges, drained

1. In a medium saucepan, cook sweet potatoes in boiling salted water just until tender, about 5-8 minutes (do not overcook). Drain; toss with the lemon juice. In a large bowl, combine mayonnaise, orange juice, honey, orange peel, ginger, salt and nutmeg. Add the warm potatoes, celery and dates. Toss to coat well.

2. Cover and chill. Before serving, gently stir in the pecans. Spoon salad onto a lettuce-lined platter. Arrange oranges around salad. **Yield:** 6-8 servings.

🎀🎀🎀
Creamy Summer Vegetable Salad
(Pictured at left)

Barbara Arneson, Creston, Washington

Mother made this salad whenever we barbecued. It's easy to fix, goes well with meat or chicken and is a good way to utilize garden vegetables.

- 4 medium tomatoes, chopped
- 3 large cucumbers, seeded and chopped
- 1 medium onion, chopped
- 10 radishes, sliced
- 2 cups (16 ounces) sour cream
- 1/4 cup lemon juice
- 1 teaspoon seasoned salt
- 1/2 teaspoon pepper
- 3/4 teaspoon celery seed, optional

1. In a large bowl, combine tomatoes, cucumbers, onion and radishes. In a small bowl, combine the remaining ingredients. Add to vegetables and toss to coat.

2. Cover and refrigerate for at least 2 hours. Serve with a slotted spoon. **Yield:** 16 servings.

Grilled Chicken Pasta Salad

(Pictured on page 22)

Lori Thon, Basin, Wyoming

During the summer, my family often requests this recipe. Simply add garlic bread for a great meal. It's wonderful, too, for a picnic or any gathering.

- 1-1/2 cups Italian salad dressing
- 1/2 cup cider vinegar
- 1/3 cup honey
- 2 teaspoons dried oregano
- 1 teaspoon dried basil
- 1/2 teaspoon pepper
- 6 boneless skinless chicken breast halves (1-1/2 pounds)
- 1 package (12 ounces) fettuccine
- 1-1/2 cups broccoli florets
- 3 medium carrots, thinly sliced
- 2 celery ribs, thinly sliced
- 1 cup chopped green pepper
- 2 cans (2-1/4 ounces *each*) sliced ripe olives, drained

DRESSING:
- 1-1/2 cups Italian salad dressing
- 1 teaspoon garlic salt
- 1 teaspoon dried oregano
- 1 teaspoon Italian seasoning

1. In a large resealable plastic bag or shallow glass container, combine the first six ingredients. Cut each chicken breast into four strips; add to dressing mixture. Seal or cover and refrigerate for 2-3 hours. Drain and discard marinade.

2. Grill chicken, uncovered, over medium heat for 4-5 minutes on each side or until juices run clear. Meanwhile, cook fettuccine according to package directions; drain and cool. Cut chicken into bite-size pieces; set aside.

3. In a large bowl, combine vegetables, olives and fettuccine. Combine dressing ingredients in a jar with a tight-fitting lid; shake well. Pour over salad and toss to coat. Top with chicken. **Yield:** 6 servings.

Grape and Cabbage Salad

(Pictured at left)

Dorothy Raymond, Mira Loma, California

This is a recipe I created using the grapes grown in our state. The flavor and texture bring many compliments, and its combination of colors add to its appeal.

- 2 cups finely shredded cabbage
- 1 cup halved red grapes
- 1/2 cup chopped green pepper
- 2 tablespoons minced fresh parsley
- 1/4 cup Italian salad dressing
- 2 tablespoons water
- 1 tablespoon cider vinegar

1. In a bowl, combine the cabbage, grapes, green pepper and parsley.

2. In another bowl, whisk together salad dressing, water and vinegar. Pour over cabbage mixture and toss to coat. Cover and refrigerate overnight. **Yield:** 4-6 servings.

🎗️🎗️🎗️
Lettuce with Hot Bacon Dressing

(Pictured at right)

Myra Innes, Auburn, Kansas

I plant lettuce in my garden, so this is a recipe I make often. It's a nice change from a regular tossed salad.

- **5 bacon strips**
- **8 cups torn salad greens**
- **2 hard-cooked eggs, chopped**
- **2 green onions, sliced**
- **1/2 cup sugar**
- **1/2 cup vinegar**
- **1/2 teaspoon seasoned salt**
- **1/2 teaspoon garlic powder**
- **1/4 teaspoon ground mustard**

1. In a skillet, cook bacon until crisp. Remove the bacon; crumble and set aside. Drain, reserving 1/4 cup drippings. In a large bowl, combine the greens, eggs, onions and bacon.

2. In the same skillet, add remaining ingredients to the reserved drippings; bring to a boil. Drizzle over the salad and toss to coat. Serve immediately. **Yield:** 8 servings.

🎗️🎗️🎗️
Creamy Cranberry Salad

(Pictured at right)

Alexandra Lypecky, Dearborn, Michigan

One of my piano students shared this recipe with me many years ago. She told me it's the perfect salad for the holidays, and she was right.

- **3 cups fresh *or* frozen cranberries, coarsely chopped**
- **1 can (20 ounces) crushed pineapple, drained**
- **1 medium apple, peeled and chopped**
- **2 cups miniature marshmallows**
- **2/3 cup sugar**
- **1/8 teaspoon salt**
- **1/4 cup chopped walnuts, optional**
- **2 cups heavy whipping cream, whipped**

1. In a bowl, combine cranberries, pineapple, apple, marshmallows, sugar, salt and walnuts if desired; mix well. Cover and refrigerate overnight.

2. Just before serving, fold in whipped cream. **Yield:** 10-12 servings.

🎗🎗🎗

Summertime Strawberry Gelatin Salad

(Pictured above)

Janet England, Chillicothe, Missouri

For years, this salad has been a "must" at family dinners, holidays and other special occasions. It's as pretty as it is good.

BOTTOM LAYER:
> 1 package (3 ounces) strawberry gelatin
> 1 cup boiling water
> 1 cup cold water

MIDDLE LAYER:
> 1 envelope unflavored gelatin
> 1/2 cup cold water
> 1 cup half-and-half cream
> 1 package (8 ounces) cream cheese, softened
> 1 cup sugar
> 1/2 teaspoon vanilla extract

TOP LAYER:
> 1 package (6 ounces) strawberry gelatin
> 1 cup boiling water
> 1 cup cold water
> 3 to 4 cups sliced fresh strawberries

1. In a bowl, dissolve strawberry gelatin in the boiling water; stir in the cold water. Pour into a 13-in. x 9-in. x 2-in. dish; chill until set. Meanwhile, place the unflavored gelatin and cold water in a small bowl; let stand until softened.

2. In a saucepan over medium heat, heat cream (do not boil). Add softened gelatin; stir until gelatin is dissolved. Cool to room temperature.

3. In a mixing bowl, beat cream cheese, sugar and vanilla until smooth. Gradually add the unflavored gelatin mixture; mix well. Carefully pour over the bottom layer. Refrigerate until set, about 1 hour.

4. For top layer, dissolve strawberry gelatin in boiling water; stir in cold water. Cool to room temperature. Stir in strawberries; carefully spoon over middle layer. Refrigerate overnight. **Yield:** 12-16 servings.

Editor's Note: This salad takes time to prepare since each layer must be set before the next layer is added.

Baked German Potato Salad

(Pictured at right)

Julie Myers, Lexington, Ohio

What makes this German potato salad so different is that it's sweet instead of tangy. The first time I took my potato salad to work, people kept coming out of their offices to find out what smelled so good. By lunch, it was gone.

- 12 medium red potatoes (about 3 pounds)
- 8 bacon strips
- 2 medium onions, chopped
- 3/4 cup packed brown sugar
- 1/3 cup vinegar
- 1/3 cup sweet pickle juice
- 2/3 cup water, *divided*
- 2 teaspoons dried parsley flakes
- 1 teaspoon salt
- 1/2 to 3/4 teaspoon celery seed
- 4-1/2 teaspoons all-purpose flour

1. In a saucepan, cook potatoes until just tender; drain. Peel and slice into an ungreased 2-qt. baking dish; set aside.

2. In a skillet, cook bacon until crisp; drain, reserving 2 tablespoons drippings. Crumble bacon and set aside.

Saute onions in drippings until tender. Stir in brown sugar, vinegar, pickle juice, 1/2 cup water, parsley, salt and celery seed. Simmer, uncovered, for 5-10 minutes.

3. Meanwhile, combine flour and remaining water until smooth; stir into onion mixture. Bring to a boil. Cook and stir for 2 minutes or until thickened. Pour over potatoes. Add bacon; gently stir to coat. Bake, uncovered, at 350° for 30 minutes or until heated through. **Yield:** 8-10 servings.

Broccoli Cauliflower Salad

(Pictured below)

Linda Kangas, Outlook, Saskatchewan

This salad has been to as many family gatherings as I have! It holds well...and leftovers are still tasty a day later. I'm an at-home mom who enjoys trying new recipes.

- 1 medium head cauliflower, broken into florets (about 7-1/2 cups)
- 1 medium bunch broccoli, cut into florets (about 4 cups)
- 2 cups seedless red grapes
- 6 green onions with tops, sliced
- 2 cups (8 ounces) shredded mozzarella cheese
- 2 cups mayonnaise
- 1/4 cup grated Parmesan cheese
- 2 tablespoons sugar
- 2 tablespoons vinegar
- 1/2 to 1 pound sliced bacon, cooked and crumbled

Leaf lettuce

Additional red grapes, optional

1. In a large bowl, combine the cauliflower, broccoli, grapes, onions and mozzarella cheese. Combine the mayonnaise, Parmesan cheese, sugar and vinegar; pour over vegetable mixture and toss to coat. Cover and refrigerate for at least 2 hours.

2. Just before serving, stir in bacon. Transfer to a lettuce-lined bowl. Garnish with grapes if desired. **Yield:** 15-20 servings.

✿✿✿ Creamy Sliced Tomatoes

(Pictured on page 23)

Doris Smith, Woodbury, New Jersey

This is a family favorite that's also popular with friends. It's a pretty presentation, perfect as a side dish. The basil and cool creamy dressing make the dish tasty and refreshing.

    1   cup mayonnaise
    1/2 cup half-and-half cream
    3/4 teaspoon dried basil *or* 1-1/2 teaspoons
        chopped fresh basil, *divided*
Lettuce leaves

    6   medium tomatoes, sliced
    1   medium red onion, thinly sliced into rings

1. In a small bowl, combine mayonnaise, cream and half of the basil; mix well. Refrigerate.

2. Just before serving, arrange lettuce, tomatoes and onions on individual salad plates. Drizzle dressing over. Sprinkle with remaining basil. **Yield:** 12 servings.

✿✿✿ Hot Chicken Salad

(Pictured above)

Michelle Wise, Spring Mills, Pennsylvania

Having my recipe selected as a winner is a special thrill for me. Baking has always been my favorite type of cooking. When I got married, I was happy to have this simple yet delicious recipe—which originated with my aunt and was passed on to my mom. It's great for a luncheon...or, served with salad and rolls, for supper.

✓ Uses less fat, sugar or salt. Includes Nutritional Analysis and Diabetic Exchanges.

    2-1/2 cups diced cooked chicken
      1   cup diced celery
      1   cup sliced fresh mushrooms
      1   tablespoon minced onion
      1   teaspoon lemon juice
      1/2 teaspoon dried rosemary, crushed
      1/4 teaspoon pepper
      1   can (8 ounces) sliced water chestnuts, drained
      2   cups cooked rice
      3/4 cup mayonnaise
      1   can (10-3/4 ounces) condensed cream of
          chicken soup, undiluted
TOPPING:
      3   tablespoons butter
      1/2 cup cornflake crumbs
      1/2 cup slivered almonds

1. In a large bowl, combine the first nine ingredients. Blend mayonnaise and soup; toss with chicken mixture. Spoon into a greased 2-qt. casserole.

2. In a skillet, melt butter and combine with the corn-flakes and almonds. Top casserole with crumb mixture. Bake at 350° for 30 minutes. **Yield:** 6 servings.

Nutritional Analysis: One serving (without topping) equals 272 calories, 522 mg sodium, 40 mg cholesterol, 29 gm carbohydrate, 21 gm protein, 12 gm fat.

Diabetic Exchanges: 2 lean meat, 1-1/2 starch, 1 vegetable, 1 fat.

🎗🎗🎗
Layered Fresh Fruit Salad
(Pictured below)

Page Alexander, Baldwin City, Kansas

People always pass along compliments when I take this salad to covered-dish suppers. It's nice on a hot day, with a winter meal or as a dessert!

CITRUS SAUCE:
- 2/3 cup fresh orange juice
- 1/3 cup fresh lemon juice
- 1/3 cup packed brown sugar
- 1 cinnamon stick
- 1/2 teaspoon grated orange peel
- 1/2 teaspoon grated lemon peel

FRUIT SALAD:
- 2 cups cubed fresh pineapple
- 1 pint fresh strawberries, hulled and sliced
- 2 kiwifruit, peeled and sliced
- 3 medium bananas, sliced
- 2 oranges, peeled and sectioned
- 1 red grapefruit, peeled and sectioned
- 1 cup seedless red grapes

1. In a saucepan, bring all sauce ingredients to a boil; simmer 5 minutes. Cool.

2. Meanwhile, in a large clear glass salad bowl, arrange fruit in layers in the order listed. Remove cinnamon stick from the sauce and pour sauce over fruit. Cover and refrigerate several hours. **Yield:** 10-12 servings.

🎗🎗🎗
Warm Mustard Potato Salad
(Pictured at right)

Tiffany Mitchell, Susanville, California

This tangy mixture is wonderful and so different from traditional potato salads. The Dijon mustard and dill spark the flavor. It's a comforting and tasty side dish that's really simple to assemble.

- 2 pounds small red potatoes
- 1 cup mayonnaise
- 1/4 cup Dijon mustard
- 1/2 to 3/4 cup chopped red onion
- 2 green onions with tops, sliced
- 2 garlic cloves, minced
- 3 tablespoons snipped fresh dill *or* 1 tablespoon dill weed
- 1/2 teaspoon salt
- 1/2 teaspoon pepper
- 1/4 teaspoon lime juice

1. Place the potatoes in a saucepan and cover with water. Cover and bring to a boil; cook until tender, about 25 minutes. Drain thoroughly and cool slightly.

2. Meanwhile, combine the remaining ingredients. Cut potatoes into chunks; place in a bowl. Add the mustard mixture and toss to coat. Serve warm. **Yield:** 8-10 servings.

Barbecued Beef Sandwiches, p. 54

Lentil Barley Soup, p. 59

Garden Harvest Chili, p. 43

Cream of Cauliflower Soup, p. 45

Soups & Sandwiches

Nothing warms up a cold day like a steaming bowl of hearty soup. In this chapter, you'll find a tempting selection of broth- and cream-based soups, chili and chowders, all of which would pair nicely with a home-style sandwich.

Baked Potato Soup, p. 46

Apple-Ham Grilled Cheese 42

Stuffed Sweet Pepper Soup 42

Halibut Chowder.................................43

Garden Harvest Chili..........................43

Chilled Cantaloupe Soup....................44

Corn and Sausage Chowder................44

Cream of Cauliflower Soup.................45

Hearty Hamburger Soup.....................45

Three-Bean Soup 46

Baked Potato Soup.............................46

Chicken Tomato Soup 47

Garden Turkey Burgers 47

Ham and Cheese Calzones..................48

Sausage Potato Soup 48

Zesty Macaroni Soup 49

Comforting Chicken Noodle Soup.......49

Baked Chili 50

Hungarian Goulash Soup....................50

Creamy Asparagus Chowder 51

Creamy Swiss Onion Soup 52

Cola Burgers......................................52

Zesty Colorado Chili..........................53

Chunky Seafood Chowder 54

Barbecued Beef Sandwiches................54

Stir-Fried Pork Soup...........................55

Super Sloppy Joes 55

Meatball Mushroom Soup...................56

Northwest Salmon Chowder 56

Corny Tomato Dumpling Soup.............57

Wild Rice Soup..................................58

Southern Chicken Rice Soup 58

Spicy Cheeseburger Soup 59

Lentil Barley Soup 59

Tasty Reuben Soup 60

Spicy White Chili 60

Tomato Dill Bisque............................61

Chunky Cheese Soup 61

Meatball Lover's Sandwich 62

Pronto Taco Soup 63

Best-Ever Potato Soup 63

Ham and Cheese Calzones, p. 48

🎗️ 🎗️ 🎗️

Apple-Ham Grilled Cheese

(Pictured at left)

Shirley Brazel, Rocklin, California

After finding this recipe years ago, I altered it to fit our tastes by adding the apples. Our whole family loves it! We look forward to fall when we go out to the orchards to gather the fresh-picked ingredients for pies, cobblers, salads…and, of course, this sandwich.

        1 cup chopped tart apples
    1/3 cup mayonnaise
    1/4 cup finely chopped walnuts
        8 slices process American cheese
        8 slices sourdough bread
        4 slices fully cooked ham
    1/4 cup butter, softened

1. Combine apples, mayonnaise and walnuts. Place a slice of cheese on four slices of bread. Layer each with 1/3 cup of the apple mixture, a slice of ham and another slice of cheese; cover with remaining bread. Butter the outsides of the sandwiches.

2. Cook in a large skillet over medium heat on each side until bread is golden brown and cheese is melted. **Yield:** 4 servings.

🎗️ 🎗️ 🎗️

Stuffed Sweet Pepper Soup

(Pictured at right)

Joseph Kendra, Coraopolis, Pennsylvania

Tomatoes, peppers, garlic and onions are the mainstays of my garden. Being the oldest of seven children, I acquired a knack for cooking from my mom.

        1 pound ground beef
        2 quarts water
        1 quart tomato juice
        3 medium sweet red *or* green peppers, diced
    1-1/2 cups chili sauce
        1 cup uncooked long grain rice
        2 celery ribs, diced
        1 large onion, diced
        2 teaspoons browning sauce, optional
        3 chicken bouillon cubes
        2 garlic cloves, minced
    1/2 teaspoon salt

1. In a large kettle or Dutch oven over medium heat, cook beef until no longer pink; drain. Add the remaining ingredients; bring to a boil.

2. Reduce heat; simmer, uncovered, for 1 hour or until the rice is tender. **Yield:** 16 servings (4 quarts).

☙ ☙ ☙
Halibut Chowder

(Pictured at right and on back cover)

Mary Davis, Palmer, Alaska

This rich, creamy chowder is so good you won't believe it starts with canned soup and frozen vegetables. It showcases tender chunks of halibut, but salmon or most any type of whitefish will do. I double the recipe for large gatherings, and guests almost lick the pot clean!

    8 to 10 green onions, thinly sliced
    2 garlic cloves, minced
    2 tablespoons butter
    4 cans (10-3/4 ounces *each*) condensed cream of
      potato soup, undiluted
    2 cans (10-3/4 ounces *each*) condensed cream of
      mushroom soup, undiluted
    4 cups milk
    2 packages (8 ounces *each*) cream cheese, cubed
1-1/2 pounds halibut *or* salmon fillets, cubed
1-1/2 cups frozen sliced carrots

1-1/2 cups frozen corn
1/8 to 1/4 teaspoon cayenne pepper, optional

1. In a Dutch oven or soup kettle, saute onions and garlic in butter until tender. Add soups, milk and cream cheese; cook and stir until cheese is melted. Bring to a boil. Stir in fish, carrots and corn.

2. Reduce heat; simmer, uncovered, for 5-10 minutes or until fish flakes easily and the vegetables are tender. Add cayenne pepper if desired. **Yield:** 16 servings (about 4 quarts).

☙ ☙ ☙
Garden Harvest Chili

(Pictured on page 40)

Debbie Cosford, Bayfield, Ontario

Any time you're looking for a way to use up your zucchini and squash, this recipe gives a different taste sensation.

 Uses less fat, sugar or salt. Includes Nutritional Analysis and Diabetic Exchanges.

    1 medium sweet red pepper, chopped
    1 medium onion, chopped
    4 garlic cloves, minced
    2 tablespoons vegetable oil
    1 tablespoon chili powder
    1 teaspoon ground cumin
    1 teaspoon dried oregano

    2 cups cubed peeled butternut squash
    1 can (28 ounces) diced tomatoes, undrained
    2 cups diced zucchini
    1 can (15 ounces) black beans, rinsed and
      drained
    1 can (8-3/4 ounces) whole kernel corn, drained
1/4 cup minced fresh parsley

1. In a 3-qt. saucepan, saute red pepper, onion and garlic in oil until tender. Stir in chili powder, cumin, oregano, butternut squash and tomatoes; bring to a boil.

2. Reduce heat; cover and simmer for 10-15 minutes or until squash is almost tender. Stir in remaining ingredients; cover and simmer 10 minutes more. **Yield:** 7 servings (1-3/4 quarts).

Nutritional Analysis: One 1-cup serving equals 193 calories, 167 mg sodium, 0 cholesterol, 33 gm carbohydrate, 8 gm protein, 5 gm fat. **Diabetic Exchanges:** 1-1/2 starch, 1 vegetable, 1 fat.

Chilled Cantaloupe Soup

(Pictured at right)

Margaret McNeil, Memphis, Tennessee

A friend in New York shared the recipe for this chilled melon soup that's pleasantly spiced with cinnamon. Most people are skeptical when I describe it, but after one spoonful, they're hooked. It's easy to prepare, pretty to serve and so refreshing.

✓ Uses less fat, sugar or salt. Includes Nutritional Analysis and Diabetic Exchanges.

- **1 medium cantaloupe, peeled, seeded and cubed**
- **2 cups orange juice, *divided***
- **1 tablespoon lime juice**
- **1/4 to 1/2 teaspoon ground cinnamon**
- **Fresh mint, optional**

1. Place cantaloupe and 1/2 cup orange juice in a blender or food processor; cover and process until smooth.

2. Transfer to a large bowl; stir in lime juice, cinnamon and remaining orange juice. Cover and refrigerate for at least 1 hour. Garnish with mint if desired. **Yield:** 6 servings.

Nutritional Analysis: One 3/4-cup serving equals 70 calories, 9 mg sodium, 0 cholesterol, 17 gm carbohydrate, 1 gm protein, trace fat. **Diabetic Exchange:** 1 fruit.

Corn and Sausage Chowder

(Pictured above)

Joanne Watts, Kitchener, Ontario

My cooking "teachers" included my Irish grandmother, my mother and the restaurant my husband and I operated years ago!

- **3 ears fresh corn, husked and cleaned**
- **4 cups heavy whipping cream**
- **2 cups chicken broth**
- **4 garlic cloves, minced**
- **10 fresh thyme sprigs**
- **1 bay leaf**
- **1-1/2 medium onions, finely chopped, *divided***
- **1/2 pound hot Italian sausage**
- **2 tablespoons butter**
- **2 teaspoons diced jalapeno peppers***
- **1/2 teaspoon ground cumin**
- **2 tablespoons all-purpose flour**
- **2 medium potatoes, peeled and cut into 1/2-inch cubes**
- **Salt and pepper to taste**
- **1-1/2 teaspoons snipped fresh *or* minced dried chives**

1. Using a small sharp knife, cut corn from cobs; set corn aside. Place the corncobs, cream, broth, garlic, thyme, bay leaf and one-third of the onions in a large saucepan. Heat almost to boiling; reduce heat and simmer, covered, for 1 hour, stirring occasionally.

2. Remove and discard corncobs. Strain cream mixture through a sieve set over a large bowl, pressing solids with back of spoon; set aside. Meanwhile, brown sausage in a large skillet. Cool and cut into 1/2-in. slices.

3. In a large saucepan, melt butter. Add jalapenos, cumin and remaining onions; cook 5 minutes. Stir in flour; cook and stir 2 minutes. Gradually add corn stock. Add sausage and potatoes. Cover; cook until potatoes are tender, about 25 minutes. Add corn and cook just until tender, about 5 minutes. Remove bay leaf. Season with salt and pepper. Sprinkle with chives before serving. **Yield:** 8 servings (2 quarts).

*Editor's Note: When cutting or seeding hot peppers, use rubber or plastic gloves to protect your hands. Avoid touching your face.

Cream of Cauliflower Soup

(Pictured on page 40)

Carol Reaves, San Antonio, Texas

Generally, my husband isn't a soup fan—but his spoon's poised and ready for this version. I adapted this rich and creamy concoction from a recipe I tasted at a local restaurant…and it's since become a popular item on my menu.

- 2 medium onions, chopped
- 2 medium carrots, grated
- 2 celery ribs, sliced
- 2 garlic cloves, minced
- 1/4 cup plus 6 tablespoons butter, *divided*
- 1 medium head cauliflower, chopped
- 5 cups chicken broth
- 1/4 cup minced fresh parsley
- 1 teaspoon salt
- 1 teaspoon coarsely ground pepper
- 1/2 teaspoon dried basil
- 1/2 teaspoon dried tarragon
- 6 tablespoons all-purpose flour
- 1 cup milk
- 1/2 cup heavy whipping cream
- 1/4 cup sour cream
- Fresh tarragon, optional

1. In a soup kettle or Dutch oven, saute the onions, carrots, celery and garlic in 1/4 cup butter until tender. Add cauliflower, broth, parsley, salt, pepper, basil and tarragon. Cover and simmer for 30 minutes or until the vegetables are tender.

2. Meanwhile, in a saucepan, melt the remaining butter. Stir in flour until smooth. Gradually stir in the milk and whipping cream. Bring to a boil; cook and stir for 2 minutes or until thickened.

3. Add to cauliflower mixture. Cook for 10 minutes or until thickened, stirring frequently. Remove from the heat; stir in sour cream. Garnish with tarragon if desired. **Yield:** 8 servings.

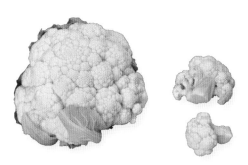

Hearty Hamburger Soup

(Pictured at right and on back cover)

Barbara Brown, Janesville, Wisconsin

At family get-togethers, our children always request this spirit-warming soup along with a fresh loaf of homemade bread and tall glasses of milk. It has robust flavor, plenty of fresh-tasting vegetables and is easy to make.

- 1 pound ground beef
- 4 cups water
- 1 can (14-1/2 ounces) diced tomatoes, undrained
- 3 medium carrots, sliced
- 2 medium potatoes, peeled and cubed
- 1 medium onion, chopped
- 1/2 cup chopped celery
- 4 beef bouillon cubes
- 1-1/2 teaspoons salt
- 1/4 teaspoon pepper
- 1/4 teaspoon dried oregano
- 1 cup cut fresh *or* frozen green beans

1. In a large saucepan over medium heat, cook beef until no longer pink; drain. Add the next 10 ingredients; bring to a boil.

2. Reduce heat; cover and simmer for 15 minutes or until potatoes and carrots are tender. Add beans. Cover and simmer 15 minutes longer or until the beans are tender. **Yield:** 8 servings (2 quarts).

> 1 medium onion, chopped
> 1 tablespoon vegetable oil
> 3 small potatoes, peeled and cubed
> 2 medium carrots, sliced
> 3 cans (14-1/2 ounces *each*) chicken broth
> 3 cups water
> 2 tablespoons parsley flakes
> 2 teaspoons dried basil
> 1 teaspoon dried oregano
> 1 garlic clove, minced
> 1/2 teaspoon pepper
> 1 can (15-1/2 ounces) great northern beans, rinsed and drained
> 1 can (15 ounces) pinto beans, rinsed and drained
> 1 can (15 ounces) garbanzo beans, rinsed and drained
> 3 cups chopped fresh spinach

🎗🎗🎗

Three-Bean Soup

(Pictured above)

Valerie Lee, Snellville, Georgia

When I was growing up, my mother prepared many different soups, each seasoned just right. She often made this colorful combination that's chock-full of harvest-fresh goodness. It showcases an assortment of beans, potatoes, carrots and spinach.

1. In a Dutch oven, saute onion in oil. Add the next nine ingredients.

2. Simmer, uncovered, until vegetables are tender. Add beans and spinach; heat through. **Yield:** 12 servings (about 3 quarts).

Nutritional Analysis: One 1-cup serving (prepared with reduced-sodium broth) equals 169 calories, 276 mg sodium, 2 mg cholesterol, 29 gm carbohydrate, 9 gm protein, 3 gm fat. **Diabetic Exchanges:** 2 starch, 1-1/2 meat.

🎗🎗🎗

Baked Potato Soup

(Pictured on page 41)

Loretha Bringle, Garland, Texas

This recipe was given to me by a dear friend with whom I taught school. She came to Texas from Michigan, and I from Oklahoma. Her entire family has become very special to me. I think of them whenever I make this rich, savory soup, which is a great way to use up leftover baked potatoes.

> 2/3 cup butter
> 2/3 cup all-purpose flour
> 7 cups milk

> 4 large baking potatoes, baked, cooled, peeled and cubed (about 4 cups)
> 4 green onions, sliced
> 12 bacon strips, cooked and crumbled
> 1-1/4 cups shredded cheddar cheese
> 1 cup (8 ounces) sour cream
> 3/4 teaspoon salt
> 1/2 teaspoon pepper

1. In a large soup kettle or Dutch oven, melt the butter. Stir in flour; heat and stir until smooth. Gradually add milk, stirring constantly until thickened. Add potatoes and onions. Bring to a boil, stirring constantly.

2. Reduce heat; simmer for 10 minutes. Add remaining ingredients; stir until cheese is melted. Serve immediately. **Yield:** 8-10 servings (2-1/2 quarts).

Chicken Tomato Soup

(Pictured at right)

Connie Johnson, Springfield, Missouri

While creating this crowd-pleasing soup, I kept in mind a variety of textures, colors and flavors. Its sweet tomato base brims with chicken, broccoli, corn and beans. It's especially tasty if you garnish it with shredded cheddar cheese and crumbled bacon.

1-1/2 cups water
    1 package (10 ounces) frozen chopped broccoli
  3/4 cup chopped onion
    1 garlic clove, minced
  3/4 pound boneless skinless chicken breast, cut into 1-inch chunks
  1/2 teaspoon seasoned salt
  1/4 teaspoon pepper
    1 can (46 ounces) tomato juice
    1 can (15-1/2 ounces) great northern beans, rinsed and drained
    1 can (15 ounces) black beans, rinsed and drained
    1 can (11 ounces) whole kernel corn, drained
    1 tablespoon ketchup
    1 teaspoon brown sugar
Crumbled bacon and shredded cheddar cheese

1. In a Dutch oven or soup kettle, combine water, broccoli, onion and garlic. Bring to a boil; boil for 8-10 minutes, stirring frequently.

2. Meanwhile, in a nonstick skillet, cook chicken until no longer pink, about 6 minutes. Sprinkle with seasoned salt and pepper. Add to broccoli mixture. Stir in tomato juice, beans, corn, ketchup and brown sugar; bring to a boil.

3. Reduce heat; cover and simmer for 10-15 minutes, stirring occasionally. Garnish with bacon and cheese. **Yield:** 12 servings (about 3 quarts).

Garden Turkey Burgers

(Pictured below)

Sandy Kitzmiller, Unityville, Pennsylvania

These moist burgers get plenty of color and flavor from onion, zucchini and red pepper. I often make the mixture ahead of time and put it in the refrigerator. Later, after helping my husband with farm chores, I can put the burgers on the grill while whipping up a salad or side dish.

☑ Uses less fat, sugar or salt. Includes Nutritional Analysis and Diabetic Exchanges.

    1 cup old-fashioned oats
  3/4 cup chopped onion
  3/4 cup finely chopped sweet red *or* green pepper
  1/2 cup shredded zucchini
  1/4 cup ketchup
    2 garlic cloves, minced
  1/4 teaspoon salt, optional
    1 pound ground turkey
    6 whole wheat hamburger buns, split and toasted

1. Coat grill rack with nonstick cooking spray before starting the grill. In a bowl, combine the first seven ingredients. Add turkey and mix well. Shape into six 1/2-in.-thick patties.

2. Grill, covered, over indirect medium heat for 6 minutes on each side or until a meat thermometer reads 165°. Serve on buns. **Yield:** 6 burgers.

Nutritional Analysis: One serving (prepared with ground turkey breast and without salt; calculated without the bun) equals 156 calories, 174 mg sodium, 37 mg cholesterol, 15 gm carbohydrate, 21 gm protein, 2 gm fat. **Diabetic Exchanges:** 2 very lean meat, 1 starch.

🎀🎀🎀
Ham and Cheese Calzones

(Pictured on page 41)

Shelby Marino, Neptune Beach, Florida

This sort of inside-out pizza is something I concocted one evening when I had leftover baked ham and needed to fix something quick and simple. My husband loved it—so did all his friends when he took some to work for lunch.

>**2 tubes (10 ounces *each*) refrigerated pizza crust**
>**1 carton (8 ounces) ricotta cheese**
>**4 to 6 ounces sliced pepperoni**
>**2 cups diced fully cooked ham**
>**2 cups (8 ounces) shredded mozzarella cheese**

Shredded Parmesan cheese, optional
Dried basil, optional
Meatless spaghetti sauce, warmed

1. Unroll one pizza crust, stretching gently to make a 14-in. x 11-in. rectangle. Spread half of the ricotta on half of the dough lengthwise, to within 1 in. of the edges. Sprinkle with half of the pepperoni, ham and mozzarella. Fold unfilled side of dough over filled half and press edges together firmly to seal. Transfer to a greased baking sheet.

2. Repeat with remaining crust and filling ingredients. Bake at 400° for 20-25 minutes or until golden brown. Sprinkle with Parmesan and basil if desired. Slice into serving-size pieces. Serve with spaghetti sauce. **Yield:** 8 servings.

🎀🎀🎀
Sausage Potato Soup

(Pictured at right)

Jennifer LeFevre, Hesston, Kansas

After a full day of teaching and coaching, I'm often too tired to spend a lot of time preparing dinner. So I rely on this thick, chunky blend that I can finish in 30 minutes. My family enjoys the wonderful flavor of the smoked sausage.

>**1/2 pound fully cooked kielbasa *or* Polish sausage, diced**
>**6 medium potatoes, peeled and cubed**
>**2 cups frozen corn**
>**1-1/2 cups chicken broth**
>**1 celery rib, sliced**
>**1/4 cup sliced carrot**
>**1/2 teaspoon garlic powder**
>**1/2 teaspoon onion powder**
>**1/2 teaspoon salt**
>**1/4 teaspoon pepper**
>**1-1/2 cups milk**
>**2/3 cup shredded cheddar cheese**
>**1 teaspoon minced fresh parsley**

1. In a large saucepan, brown sausage; drain. Set sausage aside. In the same pan, combine potatoes, corn, broth, celery, carrot and seasonings. Bring to a boil.

2. Reduce heat; cover and simmer for 15 minutes or until vegetables are tender. Add milk, cheese, parsley and sausage. Cook and stir over low heat until cheese is melted and soup is heated through. **Yield:** 6 servings.

1 pound ground beef
1 medium onion, chopped
5 cups water
1 can (15 ounces) pinto beans, rinsed and
    drained
1 can (14-1/2 ounces) diced tomatoes,
    undrained
1 can (7 ounces) whole kernel corn, drained
1 can (4 ounces) chopped green chilies, optional
1/2 teaspoon ground mustard
1/2 teaspoon salt
1/8 teaspoon pepper
1 package (7-1/2 ounces) chili macaroni dinner
    mix*
Salsa con queso dip*

1. In a saucepan, cook beef and onion over medium heat until meat is no longer pink; drain. Stir in water, beans, tomatoes, corn and chilies if desired. Stir in mustard, salt, pepper and contents of macaroni sauce mix. Bring to a boil.

2. Reduce heat; cover and simmer for 10 minutes. Stir in contents of macaroni packet. Cover and simmer 10-14 minutes longer or until macaroni is tender, stirring once. Serve with salsa con queso dip. **Yield:** 8-10 servings (about 2-1/2 quarts).

   ***Editor's Note:** This recipe was tested with Hamburger Helper brand chili macaroni. Salsa con queso dip can be found in the international food section or snack aisle of most grocery stores.

🎀 🎀 🎀

Zesty Macaroni Soup

(Pictured above)

Joan Hallford, North Richland Hills, Texas

The recipe for this thick, zippy soup first caught my attention for two reasons—it calls for ingredients that are found in my pantry, and it can be prepared in a jiffy.

🎀 🎀 🎀

Comforting Chicken Noodle Soup

(Pictured at right)

Joanna Sargent, Sandy, Utah

A good friend made us this rich, comforting soup after the birth of our son. It was such a help to have dinner taken care of until I was back on my feet. This yummy dish is so simple to fix that now I give a pot of it (along with the recipe) to other new mothers.

2 quarts water
8 chicken bouillon cubes
6-1/2 cups uncooked wide egg noodles
2 cans (10-3/4 ounces *each*) condensed cream of
    chicken soup, undiluted
3 cups cubed cooked chicken
1 cup (8 ounces) sour cream
Minced fresh parsley

1. In a large saucepan, bring water and bouillon cubes to a boil. Add the noodles; cook, uncovered, until tender, about 10 minutes. Do not drain. Add soup and chicken; heat through.

2. Remove from the heat; stir in sour cream. Sprinkle with parsley. **Yield:** 10-12 servings (about 2-1/2 quarts).

✿✿✿
Baked Chili
(Pictured at right)

Michelle Gal, Toronto, Ontario

This is wonderful the first day and makes outstanding leftovers. When I was a student, I loved savory one-pot suppers like this.

- 1 pound ground beef
- 1 large onion, chopped
- 1 large green pepper, chopped
- 1 can (16 ounces) kidney beans, rinsed and drained
- 1 can (15-1/4 ounces) whole kernel corn, drained
- 1 can (15 ounces) tomato sauce
- 1 can (14-1/2 ounces) diced tomatoes, undrained
- 1 can (4 ounces) chopped green chilies
- 2 teaspoons chili powder
- 1 teaspoon salt
- 1 teaspoon ground cumin
- 1/2 teaspoon sugar
- 1/2 teaspoon garlic powder

CORN BREAD BISCUITS:
- 1 cup all-purpose flour
- 1 cup cornmeal
- 2 teaspoons baking powder
- 1/8 teaspoon salt
- 1 egg
- 1/2 cup milk
- 1/2 cup sour cream

1. In a Dutch oven over medium heat, cook beef, onion and green pepper until meat is no longer pink; drain. Add the next 10 ingredients; bring to a boil, stirring occasionally. Reduce heat. Cover; simmer 10 minutes.

2. In a bowl, combine flour, cornmeal, baking powder and salt. Beat egg, milk and sour cream until smooth; stir into dry ingredients just until moistened.

3. Transfer chili to an ungreased 13-in. x 9-in. x 2-in. baking dish. Drop batter by heaping teaspoonfuls onto hot chili. Bake, uncovered, at 400° for 15-17 minutes or until biscuits are lightly browned. **Yield:** 8 servings (about 2 quarts).

✿✿✿
Hungarian Goulash Soup
(Pictured above)

Betty Kennedy, Alexandria, Virginia

I taught with the Defense Department in Germany where goulash soup is common. I pieced this together once I got back.

- 3 bacon strips, diced
- 1 small green pepper, seeded and chopped
- 2 medium onions, chopped
- 1 garlic clove, minced
- 1-1/2 pounds beef stew meat, cut into 1/2-inch cubes
- 2 tablespoons paprika
- 1-1/2 teaspoons salt

Pepper to taste

Dash sugar
- 1 can (14-1/2 ounces) stewed tomatoes, cut up
- 3 cups beef broth
- 2 large potatoes, peeled and diced
- 1/2 cup sour cream, optional

1. In a Dutch oven or soup kettle, cook bacon until almost crisp. Add green pepper, onion and garlic; cook until tender. Add beef cubes and brown on all sides. Sprinkle with paprika, salt, pepper and sugar; stir and cook for 2 minutes. Add tomatoes and broth.

2. Cover; simmer about 1-1/2 hours or until beef is tender. About 1/2 hour before serving, add potatoes; cook until tender. Garnish each serving with a dollop of sour cream if desired. **Yield:** 8 servings (about 2 quarts).

How to Make a Super Soup

Here are a few pointers to make homemade soups more flavorful:

- Soups that are made a day in advance and refrigerated overnight will have time to meld flavors.
- Whenever you cook meat or vegetables in liquid, save the unused liquid to make a tasty base for your next soup. Simply freeze the broth until you're ready to make soup.
- For a quick thickener for soup, add 1 tablespoon of instant mashed potato flakes. Allow soup to cook for a minute or so before checking its consistency. Add another tablespoon if needed. If you don't have instant potato flakes, puree leftover cooked potatoes or rice mixed with a little water. Add 1 tablespoon at a time, as indicated above.

- Remove as much fat from soup as you can before thickening it. Remove fat with a baster or soak it up with paper towels.
- Some herbs lose their flavor with prolonged cooking. Taste-test your soup when the cooking time is complete. Add additional herbs if necessary.
- Plan to make soup on the day after you're serving a lot of fresh vegetables with dinner. The leftover veggies can go into your soup.

Creamy Asparagus Chowder

(Pictured at right)

Shirley Beachum, Shelby, Michigan

While this soup's good with fresh asparagus, it can also be prepared with frozen or canned asparagus. In fact, I like to blanch and freeze asparagus in portions just right for the recipe—that way, I can make our favorite chowder all year.

  1/4 cup butter
    2 medium onions, chopped
    2 cups chopped celery
    1 garlic clove, minced
  1/2 cup all-purpose flour
    1 large potato, peeled and cut into 1/2-inch cubes
    4 cups milk
    4 cups chicken broth
  1/2 teaspoon dried thyme
  1/2 teaspoon dried marjoram
    4 cups chopped fresh asparagus, cooked and drained
Salt and pepper to taste
Sliced almonds
Shredded cheddar cheese
Chopped fresh tomato

1. In a Dutch oven, melt butter; saute onions, celery and garlic until tender. Stir in flour. Add potato, milk, broth and herbs; cook over low heat, stirring occasionally, until the potato is tender and soup is thickened, about 20-30 minutes.

2. Add asparagus, salt and pepper; heat through. To serve, sprinkle with almonds, cheese and chopped tomato. **Yield:** 10 servings (about 2-1/2 quarts).

7 tablespoons butter, *divided*
1-1/2 cups day-old bread cubes
3 large onions, quartered and thinly sliced
1-1/2 cups water
4-1/2 teaspoons chicken bouillon granules
1/4 cup all-purpose flour
1-3/4 cups milk, *divided*
1-1/2 cups (6 ounces) shredded Swiss cheese, *divided*
Pepper to taste
Fresh minced chives *or* parsley

🎀 🎀 🎀

Creamy Swiss Onion Soup

(Pictured above and on back cover)

I. MacKay Starr, North Saanich, British Columbia

It was a cool spring day when I came up with this sweet and creamy variation of traditional baked French onion soup. I top individual bowls with toasty buttered croutons and a sprinkling of Swiss cheese, then pop them under the broiler. The rich results are delightful!

1. Melt 3 tablespoons of butter; toss with bread cubes. Place on a lightly greased baking sheet. Bake at 350° for 7 minutes; turn and bake 7 minutes longer or until toasted.

2. Meanwhile, in a large saucepan, saute onions in remaining butter until lightly browned, about 12 minutes. Stir in water and bouillon; bring to a boil. Reduce heat; cover and simmer for 15 minutes.

3. Combine flour and 1/2 cup milk until smooth; gradually stir into onion mixture. Stir in remaining milk. Bring to a boil; boil for 2 minutes, stirring until thickened. Reduce heat to low; stir in 3/4 cup Swiss cheese and pepper.

4. Ladle into four ovenproof bowls; sprinkle with reserved croutons and remaining cheese. Broil 4 in. from the heat until cheese is melted and bubbly. Garnish with chives. **Yield:** 4 servings.

🎀 🎀 🎀

Cola Burgers

(Pictured at right)

Melva Baumer, Millmont, Pennsylvania

A friend who's an excellent cook shared this hamburger recipe with me, and it has since become a family favorite. The unusual combination of cola and French salad dressing added to the ground beef gives it fabulous flavor.

1 egg
1/2 cup cola,* *divided*
1/2 cup crushed saltines (about 15 crackers)
6 tablespoons French salad dressing, *divided*
2 tablespoons grated Parmesan cheese
1/4 teaspoon salt
1-1/2 pounds ground beef
6 hamburger buns, split

1. In a bowl, combine the egg, 1/4 cup cola, cracker crumbs, 2 tablespoons salad dressing, Parmesan cheese and salt. Add beef and mix well. Shape into six 3/4-in.-thick patties (the mixture will be moist). In a bowl, combine the remaining cola and salad dressing; set aside.

2. Grill patties, uncovered, over medium-hot heat for 3 minutes on each side. Brush with cola mixture. Grill 8-10 minutes longer or until juices run clear, basting and turning occasionally. Serve on buns. **Yield:** 6 servings.

   Editor's Note: Diet cola is not recommended for this recipe.

🎀🎀🎀
Zesty Colorado Chili
(Pictured above)

Beverly Bowman, Conifer, Colorado

Chili is a hearty winter staple up here in the mountains—especially for outdoor lovers like my husband and me!

1 pound Italian sausage
1 pound pork shoulder
2 pounds ground beef
2 medium onions, chopped
1 large green pepper, chopped
1 tablespoon minced garlic
3 cans (10-3/4 ounces *each*) tomato puree
1 can (28 ounces) diced tomatoes, undrained
1 cup beef broth
1 jalapeno pepper, seeded and minced*
2 tablespoons brown sugar
1 tablespoon vinegar
2 teaspoons chili powder

2 teaspoons ground cumin
1 to 2 teaspoons crushed red pepper flakes
1 teaspoon dried basil
1 teaspoon dried oregano
1/2 teaspoon hot pepper sauce
2 cans (16 ounces *each*) kidney beans, rinsed and drained

1. Cut sausage into 1/2-in. pieces. Trim fat from pork and cut into 1/2-in. pieces. In a 5-qt. kettle or Dutch oven over medium heat, cook sausage, pork and beef until no longer pink; drain, discarding all but 1 tablespoon of drippings. Set meat aside.

2. Saute onions, green pepper and garlic in drippings until tender. Add the next 12 ingredients. Return meat to the pan; bring to a boil. Reduce heat; cover and simmer for 1 hour. Add the beans and heat through.
Yield: 12-14 servings (3-1/2 quarts).

*Editor's Note: When cutting or seeding hot peppers, use rubber or plastic gloves to protect your hands. Avoid touching your face.

🎖🎖🎖
Chunky Seafood Chowder

(Pictured at left)

Irene Craigue, Claremont, New Hampshire

This creamy chowder, brimming with tender potato and crab, tastes so good guests will never guess it starts with canned soup. Half-and-half cream makes it rich enough for special occasions. I often serve it with crackers or French bread after a sporting event or outing.

- 1 **medium onion, chopped**
- 2 **tablespoons butter**
- 2 **pints half-and-half cream**
- 1 **can (10-3/4 ounces) condensed New England clam chowder, undiluted**
- 3 **medium potatoes, peeled and cubed**
- 1 **teaspoon salt**
- 1/4 **teaspoon white pepper**
- 1 **package (8 ounces) imitation crabmeat, flaked**

1. In a saucepan, saute onion in butter until tender. Add cream and canned chowder; bring to a boil. Stir in the potatoes, salt and pepper.

2. Reduce heat; simmer, uncovered, for 15-20 minutes or until the potatoes are tender. Stir in crab and heat through. **Yield:** 8 servings (about 2 quarts).

🎖🎖🎖
Barbecued Beef Sandwiches

(Pictured on page 40)

Denise Marshall, Bagley, Wisconsin

The great thing about this recipe—especially for non-cabbage lovers—is that you can't taste the cabbage in the meat. Yet, at the same time, it adds a nice heartiness and moistness to it. I credit my mother for my love for cooking. My grandmother, too…I remember how she made barbecued beef on weekends when grandkids visited.

- 2 **pounds beef stew meat**
- 2 **cups water**
- 4 **cups shredded cabbage**
- 1/2 **cup bottled barbecue sauce**
- 1/2 **cup ketchup**
- 1/3 **cup Worcestershire sauce**
- 1 **tablespoon prepared horseradish**
- 1 **tablespoon prepared mustard**
- 10 **hamburger *or* other sandwich buns, split**

1. In a covered Dutch oven or saucepan, simmer beef in water for 1-1/2 hours or until tender. Drain cooking liquid, reserving 3/4 cup.

2. Cool beef; shred and return to the Dutch oven. Add cabbage, barbecue sauce, ketchup, Worcestershire sauce, horseradish, mustard and the reserved cooking liquid. Cover and simmer for 1 hour. Serve warm in buns. **Yield:** 10 servings.

Add Flavor to Barbecue Sauce

This sandwich recipe calls for 1/2 cup of bottled barbecue sauce. What should you do with the rest of the bottle?

Jazz up the flavor and make it your own secret recipe by adding extra ingredients to the basic sauce, then coat chicken, ribs or other meat with the sauce and head for the grill.

Some flavor enhancers:

- Minced onion, garlic and green pepper
- Lemon (or lime) juice or zest
- Soy sauce
- Worcestershire sauce
- Maple syrup, honey, molasses or brown sugar
- Chopped fresh basil, cilantro, parsley or oregano

🎀🎀🎀
Stir-Fried Pork Soup

(Pictured at right)

Louise Johnson, Harriman, Tennessee

Especially to guests who enjoy the variety of Chinese cooking, this is a treat. I like serving it with fried noodles or rice as a side dish.

2/3 **pound boneless pork loin, cut into thin strips**
1 **cup sliced fresh mushrooms**
1 **cup chopped celery**
1/2 **cup diced carrots**
2 **tablespoons vegetable oil**
6 **cups chicken broth**
1/2 **cup chopped fresh spinach**
2 **tablespoons cornstarch**
3 **tablespoons cold water**
1 **egg, lightly beaten**
Pepper to taste

1. In a 3-qt. saucepan, stir-fry pork, mushrooms, celery and carrots in oil until pork is browned and vegetables are tender. Add broth and spinach.

2. Combine cornstarch and water to make a thin paste;

stir into the soup. Return to a boil; boil for 1 minute. Quickly stir in egg. Add pepper. Serve immediately. **Yield:** 4-6 servings.

🎀🎀🎀
Super Sloppy Joes

(Pictured below)

Ellen Stringer, Fairmont, West Virginia

Mother made these fresh-tasting sloppy joes many times when I was growing up. She passed the recipe on to me when I got married. My brother-in-law says they're the best sandwiches he's ever tasted. He ought to know—his name is Joe.

2 **pounds ground beef**
1/2 **cup chopped onion**
2 **celery ribs with leaves, chopped**
1/4 **cup chopped green pepper**
1-2/3 **cups canned crushed tomatoes**
1/4 **cup ketchup**
2 **tablespoons brown sugar**
1 **tablespoon vinegar**
1 **tablespoon Worcestershire sauce**
1 **tablespoon steak sauce**
1/2 **teaspoon garlic salt**
1/4 **teaspoon ground mustard**
1/4 **teaspoon paprika**
8 **to 10 hamburger buns, split**

1. In a Dutch oven over medium heat, cook beef, onion, celery and green pepper until the meat is no longer pink and the vegetables are tender; drain. Add the next nine ingredients; mix well.

2. Simmer, uncovered, for 35-40 minutes, stirring occasionally. Spoon 1/2 cup meat mixture onto each bun. **Yield:** 8-10 servings.

🎗🎗🎗
Meatball Mushroom Soup

(Pictured below)

JoAnn Abbott, Kerhonkson, New York

This creamy, super-thick soup is hearty with meatballs, mushrooms, barley, macaroni and rice. With dinner rolls or breadsticks, it's a simple and satisfying meal for my husband and me on a rainy day. Leftovers easily reheat for a fast, filling lunch or dinner.

1/2 pound ground beef
2 cans (10-3/4 ounces *each*) condensed cream of mushroom soup, undiluted
1-1/3 cups milk
1-1/3 cups water
1 teaspoon Italian seasoning
1 teaspoon dried minced onion
1/2 teaspoon dried minced garlic
1/4 cup quick-cooking barley
1/4 cup uncooked elbow macaroni
1/4 cup uncooked long grain rice
1 medium carrot, shredded
1 jar (4-1/2 ounces) sliced mushrooms, drained
2 tablespoons grated Parmesan cheese

1. Shape beef into 1-in. balls; set aside. In a large saucepan, combine soup, milk and water; bring to a boil. Add Italian seasoning, onion, garlic, barley, macaroni and rice. Reduce heat; simmer, uncovered, for 15 minutes.

2. Meanwhile, cook meatballs in a nonstick skillet until no longer pink. Stir carrot into soup; cover and simmer for 5 minutes. Use a slotted spoon to transfer meatballs to soup. Stir in mushrooms and Parmesan cheese; heat through. **Yield:** 6 servings.

🎗🎗🎗
Northwest Salmon Chowder

(Pictured at right)

Josephine Parton, Granger, Washington

I've lived on a farm in the Yakima Valley all my life. I have a big garden, and by the end of fall, my cellar shelves are full of canned fruits and vegetables. This recipe uses some of the root vegetables I grow...along with the delicious salmon that is so plentiful here.

1/2 cup *each* chopped celery, onion and green pepper
1 garlic clove, minced
3 tablespoons butter
1 can (14-1/2 ounces) chicken broth
1 cup uncooked diced peeled potatoes
1 cup shredded carrots
1-1/2 teaspoons salt
1/2 teaspoon pepper
1/4 to 3/4 teaspoon dill weed
1 can (14-3/4 ounces) cream-style corn
2 cups half-and-half cream
1-3/4 to 2 cups fully cooked salmon chunks *or* 1 can (14-3/4 ounces) salmon, drained, flaked, bones and skin removed

1. In a large saucepan, saute celery, onion, green pepper and garlic in butter until the vegetables are tender. Add broth, potatoes, carrots, salt, pepper and dill; bring to a boil.

2. Reduce heat; cover and simmer for 40 minutes or until the vegetables are nearly tender. Stir in the corn, cream and salmon. Simmer for 15 minutes or until heated through. **Yield:** 8 servings (2 quarts).

Corny Tomato Dumpling Soup

(Pictured above)

Jackie Ferris, Tiverton, Ontario

I have a big garden on our farm and enjoy cooking with my harvest. In this savory tomato soup, corn stars in both the broth and dumplings. Ground beef makes it a hearty first course or satisfying light main dish.

    1 pound ground beef
    3 cups fresh *or* frozen corn
    1 can (28 ounces) diced tomatoes, undrained
    2 cans (14-1/2 ounces *each*) beef broth
    1 cup chopped onion
    1 garlic clove, minced
1-1/2 teaspoons dried basil
1-1/2 teaspoons dried thyme
  1/2 teaspoon dried rosemary, crushed
Salt and pepper to taste
CORN DUMPLINGS:

    1 cup all-purpose flour
  1/2 cup cornmeal
2-1/2 teaspoons baking powder
  1/2 teaspoon salt
    1 egg
  2/3 cup milk
    1 cup fresh *or* frozen corn
  1/2 cup shredded cheddar cheese
    1 tablespoon minced fresh parsley

1. In a large saucepan or Dutch oven over medium heat, cook beef until no longer pink; drain. Stir in corn, tomatoes, broth, onion, garlic and seasonings. Bring to a boil. Reduce heat; cover and simmer for 30-45 minutes.

2. For dumplings, combine flour, cornmeal, baking powder and salt in a bowl. In another bowl, beat egg; stir in milk, corn, cheese and parsley. Stir into dry ingredients just until moistened.

3. Drop by tablespoonfuls onto simmering soup. Cover and simmer for 15 minutes or until a toothpick inserted in a dumpling comes out clean (do not lift cover while simmering). **Yield:** 8 servings (about 2 quarts).

1/3 cup uncooked wild rice
 1 tablespoon vegetable oil
 1 quart water
 1 medium onion, chopped
 1 celery rib, finely chopped
 1 carrot, finely chopped
1/2 cup butter
1/2 cup all-purpose flour
 3 cups chicken broth
 2 cups half-and-half cream
1/2 teaspoon dried rosemary, crushed
 1 teaspoon salt

1. Rinse rice; drain. In a medium saucepan, combine rice, oil and water; bring to a boil. Reduce heat; cover and simmer for 30 minutes.

2. Meanwhile, in a Dutch oven or soup kettle, cook onion, celery and carrots in butter until vegetables are almost tender. Blend in flour; cook and stir for 2 minutes. Add broth and *undrained* rice. Bring to a boil; cook and stir until slightly thickened. Stir in cream, rosemary and salt.

3. Reduce heat; simmer, uncovered, for about 20 minutes or until rice is tender. **Yield:** 8 servings (about 2 quarts).

🎀 🎀 🎀

Wild Rice Soup

(Pictured above)

Elienore Myhre, Balaton, Minnesota

As the oldest of eight girls growing up on the farm, I began cooking at an early age. This soup—which I first had at my sister's house—brings compliments wherever I serve it.

🎀 🎀 🎀

Southern Chicken Rice Soup

(Pictured at right)

Rosalie Biar, Thorndale, Texas

A favorite at soup night at our church, this recipe's one my husband concocted after he retired. I frequently find it on the table when I get home from work.

 1 broiler/fryer chicken (about 3 pounds)
10 cups water
 2 teaspoons salt
1/2 cup uncooked long grain rice
1/2 cup chopped onion
1/2 cup chopped celery
1/2 cup thinly sliced carrots
1/2 cup sliced fresh *or* frozen okra
 1 can (14-1/2 ounces) stewed tomatoes, diced
 1 tablespoon chopped green chilies
 1 garlic clove, minced
1-1/2 teaspoons chili powder
 1 teaspoon seasoned salt
1/2 teaspoon lemon-pepper seasoning
1/2 teaspoon Creole seasoning

1. Place chicken, water and salt in a soup kettle or Dutch oven. Bring to a boil; skim foam from broth. Reduce heat; cover and simmer for 1 to 1-1/2 hours or until the chicken is tender.

2. Remove chicken; when cool enough to handle, debone and dice. Skim fat from broth. Add rice, vegetables and seasonings. Cook, uncovered, over medium heat for 30 minutes. Add the chicken. Simmer for 30 minutes or until vegetables are tender. **Yield:** 10 servings (about 2-1/2 quarts).

Spicy Cheeseburger Soup

(Pictured at right)

Lisa Mast, White Cloud, Michigan

This creamy soup brings my family to the table in a hurry. I love the warming zip of cayenne, but it also tastes terrific without it if you like milder flavor. With a few simple side dishes, this soup is a full meal.

1-1/2 cups water
    2 cups cubed peeled potatoes
    2 small carrots, grated
    1 small onion, chopped
  1/4 cup chopped green pepper
    1 jalapeno pepper, seeded and chopped*
    1 garlic clove, minced
    1 tablespoon beef bouillon granules
  1/2 teaspoon salt
    1 pound ground beef, cooked and drained
2-1/2 cups milk, *divided*
    3 tablespoons all-purpose flour
    8 ounces process American cheese, cubed
  1/4 to 1 teaspoon cayenne pepper, optional
  1/2 pound sliced bacon, cooked and crumbled

1. In a large saucepan, combine the first nine ingredients; bring to a boil. Reduce heat; cover and simmer for 15-20 minutes or until potatoes are tender.

2. Stir in beef and 2 cups of milk; heat through. Combine flour and remaining milk until smooth; gradually stir into soup. Bring to a boil; cook and stir for 2 minutes or until thickened and bubbly. Reduce heat; stir in cheese until melted. Add cayenne if desired. Top with bacon just before serving. **Yield:** 6-8 servings (about 2 quarts).

*Editor's Note: When cutting or seeding hot peppers, use rubber or plastic gloves to protect your hands. Avoid touching your face.

Lentil Barley Soup

(Pictured on page 40)

Anita Warner, Mt. Crawford, Virginia

Soups are one of my favorite things to prepare—they're so easy, and nothing is better on a chilly evening with some homemade bread or biscuits.

    1 medium onion, chopped
  1/2 cup chopped green pepper
    3 garlic cloves, minced
    1 tablespoon butter
    1 can (49-1/2 ounces) chicken broth
    3 medium carrots, chopped
  1/2 cup dried lentils
1-1/2 teaspoons Italian seasoning
    1 teaspoon salt
  1/4 teaspoon pepper
    1 cup cubed cooked chicken *or* turkey
  1/2 cup quick-cooking barley
    2 medium fresh mushrooms, chopped
    1 can (28 ounces) crushed tomatoes, undrained

1. In a Dutch oven or soup kettle, saute the onion, green pepper and garlic in butter until tender. Add the broth, carrots, lentils, Italian seasoning, salt and pepper; bring to a boil. Reduce the heat; cover and simmer for 25 minutes.

2. Add chicken, barley and mushrooms; return to a boil. Reduce heat; cover and simmer for 10-15 minutes or until the lentils, barley and carrots are tender. Add tomatoes; heat through. **Yield:** 8-10 servings (about 2-1/2 quarts).

Tasty Reuben Soup

(Pictured at right)

Terry Ann Brandt, Tobias, Nebraska

I'm a working mom with limited time to feed my hungry family, so I'm always looking for quick recipes. This soup (which may remind you of a Reuben sandwich) is a favorite of ours.

 Uses less fat, sugar or salt. Includes Nutritional Analysis and Diabetic Exchanges.

- 4 cans (14-1/2 ounces *each*) chicken broth
- 4 cups shredded cabbage
- 2 cups uncooked medium egg noodles
- 1 pound fully cooked kielbasa *or* Polish sausage, halved and cut into 1-inch slices
- 1/2 cup chopped onion
- 1 teaspoon caraway seeds
- 1/4 teaspoon garlic powder
- 1 cup (4 ounces) shredded Swiss cheese

1. In a large saucepan, combine the first seven ingredients; bring to a boil.

2. Reduce heat; cover and simmer for 15 minutes or until cabbage and noodles are tender. Garnish with cheese. **Yield:** 10 servings (2-1/2 quarts).

Nutritional Analysis: One 1-cup serving (prepared with reduced-sodium chicken broth, reduced-fat turkey kielbasa and reduced-fat cheese) equals 125 calories, 455 mg sodium, 41 mg cholesterol, 9 gm carbohydrate, 12 gm protein, 5 gm fat. **Diabetic Exchanges:** 1 meat, 1 vegetable, 1/2 starch.

Spicy White Chili

(Pictured below)

Carlene Bailey, Bradenton, Florida

I thought the original version of this dish was fine. But my son can't get enough spice, so I added green chilies and other seasonings until I created a quick and easy chili he's wild about.

- 2 medium onions, chopped
- 1 tablespoon vegetable oil
- 4 garlic cloves, minced
- 2 cans (4 ounces *each*) chopped green chilies
- 2 teaspoons ground cumin
- 1 teaspoon dried oregano
- 1/4 teaspoon cayenne pepper
- 1/4 teaspoon ground cloves
- 2 cans (14-1/2 ounces *each*) chicken broth
- 4 cups cubed cooked chicken
- 3 cans (15-1/2 ounces *each*) great northern beans, rinsed and drained
- 2 cups (8 ounces) shredded Monterey Jack cheese

Sour cream and sliced jalapeno peppers*, optional

1. In a large saucepan, saute onions in oil until tender. Stir in garlic, chilies, cumin, oregano, cayenne and cloves; cook and stir 2-3 minutes more. Add broth, chicken and beans; simmer, uncovered, for 15 minutes.

2. Remove from the heat. Stir in cheese until melted. Garnish with sour cream and jalapeno peppers if desired. **Yield:** 6-8 servings (2-1/4 quarts).

*Editor's Note: When cutting or seeding hot peppers, use rubber or plastic gloves to protect your hands. Avoid touching your face.

Tomato Dill Bisque

(Pictured at right)

Susan Breckbill, Lincoln University, Pennsylvania

My family really enjoys this soup when we make it from our garden tomatoes. When those tomatoes are plentiful, I make a big batch (without mayonnaise) and freeze it. Then we can enjoy it even after the garden is gone for the season.

✓ Uses less fat, sugar or salt. Includes Nutritional Analysis and Diabetic Exchanges.

- 2 medium onions, chopped
- 1 garlic clove, minced
- 2 tablespoons butter
- 2 pounds tomatoes, peeled and chopped
- 1/2 cup water
- 1 chicken bouillon cube
- 1 teaspoon sugar
- 1 teaspoon dill weed
- 1/2 teaspoon salt
- 1/4 teaspoon pepper
- 1/2 cup mayonnaise, optional

1. In a large saucepan, saute onions and garlic in butter until tender. Add tomatoes, water, bouillon, sugar and seasonings. Cover and simmer 10 minutes or until

tomatoes are tender. Remove from heat; cool.

2. Puree in a blender or food processor. Return to saucepan. If a creamy soup is desired, stir in mayonnaise. Cook and stir over low heat until heated through. Serve warm. **Yield:** 5 servings (5 cups).

Nutritional Analysis: One serving (prepared without mayonnaise) equals 108 calories, 572 mg sodium, 0 cholesterol, 14 gm carbohydrate, 3 gm protein, 5 gm fat. **Diabetic Exchanges:** 2 vegetable, 1 fat.

Chunky Cheese Soup

(Pictured below)

Gertrude Slabach, Virgilina, Virginia

Although winters in Virginia are not necessarily harsh, it still gets cold enough to chill you to the bones. This tasty soup warms you through and through.

- 2 cups water
- 2 cups diced peeled potatoes
- 1/2 cup diced carrot
- 1/2 cup chopped celery
- 1/4 cup chopped onion
- 1-1/2 teaspoons salt
- 1/4 teaspoon pepper
- 1 cup cubed fully cooked ham*
- 1/4 cup butter
- 1/4 cup all-purpose flour
- 2 cups milk
- 2 cups (8 ounces) shredded cheddar cheese

1. In a large saucepan, combine the first seven ingredients; bring to a boil. Reduce heat; cover and simmer until the vegetables are tender. Add ham.

2. In another saucepan, melt the butter; stir in flour until smooth. Gradually add milk. Bring to a boil; cook and stir for 2 minutes or until thickened. Stir in cheese until melted; add to the soup. **Yield:** 6-8 servings.

*Editor's Note: In place of the ham, one of the following can be substituted—6 ounces of tuna or salmon; 1 cup of cooked ground beef or bulk pork sausage; or 1 pound of bacon, cooked and crumbled.

Meatball Lover's Sandwich

(Pictured above)

Kelly Gerhardt, Council Bluffs, Iowa

You'll find that these hearty sandwiches will satisfy even the healthiest appetites. My husband and our three children love them! I like the fact that the recipe makes a big batch of meatballs with tangy sauce.

      2 eggs
  1/3 cup milk
      2 cups soft bread crumbs
  1/2 cup finely chopped onion
1-1/2 teaspoons salt
      2 pounds ground beef
      2 garlic cloves, minced
      1 teaspoon butter
      1 cup ketchup
  2/3 cup chili sauce
  1/4 cup packed brown sugar
      2 tablespoons Worcestershire sauce
      2 tablespoons prepared mustard
      2 teaspoons celery seed
  1/2 teaspoon salt
  1/4 teaspoon hot pepper sauce
      8 hoagie buns *or* submarine rolls, split
      1 large onion, sliced

1. In a bowl, beat eggs and milk. Stir in bread crumbs, chopped onion and salt. Add beef; mix well. Shape into 1-in. balls. Place in a lightly greased 15-in. x 10-in. x 1-in. baking pan. Bake, uncovered, at 375° for 15-20 minutes or until meat is no longer pink.

2. In a saucepan, saute garlic in butter. Add ketchup, chili sauce, brown sugar, Worcestershire sauce, mustard, celery seed, salt and hot pepper sauce. Bring to a boil; add meatballs. Reduce heat; cover and simmer for 20 minutes or until heated through, stirring occasionally.

3. Carefully hollow out buns, leaving a 1/2-in. shell. Spoon meatball mixture into buns; top with sliced onion. **Yield:** 8 servings.

Pronto Taco Soup

(Pictured at right and on back cover)

Priscilla Gilbert, Indian Harbour Beach, Florida

When out-of-state friends dropped by, I invited them to stay for dinner, knowing that I could put together this mild, chili-flavored soup in a jiffy. I served it with cornmeal muffins and a crisp salad for a filling meal everyone loved. My guests even asked for the recipe before leaving!

  1 **pound ground beef**
  1 **medium onion, chopped**
  2 **garlic cloves, minced**
  2 **cans (14-1/2 ounces *each*) beef broth**
  1 **can (14-1/2 ounces) diced tomatoes, undrained**
1-1/2 **cups picante sauce**
  1 **cup uncooked spiral *or* small shell pasta**
  1 **medium green pepper, chopped**
  2 **teaspoons chili powder**
  1 **teaspoon dried parsley flakes**
Shredded cheddar cheese and tortilla chips

1. In a large saucepan, cook beef, onion and garlic until meat is no longer pink; drain. Add the broth, tomatoes, picante sauce, pasta, green pepper, chili powder and parsley. Bring to a boil, stirring occasionally.

2. Reduce heat; cover and simmer for 10-15 minutes or until pasta is tender. Garnish with cheese and tortilla chips. **Yield:** 8 servings (2 quarts).

Best-Ever Potato Soup

(Pictured below)

Coleen Morrissey, Sweet Valley, Pennsylvania

You'll be surprised at the taste of this rich, cheesy concoction— it's not a typical potato soup. I came up with the recipe after enjoying baked potato soup at one of our favorite restaurants. I added bacon, and we think that makes it even better.

  6 **bacon strips, diced**
  3 **cups cubed peeled potatoes**
  1 **can (14-1/2 ounces) chicken broth**
  1 **small carrot, grated**
1/2 **cup chopped onion**
  1 **tablespoon dried parsley flakes**
1/2 **teaspoon *each* celery seed, salt and pepper**
  3 **tablespoons all-purpose flour**
  3 **cups milk**
  8 **ounces process American cheese, cubed**
  2 **green onions, thinly sliced, optional**

1. In a large saucepan, cook bacon until crisp; drain. Add potatoes, broth, carrot, onion, parsley, celery seed, salt and pepper. Cover and simmer until potatoes are tender, about 15 minutes.

2. Combine flour and milk until smooth; add to soup. Bring to a boil; boil and stir for 2 minutes. Add cheese; stir until cheese is melted and the soup is heated through. Garnish with green onions if desired. **Yield:** 8 servings (2 quarts).

Sweet Raspberry Muffins, p. 66

Burst o' Lemon Muffins, p. 74

Bacon Potato
Pancakes, p. 73

Breakfast Wassail, p. 69

Breakfast & Brunch

You'll find this chapter especially helpful when you have weekend guests and you want to treat them to a memorable breakfast. Any of the winners from our national muffin contest is sure to do the trick. Or how about some warm, gooey rolls?

Dijon Ham Muffins, p. 70

Chocolate Cookie Muffins...................66
Sweet Raspberry Muffins.................66
Caramel Pecan Rolls 67
Cinnamon Rolls in a Snap 68
Egg and Corn Quesadilla 68
Cherry Almond Muffins 69
Breakfast Wassail..............................69
Orange-Raisin Sticky Muffins 70
Dijon Ham Muffins 70
Morning Orange Drink......................71
Cappuccino Mix 72
Morning Maple Muffins 72

Mashed Potato Cinnamon Rolls 73
Bacon Potato Pancakes......................73
Burst o' Lemon Muffins 74
Apple Nut Muffins 74
Hash Brown Egg Dish 75
Cocoa Macaroon Muffins 75
Cappuccino Muffins 76
Fudgy Banana Muffins 77
Crustless Swiss Quiche......................77
Sunrise Mini Pizzas 78
Spiced Pear Muffins 78
Sticky Bun Coffee Ring 79

🎀 🎀 🎀

Chocolate Cookie Muffins

(Pictured above)

Jan Blue, Cuyahoga Falls, Ohio

These fun muffins are a double treat—like eating muffins and cookies at the same time.

1-3/4 cups all-purpose flour
1/4 cup sugar

---

3 teaspoons baking powder
1/3 cup cold butter
1 egg
1 cup milk
16 cream-filled chocolate sandwich cookies, coarsely chopped
TOPPING:
3 tablespoons all-purpose flour
3 tablespoons sugar
5 cream-filled chocolate sandwich cookies, finely crushed
2 tablespoons cold butter
1 cup vanilla *or* white chips
1 tablespoon shortening

1. In a large bowl, combine flour, sugar and baking powder. Cut in butter until mixture resembles coarse crumbs.

2. Beat egg and milk; stir into dry ingredients just until moistened. Fold in chopped cookies. Fill greased muffin cups two-thirds full.

3. For topping, combine the flour, sugar and crushed cookies. Cut in the butter until crumbly; sprinkle about 1 tablespoon over each muffin.

4. Bake at 400° for 16-18 minutes or until a toothpick comes out clean. Cool for 5 minutes before removing from pan to a wire rack.

5. In a heavy saucepan over low heat, melt vanilla chips and shortening until smooth. Drizzle over cooled muffins. **Yield:** 1 dozen.

🎀 🎀 🎀

Sweet Raspberry Muffins

(Pictured on page 64)

Teresa Raab, Tustin, Michigan

I like to linger over a cup of coffee and a warm sweet treat on weekend mornings. These moist muffins are perfect because making them ties up so little time in the kitchen.

2 cups biscuit/baking mix
2 tablespoons sugar
1/4 cup cold butter
2/3 cup milk
1/4 cup raspberry jam
GLAZE:
1/2 cup confectioners' sugar
2 teaspoons warm water
1/4 teaspoon vanilla extract

1. In a bowl, combine biscuit mix and sugar. Cut in butter until the mixture resembles coarse crumbs. Stir in milk just until moistened (batter will be thick).

2. Spoon about 1 tablespoon of batter into 12 paper-lined muffin cups. Top with 1 teaspoon jam. Spoon the remaining batter (about 1 tablespoon each) over jam.

3. Bake at 425° for 12-14 minutes or until lightly browned. Cool in pans for 5 minutes.

4. Meanwhile, in a small bowl, combine glaze ingredients until smooth. Remove muffins to a wire rack. Drizzle with glaze. **Yield:** 1 dozen.

Caramel Pecan Rolls

(Pictured above)

Carolyn Buschkamp, Emmetsburg, Iowa

There's not a better Christmas morning treat than these outstanding rolls. I make them every year.

- **2 cups milk**
- **1/2 cup water**
- **1/2 cup sugar**
- **1/2 cup butter**
- **1/3 cup cornmeal**
- **2 teaspoons salt**
- **7 to 7-1/2 cups all-purpose flour,** *divided*
- **2 packages (1/4 ounce** *each***) active dry yeast**
- **2 eggs**

TOPPING:
- **2 cups packed brown sugar**
- **1/2 cup butter**
- **1/2 cup milk**
- **1/2 to 1 cup chopped pecans**

FILLING:
- **1/4 cup butter, softened**
- **1/2 cup sugar**
- **2 teaspoons ground cinnamon**

1. In a saucepan, combine first six ingredients; bring to a boil, stirring frequently. Set aside to cool to 120°-130°.

2. In a mixing bowl, combine 2 cups flour and yeast. Add cooled cornmeal mixture; beat on low until smooth. Add eggs and 1 cup of flour; mix for 1 minute. Stir in enough remaining flour to form a soft dough. Turn onto a floured surface; knead until smooth and elastic, about 6-8 minutes. Place in a greased bowl, turning once to grease top. Cover and let rise in a warm place until doubled, about 1 hour.

3. Combine the first three topping ingredients in a saucepan; bring to a boil, stirring occasionally. Pour into two greased 13-in. x 9-in. x 2-in. baking pans. Sprinkle with pecans; set aside.

4. Punch dough down; divide in half. Roll each into a 12-in. x 15-in. rectangle; spread with butter. Combine sugar and cinnamon; sprinkle over butter. Roll up dough from one long side; pinch seams and turn ends under. Cut each roll into 12 slices. Place 12 slices, cut side down, in each baking pan. Cover and let rise in a warm place until nearly doubled, about 30 minutes.

5. Bake at 375° for 20-25 minutes or until golden brown. Let cool 1 minute; invert onto a serving platter. **Yield:** 2 dozen.

Cinnamon Rolls in a Snap

(Pictured above)

Laura McDermott, Big Lake, Minnesota

I turned biscuits into hot cinnamon rolls one morning because a friend was stopping by. She was impressed.

4-1/2 cups biscuit/baking mix
1-1/3 cups milk
FILLING:
  2 tablespoons butter, softened
  1/4 cup sugar
  1 teaspoon ground cinnamon
  1/3 cup raisins, optional
ICING:
  2 cups confectioners' sugar
  2 tablespoons milk
  2 tablespoons butter, melted
  1 teaspoon vanilla extract

1. In a bowl, combine biscuit mix and milk. Turn onto a floured surface; knead 8-10 times. Roll the dough into a 12-in. x 10-in. rectangle. Spread with butter. Combine sugar, cinnamon and raisins if desired; sprinkle over butter. Roll up from a long side; pinch seam to seal.

2. Cut into 12 slices; place with cut side down on a large greased baking sheet. Bake at 450° for 10-12 minutes or until golden brown.

3. Meanwhile, combine the icing ingredients; spread over rolls. Serve warm. **Yield:** 1 dozen.

Egg and Corn Quesadilla

(Pictured at right)

Stacy Joura, Stoneboro, Pennsylvania

For a deliciously different breakfast or brunch, try this excellent quesadilla. It's also great for a light lunch or supper. Corn is a natural in Southwestern cooking and a tasty addition to this zippy egg dish.

1 medium onion, chopped
1 medium green pepper, chopped
1 garlic clove, minced
2 tablespoons olive oil
3 cups fresh *or* frozen corn
1 teaspoon minced chives
1/2 teaspoon dried cilantro flakes
1/2 teaspoon salt
1/4 teaspoon pepper
4 eggs, beaten
4 flour tortillas (10 inches)
1/2 cup salsa
1 cup (8 ounces) sour cream
1 cup (4 ounces) shredded cheddar cheese
1 cup (4 ounces) shredded mozzarella cheese
Additional salsa and sour cream, optional

1. In a skillet, saute onion, green pepper and garlic in oil until tender. Add the corn, chives, cilantro, salt and pepper. Cook until heated through, about 3 minutes. Stir in eggs; cook until completely set, stirring occasionally. Remove from the heat.

2. Place one tortilla on a lightly greased baking sheet or pizza pan; top with a third of the corn mixture, salsa and sour cream. Sprinkle with a fourth of the cheeses. Repeat layers twice. Top with remaining tortilla and cheeses.

3. Bake at 350° for 10 minutes or until the cheese is melted. Cut into wedges. Serve with salsa and sour cream if desired. **Yield:** 6-8 servings.

Cherry Almond Muffins

(Pictured at right)

John Montgomery, Fortuna, California

As a kid, I loved doughnuts filled with custard or jelly. So I decided to experiment with fillings in muffins. The result was this terrific recipe with a creamy center and a nutty topping.

1-3/4 cups all-purpose flour
1/2 cup plus 1 tablespoon sugar
1/2 teaspoon baking powder
1/2 teaspoon baking soda
1/4 teaspoon salt
1/2 cup cold butter
1 egg
3/4 cup sour cream
1 teaspoon almond extract

FILLING:
1 package (8 ounces) cream cheese, softened
1 egg
1/4 cup sugar
1/2 teaspoon vanilla extract
3/4 cup cherry preserves, warmed

TOPPING:
1/3 cup all-purpose flour
2 tablespoons sugar
2 tablespoons cold butter
1/3 cup chopped sliced almonds

1. In a bowl, combine flour, sugar, baking powder, baking soda and salt. Cut in butter until the mixture resembles coarse crumbs. In another bowl, beat the egg, sour cream and extract until smooth; stir into dry ingredients just until moistened (batter will be thick).

2. In a mixing bowl, beat cream cheese, egg, sugar and vanilla until smooth. In a saucepan over low heat, warm preserves.

3. For topping, combine flour and sugar in a small bowl; cut in butter until crumbly. Stir in nuts; set aside.

4. Fill greased jumbo muffin cups half full with batter. Divide cream cheese filling and preserves evenly between muffin cups; swirl gently. Cover with remaining batter. Sprinkle with topping.

5. Bake at 350° for 30-35 minutes or until a toothpick comes out clean. Cool for 5 minutes before removing from pans to wire racks. **Yield:** 7 jumbo muffins or 14 regular muffins.

Editor's Note: If using regular-size muffin cups, bake for 20-25 minutes.

Breakfast Wassail

(Pictured on page 64)

Amy Holtsclaw, Carbondale, Illinois

This fruity beverage is great all year-round, and it's tasty hot or chilled. I got the recipe from a co-worker and made it one Christmas for a family gathering. Now whenever we get together for the holidays, I'm the designated wassail-maker.

1 bottle (64 ounces) cranberry juice
1 bottle (32 ounces) apple juice
1 can (12 ounces) frozen pineapple juice concentrate, undiluted
1 can (12 ounces) frozen lemonade concentrate, undiluted
3 to 4 cinnamon sticks
1 quart water, optional

1. In a large saucepan or Dutch oven, combine juices, lemonade and cinnamon sticks. Bring to a boil.

2. Reduce heat; cover and simmer for 1 hour. Add water if desired. Serve hot or cold. **Yield:** about 4 quarts.

1/4 cup chopped raisins
1 tablespoon sugar
1/2 teaspoon ground cinnamon
TOPPING:
1/2 cup chopped nuts
1/3 cup packed brown sugar
2 tablespoons butter, melted
2 tablespoons honey
1/4 teaspoon ground cinnamon
MUFFINS:
2 cups all-purpose flour
3 teaspoons baking powder
1/2 teaspoon salt
1 egg
2/3 cup milk
1/4 cup honey
1/3 cup butter, melted
2 tablespoons grated orange peel

1. Combine raisins, sugar and cinnamon; set aside. Combine the topping ingredients and spoon 1 teaspoonful into 12 greased muffin cups. Set aside.

2. In a bowl, combine the flour, baking powder and salt. Beat egg, milk, honey, butter and orange peel; stir into dry ingredients just until moistened. Spoon 1 tablespoon of batter into the prepared muffin cups; sprinkle with raisin mixture. Top with remaining batter.

3. Bake at 375° for 16-20 minutes or until a toothpick comes out clean. Cool for 5 minutes; invert pan onto a lightly buttered foil-lined shallow baking pan. Serve warm. **Yield:** 1 dozen.

Orange-Raisin Sticky Muffins

(Pictured above)

Sandi Ritchey, Silverton, Oregon

These finger-licking muffins have the appeal of old-fashioned sticky buns without the fuss of yeast dough. Their delightful blend of flavors comes from walnuts, raisins, cinnamon, honey and sunny orange zest. They're a sure morning eye-opener and a treat anytime.

Dijon Ham Muffins

(Pictured on page 65)

Karen Davis, Springfield, Missouri

For a nice change from sweet muffins, try this delightful hearty variety. They're easy to fix and great for breakfast with scrambled eggs or on a brunch buffet. They're also super for lunch with soup.

1-2/3 cups all-purpose flour
1/3 cup cornmeal
1/4 cup sugar
2 teaspoons baking powder
1 to 2 teaspoons ground mustard
1/2 teaspoon salt
1/2 teaspoon baking soda
1/8 teaspoon ground cloves
2 eggs
1 cup buttermilk
1/3 cup vegetable oil
3 tablespoons Dijon mustard
1 cup finely chopped fully cooked ham

1. In a bowl, combine the first eight ingredients. Combine the eggs, buttermilk, oil and mustard; stir into dry ingredients just until moistened. Fold in the ham.

2. Fill greased or paper-lined muffin cups three-fourths full. Bake at 375° for 20-25 minutes or a toothpick comes out clean. Cool for 5 minutes before removing from pans to wire racks. **Yield:** 14 muffins.

Morning Orange Drink

(Pictured above)

Joyce Mummau, Mt. Airy, Maryland

Although it requires only a few basic ingredients and little preparation, this drink always draws raves from overnight guests about its "wake-up" taste.

1 can (6 ounces) frozen orange juice concentrate
1 cup cold water
1 cup milk
1/3 cup sugar
1 teaspoon vanilla extract
10 ice cubes

Combine the first five ingredients in a blender; process at high speed. Add ice cubes, a few at a time, blending until smooth. Serve immediately. **Yield:** 4-6 servings.

Cappuccino Mix

(Pictured at left)

Susan Prillhart, Rockledge, Florida

One day, friends and I were swapping recipes for hot choco-late, and someone came up with this mix. I put it in jars as gifts for Christmas. I also keep a big batch in a large tin for us and so visitors can help themselves if they want! I've always liked to cook.

- 1 cup instant coffee creamer
- 1 cup instant chocolate drink mix
- 2/3 cup instant coffee crystals
- 1/2 cup sugar
- 1/2 teaspoon ground cinnamon
- 1/4 teaspoon ground nutmeg

1. Combine all ingredients; mix well. Store in an air-tight container.

2. To prepare one serving, add 3 tablespoons mix to 6 ounces hot water; stir well. **Yield:** 3 cups dry mix.

★ ★ ★

Morning Maple Muffins

(Pictured at right)

Elizabeth Talbot, Lexington, Kentucky

Maple combines with a subtle touch of cinnamon and nuts to give these muffins the flavor of a hearty pancake breakfast.

- 2 cups all-purpose flour
- 1/2 cup packed brown sugar
- 2 teaspoons baking powder
- 1/2 teaspoon salt
- 3/4 cup milk
- 1/2 cup butter, melted
- 1/2 cup maple syrup
- 1/4 cup sour cream
- 1 egg
- 1/2 teaspoon vanilla extract

TOPPING:

- 3 tablespoons all-purpose flour
- 3 tablespoons sugar
- 2 tablespoons chopped nuts
- 1/2 teaspoon ground cinnamon
- 2 tablespoons cold butter

1. In a large bowl, combine the flour, brown sugar, baking powder and salt. In another bowl, combine the milk, butter, syrup, sour cream, egg and vanilla. Stir into the dry ingredients just until moistened. Fill greased or paper-lined muffin cups two-thirds full.

2. For topping, combine the flour, sugar, nuts and cinnamon; cut in the butter until crumbly. Sprinkle mixture over muffins.

3. Bake at 400° for 16-20 minutes or until a toothpick comes out clean. Cool for 5 minutes before removing from pans to wire racks. **Yield:** 16 muffins.

Mashed Potato Cinnamon Rolls

(Pictured at right)

Christine Duncan, Ellensburg, Washington

Potatoes are the surprise ingredient that help keep these tempting rolls moist and yummy.

- 1/2 **pound russet potatoes, peeled and quartered**
- 2 **packages (1/4 ounce *each*) active dry yeast**
- 2 **tablespoons sugar**
- 2 **cups warm water (110° to 115°)**
- 3/4 **cup butter, melted**
- 2 **eggs, beaten**
- 3/4 **cup sugar**
- 2/3 **cup instant nonfat dry milk powder**
- 1 **tablespoon salt**
- 2 **teaspoons vanilla extract**
- 8 **cups all-purpose flour**

FILLING:
- 1/2 **cup butter, melted**
- 3/4 **cup packed brown sugar**
- 3 **tablespoons ground cinnamon**

ICING:
- 2 **cups confectioners' sugar**
- 1/4 **cup milk**
- 2 **tablespoons butter, melted**
- 1/2 **teaspoon vanilla extract**

1. Place potatoes in a saucepan and cover with water. Bring to a boil; cook until tender. Drain, reserving 1/2 cup cooking liquid; set aside. Mash potatoes; set aside 1 cup. (Save remaining potatoes for another use.) Heat reserved potato liquid to 110°-115°.

2. In a mixing bowl, dissolve yeast and sugar in potato liquid; let stand 10 minutes. Add warm water, mashed potatoes, butter, eggs, sugar, milk powder, salt, vanilla and 5 cups flour; beat until smooth. Add enough remaining flour to form a soft dough. Turn onto a floured surface; knead until smooth and elastic, about 6-8 minutes. Place in a greased bowl, turning once to grease top. Cover and chill overnight.

3. Punch dough down; divide into thirds. On a floured surface, roll each portion into a 12-in. x 8-in. rectangle; spread with butter. Combine brown sugar and cinnamon; sprinkle over the dough. Roll up from a long side; pinch seam to seal. Cut each into 12 slices; place cut side down in three greased 13-in. x 9-in. x 2-in. baking pans. Cover and let rise until almost doubled, about 45 minutes.

4. Bake at 350° for 25-30 minutes. Combine icing ingredients; drizzle over rolls. **Yield:** 3 dozen.

Bacon Potato Pancakes

(Pictured on page 64)

Linda Hall, Hazel Green, Wisconsin

Potatoes are something I can eat any time of day and almost any way. This recipe's one I came up with to go along with pigs in blankets several years ago.

- 5 to 6 **medium uncooked red potatoes, peeled and shredded (3 cups)**
- 5 **bacon strips, cooked and crumbled**
- 1/2 **cup chopped onion**
- 2 **eggs, beaten**
- 2 **tablespoons all-purpose flour**
- **Salt and pepper to taste**
- **Dash ground nutmeg**
- **Oil for frying**

1. Rinse and thoroughly drain potatoes. In a bowl, combine the potatoes, bacon, onion, eggs, flour, salt, pepper and nutmeg. In an electric skillet, heat 1/8 in. of oil to 375°.

2. Drop batter by 2 heaping tablespoonfuls into hot oil. Flatten to form patties. Fry pancakes until golden brown; turn and cook the other side. Drain on paper towels. **Yield:** 2 dozen.

🎖🎖🎖
Burst o' Lemon Muffins
(Pictured on page 64)

Nancy Rader, Westerville, Ohio

While I visited my sister in Florida, she baked a batch of these incredible muffins. I went home with the recipe.

- 1-3/4 cups all-purpose flour
- 3/4 cup sugar
- 1 teaspoon baking powder
- 3/4 teaspoon baking soda
- 1/4 teaspoon salt
- 1 cup (8 ounces) lemon *or* vanilla yogurt
- 1 egg
- 1/3 cup butter, melted
- 1 to 2 tablespoons grated lemon peel
- 1 tablespoon lemon juice
- 1/2 cup flaked coconut

TOPPING:
- 1/3 cup lemon juice
- 1/4 cup sugar
- 1/4 cup flaked coconut, toasted

1. In a large bowl, combine the flour, sugar, baking powder, baking soda and salt. In another bowl, beat the yogurt, egg, butter, lemon peel and lemon juice until smooth; stir into dry ingredients just until moistened. Fold in the coconut.

2. Fill greased muffin cups two-thirds full. Bake at 400° for 18-22 minutes or until golden brown and a toothpick comes out clean. Cool for 5 minutes before removing from pan to a wire rack.

3. In a saucepan, combine the lemon juice and sugar; cook and stir until sugar is dissolved. Stir in coconut. Using a toothpick, poke 6-8 holes in each muffin. Spoon the coconut mixture over muffins. Serve warm or cool to room temperature. **Yield:** 1 dozen.

🎖🎖🎖
Apple Nut Muffins
(Pictured at right)

Hollie Gregory, Mount Vision, New York

The inspiration for these muffins came from a favorite coffee cake. For variety, I'll sometimes substitute prepared blueberry or lemon pie filling for the from-scratch apple filling.

- 2 tablespoons butter
- 1/3 cup packed brown sugar
- 1 tablespoon all-purpose flour
- 1/2 teaspoon ground cinnamon
- 1/8 to 1/4 teaspoon ground nutmeg
- 2 cups finely chopped peeled apples
- 1/2 cup finely chopped nuts

MUFFINS:
- 3/4 cup butter, softened
- 1-1/2 cups sugar
- 3 eggs
- 1-1/2 teaspoons vanilla extract
- 3-1/2 cups all-purpose flour
- 1-1/2 teaspoons baking powder
- 1-1/2 teaspoons baking soda
- 3/4 teaspoon salt
- 1-1/2 cups (12 ounces) sour cream

Cinnamon-sugar

1. In a saucepan, melt butter. Stir in brown sugar, flour, cinnamon and nutmeg until smooth. Add apples; cook over medium-low heat for 10 minutes or until tender, stirring frequently. Remove from the heat; stir in nuts. Set aside to cool.

2. In a mixing bowl, cream butter and sugar. Add eggs, one at a time, beating well after each addition. Beat in vanilla. Combine dry ingredients; add to creamed mixture alternately with sour cream.

3. Spoon 1/4 cupfuls of batter into greased jumbo muffin cups. Spoon apple mixture into the center of each (do not spread). Top with remaining batter. Sprinkle with cinnamon-sugar.

4. Bake at 350° for 25-27 minutes or until a toothpick comes out clean. Cool for 5 minutes before removing from pans to wire racks. **Yield:** 1 dozen jumbo muffins or 2 dozen regular muffins.

Editor's Note: If using regular-size muffin cups, fill cups half full with batter; add a rounded teaspoonful of apple mixture and remaining batter. Bake for 16-18 minutes.

Hash Brown Egg Dish

(Pictured above)

Diann Sivley, Signal Mountain, Tennessee

I cook the bacon and chop up the vegetables for this hearty casserole the night before, so it takes only a few minutes to finish in the morning. I serve it along with blueberry muffins.

3/4 to 1 pound sliced bacon
6 cups frozen shredded hash brown potatoes
1 small onion, chopped
1 medium green pepper, chopped
1 jar (4-1/2 ounces) sliced mushrooms, drained
3 tablespoons butter
6 eggs
1/4 cup milk
3/4 teaspoon salt
1/4 teaspoon dried basil
1/8 teaspoon pepper
2 cups (8 ounces) shredded cheddar cheese

1. Layer paper towels on a microwave-safe plate. Top with four bacon strips; cover with more paper towels. Microwave on high for 4 minutes. Repeat with remaining bacon. Cool; crumble and set aside.

2. In a 2-1/2-qt. microwave-safe dish, combine potatoes, onion, green pepper, mushrooms and butter. Cover and microwave on high for 7-8 minutes or until the vegetables are tender, stirring once.

3. Beat eggs, milk, salt, basil and pepper; stir into vegetable mixture. Cover; cook at 70% power for 6-8 minutes or until eggs are almost set, stirring every 2 minutes. Sprinkle with cheese and bacon. Cook, uncovered, on high for 1-2 minutes or until cheese is melted. Let stand 5 minutes before serving. **Yield:** 6-8 servings.

Editor's Note: This recipe was tested in an 850-watt microwave.

Cocoa Macaroon Muffins

(Pictured at right)

Carol Wilson, Rio Rancho, New Mexico

This recipe is a favorite that I've modified over the years depending on whether I served them for breakfast, a snack or dessert.

2 cups all-purpose flour
1/2 cup sugar
3 tablespoons baking cocoa
3 teaspoons baking powder
1 teaspoon salt
1 cup milk
1 egg
1/3 cup vegetable oil
1-1/4 cups flaked coconut, *divided*
1/4 cup sweetened condensed milk
1/4 teaspoon almond extract

1. In a bowl, combine flour, sugar, cocoa, baking powder and salt. Combine milk, egg and oil; mix well. Stir into dry ingredients just until moistened. Spoon 2 tablespoonfuls into 12 greased or paper-lined muffin cups.

2. Combine 1 cup coconut, condensed milk and extract; place 2 teaspoonfuls in the center of each cup (do not spread). Top with remaining batter; sprinkle with remaining coconut.

3. Bake at 400° for 20-22 minutes or until a toothpick comes out clean. Cool for 5 minutes before removing from pan to a wire rack. **Yield:** 1 dozen.

🎗️ 🎗️ 🎗️

Cappuccino Muffins

(Pictured above)

Janice Bassing, Racine, Wisconsin

These are my favorite muffins to serve with a cup of coffee or a tall glass of cold milk. Not only are they great for breakfast, they make a tasty dessert or midnight snack. The espresso spread is also super on a bagel.

ESPRESSO SPREAD:
- 4 ounces cream cheese, cubed
- 1 tablespoon sugar
- 1/2 teaspoon instant coffee granules
- 1/2 teaspoon vanilla extract
- 1/4 cup miniature semisweet chocolate chips

MUFFINS:
- 2 cups all-purpose flour
- 3/4 cup sugar
- 2-1/2 teaspoons baking powder
- 1 teaspoon ground cinnamon
- 1/2 teaspoon salt
- 1 cup milk
- 2 tablespoons instant coffee granules
- 1/2 cup butter, melted
- 1 egg, beaten
- 1 teaspoon vanilla extract
- 3/4 cup miniature semisweet chocolate chips

1. In a food processor or blender, combine the spread ingredients; cover and process until well blended. Cover and refrigerate until serving.

2. In a bowl, combine the flour, sugar, baking powder, cinnamon and salt. In another bowl, stir milk and coffee granules together until coffee is dissolved. Add the butter, egg and vanilla; mix well. Stir into dry ingredients just until moistened. Fold in the chocolate chips.

3. Fill greased or paper-lined muffin cups two-thirds full. Bake at 375° for 17-20 minutes or until a toothpick comes out clean. Cool for 5 minutes before removing from pans to wire racks. Serve with espresso spread. **Yield:** about 14 muffins (1 cup spread).

Fudgy Banana Muffins

(Pictured at right)

Kristin Wagner, Spokane, Washington

We love the taste of chocolate and banana. Once when I had no chocolate chips on hand, I made these moist muffins with chunks of chocolate bars instead.

- 1-1/4 cups all-purpose flour
- 1 cup whole wheat flour
- 3/4 cup packed brown sugar
- 1-1/2 teaspoons baking powder
- 1 teaspoon baking soda
- 1/4 teaspoon salt
- 3 medium ripe bananas, mashed
- 1-1/4 cups milk
- 1 egg
- 1 tablespoon vegetable oil
- 2 teaspoons vanilla extract
- 6 milk chocolate candy bars (1.55 ounces *each*)

1. In a mixing bowl, combine the flours, brown sugar, baking powder, baking soda and salt. In another bowl, combine bananas, milk, egg, oil and vanilla; stir into dry ingredients just until moistened.

2. Fill greased or paper-lined muffin cups one-third full. Break each candy bar into 12 pieces; place two pieces in each muffin cup. Top with remaining batter.

3. Chop remaining candy bar pieces; sprinkle over batter. Bake at 400° for 15 minutes or until a toothpick comes out clean. Cool for 5 minutes before removing from pans to wire racks. **Yield:** 1-1/2 dozen.

Crustless Swiss Quiche

(Pictured below)

Marlene Kole, Highland Heights, Ohio

I received this recipe from my mother-in-law, an all-around great cook. Everyone raves about her rich quiche when she serves it at card parties and other occasions.

- 1/2 cup butter
- 1/2 cup all-purpose flour
- 1-1/2 cups milk
- 2-1/2 cups cottage cheese
- 1 teaspoon baking powder
- 1 teaspoon salt
- 1 teaspoon Dijon mustard
- 9 eggs
- 2 packages (one 8 ounces, one 3 ounces) cream cheese, softened
- 3 cups (12 ounces) shredded Swiss cheese
- 1/3 cup grated Parmesan cheese

1. In a medium saucepan, melt the butter. Stir in the flour; cook and stir until bubbly. Gradually add the milk; cook over medium heat, stirring occasionally, until sauce thickens. Remove from the heat; set aside to cool, about 15-20 minutes.

2. Meanwhile, combine cottage cheese, baking powder, salt and mustard; set aside. In a large mixing bowl, beat the eggs. Slowly add cream cheese, cottage cheese mixture and cooled cream sauce. Fold in Swiss and Parmesan cheeses.

3. Pour into two greased 10-in. pie plates. Bake at 350° for 40 minutes or until puffed and lightly browned. Serve immediately. **Yield:** 16-20 servings.

🎀🎀🎀
Sunrise Mini Pizzas

(Pictured at right)

Teresa Silver, Melba, Idaho

I created this recipe for "something different" at breakfast. Even though they look like I went to a lot of trouble, these little pizzas do go together quickly—I even make them for our three children on rushed school mornings.

> 8 to 10 eggs
> 3 tablespoons milk
> Salt and pepper to taste
> 1 tablespoon butter
> 10 frozen white dinner rolls, thawed
> 10 bacon strips, cooked and crumbled
> 2 cups (8 ounces) shredded cheddar cheese

1. In a bowl, beat the eggs. Add milk, salt and pepper. Melt butter in a skillet; add the egg mixture. Cook and stir over medium heat until the eggs are set. Remove from the heat and set aside.

2. Roll each dinner roll into a 5-in. circle. Place on greased baking sheets. Spoon egg mixture evenly over crusts. Sprinkle with bacon and cheese. Bake at 350° for 15 minutes or until the cheese is melted. **Yield:** 10 pizzas.

🎀🎀🎀
Spiced Pear Muffins

(Pictured at right)

Linda Jachimstal, Manitowoc, Wisconsin

I got this delightful recipe from the custodian at our church, who fixes these moist, fruity muffins and shares them with friends. The combination of pears and spices is irresistible.

> 2 cups all-purpose flour
> 1/2 cup packed brown sugar
> 2 teaspoons ground ginger
> 1 teaspoon baking soda
> 1 teaspoon ground cinnamon
> 1/2 teaspoon salt
> 1/8 teaspoon ground nutmeg
> 1/8 teaspoon ground cloves
> 1 egg
> 1 cup (8 ounces) plain yogurt
> 1/2 cup vegetable oil
> 3 tablespoons molasses
> 1-1/2 cups finely chopped peeled pears (about 2 medium)
> 1/2 cup raisins
> 1/3 cup chopped walnuts

1. In a large bowl, combine the first eight ingredients. In another bowl, beat the egg, yogurt, oil and molasses until smooth. Stir into dry ingredients just until moistened. Fold in pears, raisins and walnuts.

2. Fill greased or paper-lined miniature muffin cups two-thirds full. Bake at 400° for 10-12 minutes or until a toothpick comes out clean. Cool for 5 minutes before removing from pans to wire racks. Serve warm. **Yield:** 2 dozen mini muffins or 16 regular muffins.

Editor's Note: If using regular-size muffin cups, bake for 18-22 minutes.

Sticky Bun Coffee Ring

(Pictured above)

Viola Shephard, Bay City, Michigan

Guests will think you went to a lot of trouble when you bring out this pretty nut-topped ring of scrumptious caramel rolls. In fact, these tasty treats are easy to put together using refrigerated biscuits. They taste best when warm and chewy.

3 tablespoons butter, melted, *divided*
3 tablespoons maple syrup
1/4 cup packed brown sugar
1/4 cup chopped pecans
1/4 cup chopped almonds
1/2 teaspoon ground cinnamon
1 tube (12 ounces) refrigerated buttermilk biscuits

1. Brush a 10-in. fluted tube pan with 1 tablespoon butter. In a small bowl, combine syrup and remaining butter. Drizzle 2 tablespoons into pan.

2. Combine brown sugar, nuts and cinnamon; sprinkle 1/3 cupful over syrup mixture. Separate biscuits; place in prepared pan with edges overlapping. Top with remaining syrup and nut mixtures.

3. Bake at 375° for 15 minutes or until golden brown. Cool for 1-2 minutes; invert onto a serving platter. Serve warm. **Yield:** 10 servings.

Mom's Chicken 'n' Buttermilk
Dumplings, p. 87

Roasted Veggie Pizza, p. 82

Stuffed Duckling, p. 89

Pot Roast with Cranberry Sauce, p. 91

Corn Tortilla Pizzas, p. 95

Main Dishes

The choices are almost endless in this chapter of family-pleasing entrees. Whether you want to serve chicken, beef, pork, seafood or lamb, you'll find the perfect recipe right here.

Skillet Bow Tie Lasagna, p. 85

Classic Cabbage Rolls.....................................82
Roasted Veggie Pizza......................................82
Pork Chops with Mushroom Gravy.................83
Glazed Ham Balls 83
Shrimp Monterey 84
Saucy Skillet Fish 84
Skillet Bow Tie Lasagna..................................85
Summertime Chicken Tacos............................85
Surprise Meatball Skewers..............................86
Bacon Cheeseburger Pizza..............................86
Creamy Sausage Stew......................................87
Mom's Chicken 'n' Buttermilk Dumplings............87
Gingered Honey Salmon..................................88
Spinach Turkey Meatballs................................88
Stuffed Duckling...89
Chicken Corn Fritters......................................89
Maryland Crab Cakes......................................90
Pleasing Potato Pizza......................................90
Meatball Hash Brown Bake..............................91
Pot Roast with Cranberry Sauce.....................91
Microwave Tuna Casserole..............................92
Broccoli Fish Bundles......................................92
Marinated Catfish Fillets 93
Deep-Dish Sausage Pizza................................93
Spinach Beef Biscuit Bake...............................94
Peanutty Pork Kabobs....................................94
Reuben Meatballs..95
Corn Tortilla Pizzas...95
Chicken Fajita Pizza 96
French Country Casserole................................96
Cool-Kitchen Meat Loaf.................................97
Irish Lamb Stew 97
Broccoli Ham Stroganoff.................................98
Au Gratin Sausage Skillet................................99
Firecracker Casserole 99
Fiesta Meatballs..100
Chicken 'n' Chips 100
Marinated Flank Steak...................................101
Four-Cheese Chicken Fettuccine...................101
Garlic Beef Enchiladas...................................102
Zucchini Con Carne......................................102
Chicken with Apple Cream Sauce.................103
Mushroom Salisbury Steak............................104

Creamy Chicken and Rice.............................104
Ham and Sweet Potato Cups.........................105
Pizza with Stuffed Crust 105
Quick Chicken Cordon Bleu.........................106
Meatballs with Cream Sauce 107
Salsa Beef Skillet 107
Stew with Confetti Dumplings 108
Southern Chicken Roll-Ups...........................108
Old-Fashioned Chicken Potpie.....................109
Meaty Mac 'n' Cheese...................................109
Sloppy Joe Under a Bun................................110
Chicken Stroganoff..110
Turkey Dressing Pie......................................111
Great Pork Chop Bake..................................112
Oven-Fried Chicken......................................112
Tangy Beef Brisket..113
Colorful Stuffed Peppers...............................113
Meatball Shish Kabobs..................................114
Chicken with Pineapple Sauce......................115
Mashed Potato Beef Casserole......................115
Two-Meat Pizza with Wheat Crust 116
Pizza Tot Casserole.......................................116
Western-Style Beef 'n' Beans 117
No-Fuss Pork Chops......................................117
Tasty Meat Pie..118
Cajun Cabbage 118
Spaghetti 'n' Meatballs..................................119
Chicken Wild Rice Casserole........................120
Sesame Chicken with Mustard Sauce.............120
Tenderloin with Creamy Garlic Sauce...............121
Green Chili Pork Stew...................................121
Apple Beef Stew..122
Chili Nacho Supper.......................................123
Southwestern Veggie Bake.............................123
Blue Plate Beef Patties..................................124
Pork and Apple Supper 124
Beef Stroganoff Meatballs 125
Crab-Stuffed Chicken Breasts 126
Pepperoni Pan Pizza......................................127
Lemon-Batter Fish..127
Glazed Country Ribs.....................................128
Li'l Cheddar Meat Loaves..............................129
Meatball Sub Casserole 129

2 cans (14-1/2 ounces *each*) Italian stewed
  tomatoes
4 garlic cloves, minced
2 tablespoons brown sugar
1-1/2 teaspoons salt, *divided*
1 cup cooked rice
1/4 cup ketchup
2 tablespoons Worcestershire sauce
1/4 teaspoon pepper
1 pound lean ground beef
1/4 pound bulk Italian sausage
1/2 cup V-8 juice, optional

🏵 🏵 🏵

Classic Cabbage Rolls

(Pictured above)

Beverly Zehner, McMinnville, Oregon

I've always enjoyed cabbage rolls but didn't make them since most methods were too complicated. This recipe is fairly simple and results in the best tasting rolls.

1 medium head cabbage, cored
1-1/2 cups chopped onion, *divided*
1 tablespoon butter

1. In a Dutch oven, cook cabbage in boiling water for 10 minutes or until outer leaves are tender; drain. Rinse in cold water; drain. Remove eight large outer leaves (refrigerate remaining cabbage for another use); set aside.

2. In a saucepan, saute 1 cup onion in butter until tender. Add tomatoes, garlic, brown sugar and 1/2 teaspoon salt. Simmer for 15 minutes, stirring occasionally.

3. Meanwhile, in a bowl, combine rice, ketchup, Worcestershire sauce, pepper and remaining onion and salt. Add beef and sausage; mix well. Remove thick vein from cabbage leaves for easier rolling. Place about 1/2 cup meat mixture on each leaf; fold in sides. Starting at an unfolded edge, roll up leaf to completely enclose filling. Place seam side down in a skillet. Top with the sauce.

4. Cover and cook over medium-low heat for 1 hour. Add V-8 juice if desired. Reduce heat to low; cook 20 minutes longer or until rolls are heated through and meat is no longer pink. **Yield:** 4 servings.

🏵 🏵 🏵

Roasted Veggie Pizza

(Pictured on page 80)

Cindy Elsbernd, Des Moines, Iowa

A bold, flavorful garlic and basil pesto sauce is an awesome change of pace from traditional tomato-based pizza sauce. Roasted vegetables are a fantastic topping. Whenever I serve it alongside a standard meat pizza, this one's always the first to go!

8 to 10 medium fresh mushrooms, sliced
1 small onion, sliced
1/2 cup sliced green pepper
1/2 cup sliced sweet red pepper
2 teaspoons olive oil
2 garlic cloves, minced
1/4 teaspoon *each* dried rosemary, oregano and
  thyme
PESTO SAUCE:
1/2 cup coarsely chopped fresh basil

1/4 cup olive oil
1/4 cup grated Parmesan cheese
4 garlic cloves, minced
1 prebaked Italian bread shell crust (1 pound)
1 large tomato, thinly sliced
2 cups (8 ounces) shredded mozzarella cheese

1. Place mushrooms, onion and peppers in a roasting pan or baking pan lined with heavy-duty foil. Combine oil, garlic, rosemary, oregano and thyme; drizzle over vegetables and toss to coat. Cover and bake at 400° for 20 minutes.

2. Meanwhile, for sauce, combine basil, oil, Parmesan cheese and garlic in a food processor or blender; cover and process until smooth, scraping sides often. Set aside.

3. Place crust on an ungreased 12-in. pizza pan. Spread with sauce; top with the tomato slices. Sprinkle with mozzarella cheese. Top with roasted vegetables. Bake for 15 minutes or until the cheese is melted and bubbly. **Yield:** 8 slices.

🎗🎗🎗
Pork Chops with Mushroom Gravy

(Pictured at right)

Nancy Schilling, Berkeley Springs, West Virginia

This recipe is based on the method of preparation my grand-mother used to keep meat moist and tender. I serve it with mashed potatoes, peas and cranberry sauce.

- **1/2 cup all-purpose flour,** *divided*
- **1/2 cup Italian-seasoned bread crumbs,** *divided*
- **4 pork chops (1/2 inch thick)**
- **2 tablespoons vegetable oil**
- **1 medium onion, sliced**
- **2 garlic cloves, minced**
- **1/4 teaspoon pepper**
- **3 cups water**
- **2 tablespoons instant beef bouillon granules**
- **1 teaspoon browning sauce**
- **2 bay leaves**
- **1 jar (4-1/2 ounces) sliced mushrooms, drained**
- **1/2 cup cold water**

1. In a shallow bowl, combine half of the flour and bread crumbs; coat the pork chops.

2. In a large skillet over medium heat, brown pork chops on both sides in oil. Add onion, garlic, pepper and water. Stir in bouillon, browning sauce and bay leaves; bring to a boil. Reduce heat; cover and simmer for 1-1/2 hours or until pork is tender. Remove bay leaves.

3. Remove pork to serving platter and keep warm. Add mushrooms to skillet. Combine cold water and remaining flour until smooth; stir into pan juices. Bring to a boil, stirring constantly until thickened and bubbly. Stir in the remaining bread crumbs. Serve over pork chops. **Yield:** 4 servings.

🎗🎗🎗
Glazed Ham Balls

(Pictured below)

Esther Leitch, Fredericksburg, Virginia

Over the years, I have found this recipe ideal for using left-overs from a baked ham. The pleasantly soft ham balls are glazed with a thick sauce that's slightly sweet with a hint of cloves. I frequently take them to church potlucks.

- **3 eggs**
- **1 cup milk**
- **1-1/4 cups quick-cooking oats**
- **2-1/2 pounds ground fully cooked ham**
- **SAUCE:**
- **1 cup plus 2 tablespoons packed brown sugar**
- **3 tablespoons cornstarch**
- **1/2 teaspoon ground cloves, optional**
- **1-3/4 cups pineapple juice**
- **1/2 cup light corn syrup**
- **3 tablespoons cider vinegar**
- **4-1/2 teaspoons Dijon mustard**

1. In a bowl, combine the eggs, milk, oats and ham; mix well. Shape into 1-1/2-in. balls. Place in a greased 15-in. x 10-in. x 1-in. baking pan.

2. In a saucepan, combine the brown sugar, cornstarch and cloves if desired. Stir in pineapple juice, corn syrup, vinegar and mustard until smooth. Bring to a boil over medium heat; cook and stir for 2 minutes. Pour over ham balls. Bake, uncovered, at 350° for 35-40 minutes or until browned. **Yield:** 10 servings.

Shrimp Monterey

(Pictured at right)

Jane Birch, Edison, New Jersey

For a special occasion or when company's coming, this delicious seafood dish makes a lasting impression. You'll be surprised at how fast you can prepare it. A mild, fresh-tasting sauce and the Monterey Jack cheese nicely complement the shrimp. I serve it over pasta or rice.

- **2 garlic cloves, minced**
- **2 tablespoons butter**
- **2 pounds uncooked medium shrimp, peeled and deveined**
- **1/2 cup white wine *or* chicken broth**
- **2 cups (8 ounces) shredded Monterey Jack cheese**
- **2 tablespoons minced fresh parsley**

1. In a skillet over medium heat, saute garlic in butter for 1 minute. Add shrimp; cook 4-5 minutes or until pink.

2. Using a slotted spoon, transfer shrimp to a greased 11-in. x 7-in. x 2-in. baking dish; set aside and keep warm. Add wine or broth to the skillet; bring to a boil.

3. Cook and stir for 5 minutes or until sauce is reduced. Pour over shrimp; top with cheese and parsley. Bake, uncovered, at 350° for 10 minutes or until cheese is melted. **Yield:** 6 servings.

Saucy Skillet Fish

(Pictured below)

Merle Powell, Kodiak, Alaska

The main industry here on Kodiak Island is fishing, so I'm always on the lookout for new seafood recipes. This is my favorite way to fix halibut since it's quick and tasty. I often get recipe requests when I serve this to guests.

- **1/2 cup all-purpose flour**
- **1-1/4 teaspoons salt**
- **1 teaspoon paprika**
- **1/8 teaspoon pepper**
- **2 pounds halibut, haddock *or* salmon fillets *or* steaks**
- **1 medium onion, sliced**
- **1/3 cup butter**
- **1-1/2 cups (12 ounces) sour cream**
- **1 teaspoon dried basil**
- **1 tablespoon minced fresh parsley**

1. In a large resealable plastic bag, combine the flour, salt, paprika and pepper. Add fish and shake to coat (if using fillets, cut into serving-size pieces first).

2. In a skillet, saute onion in butter until tender; remove and set aside. Add fish to the skillet; cook over medium heat for 3-5 minutes on each side or until the fish flakes easily with a fork. Remove fish to a serving plate and keep warm.

3. Add sour cream, basil and onion to the skillet; heat through (do not boil). Serve over fish. Garnish with parsley. **Yield:** 6-8 servings.

Skillet Bow Tie Lasagna

(Pictured on page 81)

Arleta Schurle, Clay Center, Kansas

This quick recipe tastes just like lasagna, but you make it on the stove. It's very tasty and is always a hit with my family.

- 1 pound ground beef
- 1 small onion, chopped
- 1 garlic clove, minced
- 1 can (14-1/2 ounces) diced tomatoes, undrained
- 1-1/2 cups water
- 1 can (6 ounces) tomato paste
- 1 tablespoon dried parsley flakes
- 2 teaspoons dried oregano
- 1 teaspoon salt
- 2-1/2 cups uncooked bow tie pasta
- 3/4 cup small-curd cottage cheese
- 1/4 cup grated Parmesan cheese

1. In a large skillet, cook beef, onion and garlic until meat is no longer pink; drain. Add the tomatoes, water, tomato paste, parsley, oregano and salt; mix well. Stir in pasta; bring to a boil. Reduce heat; cover and simmer 20-25 minutes or until pasta is tender, stirring once.

2. Combine cheeses; drop by rounded tablespoonfuls onto pasta mixture. Cover and cook for 5 minutes. **Yield:** 4 servings.

Summertime Chicken Tacos

(Pictured at right)

Susan Scott, Asheville, North Carolina

Try these tempting tacos when you're looking for a change of pace from regular tacos. A mild zing from the lime juice in the marinade for the chicken comes through after grilling.

 Uses less fat, sugar or salt. Includes Nutritional Analysis and Diabetic Exchanges.

- 1/3 cup olive oil
- 1/4 cup lime juice
- 4 garlic cloves, minced
- 1 tablespoon minced fresh parsley *or* 1 teaspoon dried parsley flakes
- 1 teaspoon ground cumin
- 1 teaspoon dried oregano
- 1/2 teaspoon salt, optional
- 1/4 teaspoon pepper
- 4 boneless skinless chicken breast halves (1-1/4 pounds)
- 6 flour tortillas (8 inches) *or* taco shells, warmed

Toppings of your choice

1. In a large resealable plastic bag or shallow glass container, combine the first eight ingredients. Add chicken and turn to coat. Seal or cover and refrigerate 8 hours or overnight, turning occasionally.

2. Drain and discard marinade. Grill chicken, uncovered, over medium heat for 5-7 minutes on each side or until juices run clear. Cut into thin strips; serve in tortillas or taco shells with toppings. **Yield:** 6 servings.

Nutritional Analysis: One serving (prepared with flour tortillas and without salt; calculated without toppings) equals 338 calories, 289 mg sodium, 63 mg cholesterol, 28 gm carbohydrate, 27 gm protein, 12 gm fat. **Diabetic Exchanges:** 3 lean meat, 2 starch, 1/2 fat.

1 egg
1/4 cup dry bread crumbs
1 tablespoon minced fresh parsley
1 teaspoon Italian seasoning
1/4 teaspoon salt
Pepper to taste
1 pound ground beef
1 block (1-1/2 ounces) Monterey Jack *or* Swiss cheese, cut into 12 cubes
12 small mushrooms, stems removed
1 medium green pepper, cut into pieces
1 medium sweet yellow *or* red pepper, cut into pieces
1 medium onion, cut into wedges

1. In a saucepan, combine the first five ingredients. Bring to a boil. Reduce heat; simmer, uncovered, for 5-7 minutes or until onion is tender and sauce is slightly thickened. Remove from the heat; set aside.

2. In a large bowl, combine the egg, bread crumbs, parsley, Italian seasoning, salt and pepper. Crumble beef over mixture and mix well. Divide into 12 portions. Place a cube of cheese in each mushroom cap; shape each meat portion around a mushroom.

3. On six metal or soaked bamboo skewers, alternate meatballs, peppers and onion wedges.

4. Grill, uncovered, over medium heat for 3 minutes on each side. Grill 10-12 minutes longer or until meat juices run clear, turning occasionally. Brush with reserved glaze during the last 2 minutes. **Yield:** 6 servings.

Surprise Meatball Skewers

(Pictured above)

Kristen Wondra, Hudson, Kansas

I still remember the first time I served these colorful kabobs—my family was thrilled to find a surprise in the meatballs. I sometimes substitute different vegetables or cheeses for variety.

1/3 cup honey
3 tablespoons Dijon mustard
2 tablespoons finely chopped onion
2 tablespoons apple juice *or* cider
Dash cayenne pepper

Bacon Cheeseburger Pizza

(Pictured at right)

Cherie Ackerman, Lakeland, Minnesota

Kids of all ages love pizza and cheeseburgers, and this recipe combines them both. My grandchildren usually request pizza for supper when they visit me. They like to help me assemble this version—and they especially enjoy eating it!

1/2 pound ground beef
1 small onion, chopped
1 prebaked Italian bread shell crust (1 pound)
1 can (8 ounces) pizza sauce
6 bacon strips, cooked and crumbled
20 dill pickle coin slices
2 cups (8 ounces) shredded mozzarella cheese
2 cups (8 ounces) shredded cheddar cheese
1 teaspoon pizza *or* Italian seasoning

1. In a skillet, cook beef and onion until meat is no longer pink; drain and set aside.

2. Place crust on an ungreased 12-in. pizza pan. Spread with pizza sauce. Top with beef mixture, bacon, pickles and cheeses. Sprinkle with pizza seasoning.

3. Bake at 450° for 8-10 minutes or until cheese is melted. **Yield:** 8 slices.

🎗🎗🎗
Creamy Sausage Stew

(Pictured at right)

Rosemary Jesse, Cabool, Missouri

Depending on the time of year, I serve my stew with bread or sweet corn muffins and fresh butter, and with salad or fruit.

    8 **to 10 medium red potatoes, cut into 1-1/2-inch pieces**
    2 **large white onions, quartered**
    1 **large green pepper, cut into 1-inch pieces**
    1 **large sweet red pepper, cut into 1-inch pieces**
    2 **pounds smoked Polish sausage, cut into 1-inch slices**
1/3 **cup vegetable oil**
    1 **tablespoon dried basil**
    2 **teaspoons salt**
    1 **teaspoon pepper**
    1 **pint heavy whipping cream**
    3 **tablespoons cornstarch**
    3 **tablespoons water**

1. Place potatoes in a 5-qt. roasting pan. Add onions, peppers and sausage; toss gently. Combine oil, basil, salt and pepper. Pour over the meat and vegetables; toss well.

2. Cover and bake at 350° for 45 minutes; stir. Add the cream; cover and bake 30-40 minutes longer or until potatoes are tender.

3. Combine cornstarch and water; stir into stew. Place on stovetop and bring to a boil, stirring constantly until thickened. **Yield:** 10-12 servings.

🎗🎗🎗
Mom's Chicken 'n' Buttermilk Dumplings

(Pictured on page 80)

Ellen Proefrock, Brodhead, Wisconsin

I serve this—with a tossed or cucumber salad—to friends dining with us or on visits by our two sons and their families.

    1 **stewing chicken (about 5 pounds), cut up**
10 **cups water**
    1 **large onion, chopped**
    2 **medium carrots, sliced**
    3 **celery ribs, chopped**
    4 **garlic cloves, minced**
    1 **teaspoon salt**
1/4 **cup butter**
    6 **tablespoons all-purpose flour**
1/8 **teaspoon *each* paprika and pepper**
1/2 **cup half-and-half cream**
DUMPLINGS:
    2 **cups all-purpose flour**
    4 **teaspoons baking powder**
    4 **teaspoons sugar**
    1 **teaspoon salt**
    2 **eggs**
1/2 **cup buttermilk**
1/4 **cup butter, melted**

1. In a soup kettle or Dutch oven, combine the first seven ingredients. Bring to a boil; skim foam from broth. Reduce heat; cover and simmer for 1-1/2 hours or until chicken is tender. Remove chicken; when cool enough to handle, debone and dice. Strain broth, reserving broth and vegetables.

2. In the same kettle, melt butter. Stir in flour, paprika and pepper until smooth. Gradually stir in 6 cups reserved broth (save remaining broth for another use). Bring to a boil; boil and stir for 2 minutes. Reduce heat; stir in the cream, reserved vegetables and chicken. Cover and bring to a boil; reduce the heat to simmer.

3. For dumplings, combine flour, baking powder, sugar and salt in a bowl. Combine eggs, buttermilk and butter; stir into dry ingredients to form a stiff batter. Drop by tablespoonfuls onto simmering mixture. Cover and simmer for 20 minutes or until a toothpick inserted in a dumpling comes out clean (do not lift cover while simmering). Serve immediately. **Yield:** 6-8 servings.

Gingered Honey Salmon

(Pictured at right)

Dan Strumberger, Farmington, Minnesota

Ginger, garlic powder and green onion blend nicely in an easy marinade that gives pleasant flavor to salmon. We also like to use this versatile mixture when grilling chicken.

- 1/3 cup orange juice
- 1/3 cup soy sauce
- 1/4 cup honey
- 1 green onion, chopped
- 1 teaspoon ground ginger
- 1 teaspoon garlic powder
- 1 salmon fillet (1-1/2 pounds and 3/4 inch thick)

1. Coat grill rack with nonstick cooking spray before starting the grill.

2. In a bowl, combine the first six ingredients; mix well. Set aside 1/3 cup for basting; cover and refrigerate. Pour remaining marinade into a large resealable plastic bag or shallow glass container; add salmon and turn to coat. Seal or cover and refrigerate for 30 minutes, turning once or twice. Drain and discard marinade.

3. Place salmon fillet skin side down on grill. Grill, covered, over medium-hot heat for 5 minutes. Baste with the reserved marinade. Grill 10-15 minutes longer or until the fish flakes easily with a fork, basting frequently. **Yield:** 4-6 servings.

Spinach Turkey Meatballs

(Pictured at left)

Mimi Blanco, Bronxville, New York

Our children call these "Gramby Meatballs" because the recipe came from my dear mother-in-law. It's a great way to make spinach palatable. I usually make a triple batch, bake them all and freeze the extras for a quick meal later.

- 1 package (10 ounces) frozen chopped spinach, thawed and squeezed dry
- 1 egg, beaten
- 1 cup soft bread crumbs
- 2 tablespoons grated onion
- 1 teaspoon seasoned salt
- 1 pound ground turkey

Tomato wedges, optional

1. In a bowl, combine spinach, egg, bread crumbs, onion and seasoned salt. Crumble turkey over mixture and mix well. Shape into 2-in. balls. Place in a lightly greased 15-in. x 10-in. x 1-in. baking pan.

2. Bake, uncovered, at 400° for 20 minutes or until the meat is no longer pink. Drain on paper towels. Garnish with tomato wedges if desired. **Yield:** 4 servings.

Stuffed Duckling

(Pictured on page 80)

Joanne Callahan, Far Hills, New Jersey

I enjoy experimenting in the kitchen. I started with a basic bread stuffing, then began adding different things from my cupboard. The stuffing disappears long before the bird is gone!

- 1 domestic duckling (4 to 5 pounds)
- 1 teaspoon salt, *divided*
- 1/2 cup chopped onion
- 1 garlic clove, minced
- 1 tablespoon butter
- 2 cups cubed day-old bread
- 1 cup cooked rice
- 1 teaspoon *each* dried basil, rubbed sage, dried parsley flakes and dried rosemary, crushed
- 1/8 teaspoon pepper
- 1/2 cup raisins
- 1/2 cup chopped pecans
- 1/4 to 1/3 cup chicken broth

1. Sprinkle inside duckling cavity with 1/2 teaspoon salt. Prick skin in several places; set aside.

2. In a skillet, saute onion and garlic in butter until tender. In a bowl, combine bread cubes, rice, basil, sage, parsley, rosemary, pepper and remaining salt. Add raisins, pecans and enough broth to moisten; toss gently. Stuff into duckling.

3. Place breast side up on rack in shallow roasting pan. Bake, uncovered, at 350° for 1-3/4 to 2 hours or until a meat thermometer reads 180° for duck and 165° for stuffing. Drain fat several times during roasting.

4. Cover and let stand for 20 minutes before removing stuffing and carving. **Yield:** 2-4 servings.

Chicken Corn Fritters

(Pictured at right)

Marie Greene, Scottsbluff, Nebraska

I've always loved corn fritters, but they weren't satisfying as a main dish. I came up with this recipe and was thrilled when my husband and our three young boys gave it rave reviews.

- 1 can (15-1/4 ounces) whole kernel corn, drained
- 1 cup finely chopped cooked chicken
- 1 egg, lightly beaten
- 1/2 cup milk
- 2 tablespoons butter, melted
- 1/2 teaspoon salt
- 1/8 teaspoon pepper
- 1-3/4 cups all-purpose flour
- 1 teaspoon baking powder

Oil for deep-fat frying

GREEN CHILI SAUCE:
- 1/3 cup butter
- 1/4 cup all-purpose flour
- 1/4 teaspoon salt
- 1/8 teaspoon pepper
- 1/8 teaspoon garlic powder
- 1/8 teaspoon ground cumin
- 1 can (4 ounces) chopped green chilies
- 1 cup milk

Shredded cheddar cheese, optional

1. Place corn in a bowl; lightly crush with a potato masher. Stir in chicken, egg, milk, butter, salt and pepper. Combine flour and baking powder; stir into the corn mixture just until combined.

2. In a deep-fat fryer or skillet, heat 2 in. of oil to 375°. Drop batter by 1/4 cupfuls into oil. Fry for 3 minutes on each side or until golden brown. Drain on paper towels; keep warm.

3. In a saucepan, melt butter over medium-low heat. Stir in flour and seasonings until smooth. Add chilies. Gradually stir in milk. Bring to a boil; cook and stir for 2 minutes or until thickened. Serve with the corn fritters; sprinkle with the cheese if desired. **Yield:** 1 dozen.

I've lived in Maryland for more than 50 years, so I know how much folks around here love crab cakes. I came up with this recipe, which my family really likes.

- 1 egg
- 1/4 cup milk
- 3 tablespoons mayonnaise
- 1 tablespoon all-purpose flour
- 1 tablespoon Worcestershire sauce
- 1 teaspoon prepared mustard
- 1 teaspoon salt
- 1/4 teaspoon pepper
- 1 pound cooked crabmeat *or* 3 cans (6 ounces *each*) crabmeat, drained, flaked and cartilage removed
- 1/2 cup dry bread crumbs
- 2 tablespoons butter

1. In a large bowl, whisk together the first eight ingredients. Fold in crab.

2. Place the bread crumbs in a shallow dish. Drop 1/3 cup crab mixture into crumbs; shape into a 3/4-in.-thick patty. Carefully turn to coat. Repeat with the remaining crab mixture.

3. In a skillet, cook patties in butter for 3 minutes on each side or until golden brown. **Yield:** 6 patties.

🎀 🎀 🎀

Maryland Crab Cakes

(Pictured above)

Catherine Tocha, Silver Spring, Maryland

🎀 🎀 🎀

Pleasing Potato Pizza

(Pictured at right)

Barbara Zimmer, Wanless, Manitoba

I first heard of this delicious and distinctive pizza when a friend tried it at a restaurant. It sounded great, so I experimented to come up with my own recipe. The way the slices disappear, there's no doubt about their popularity.

- 3 large potatoes, peeled and cubed
- 1 tube (10 ounces) refrigerated pizza crust
- 1/4 cup milk
- 1/2 teaspoon salt
- 1 pound sliced bacon, diced
- 1 large onion, chopped
- 1/2 cup chopped sweet red pepper
- 1-1/2 cups (6 ounces) shredded cheddar cheese
- 1-1/2 cups (6 ounces) shredded mozzarella cheese

Sour cream, optional

1. Place potatoes in a saucepan and cover with water. Bring to a boil; cook for 20-25 minutes or until very tender.

2. Meanwhile, unroll the pizza crust onto an ungreased 14-in. pizza pan; flatten dough and build up edges slightly. Prick dough several times with a fork.

Bake at 350° for 15 minutes or until lightly browned. Cool on a wire rack.

3. Drain potatoes and transfer to a mixing bowl. Mash with milk and salt until smooth. Spread over crust. In a skillet, partially cook the bacon. Add onion and red pepper; cook until bacon is crisp and vegetables are tender. Drain well; sprinkle over potatoes. Top with cheeses.

4. Bake at 375° for 20 minutes or until cheese is melted. Serve with sour cream if desired. **Yield:** 8 slices.

Meatball Hash Brown Bake

(Pictured at right)

Jo Ann Fritzler, Belen, New Mexico

For a seniors potluck at church, I wanted to create a recipe that would incorporate a meat dish and side dish in one. This casserole proved to be a crowd-pleaser.

    2 eggs
  3/4 cup crushed saltines (about 20 crackers)
    6 to 8 garlic cloves, minced
    2 teaspoons salt, *divided*
1-1/2 teaspoons pepper, *divided*
    1 pound lean ground beef
    1 can (10-3/4 ounces) condensed cream of
      chicken soup, undiluted
    1 cup (8 ounces) sour cream
    1 cup (4 ounces) shredded cheddar cheese
    1 large onion, chopped
    1 package (30 ounces) frozen shredded hash
      brown potatoes, thawed

1. In a bowl, lightly beat the eggs. Stir in the cracker crumbs, garlic, 1 teaspoon salt and 1/2 teaspoon pepper. Crumble beef over mixture and mix well. Shape into 1-in. balls.

2. In a covered skillet over low heat, cook meatballs in a small amount of water until browned; drain. In a bowl, combine the soup, sour cream, cheese, onion and remaining salt and pepper. With paper towels, pat hash browns dry. Stir into the soup mixture.

3. Transfer to a greased 13-in. x 9-in. x 2-in. baking dish. Arrange meatballs over top, pressing lightly into mixture. Cover and bake at 350° for 45 minutes. Uncover; bake 15 minutes longer or until meat is no longer pink and potatoes are tender. **Yield:** 8 servings.

Pot Roast with Cranberry Sauce

(Pictured on page 80)

Elinor Muller, Vineyard Haven, Massachusetts

My friends rave about the different taste the cranberry sauce gives to this roast, and I couldn't agree more. I've made the sauce ahead of time and frozen it, which saves preparation time on a busy schedule.

  1/2 cup all-purpose flour
    1 garlic clove, minced
    1 teaspoon salt
  1/2 teaspoon pepper
    1 boneless rump *or* chuck roast (about 3-1/2
      pounds)
    3 tablespoons vegetable oil
    2 cups beef broth
    1 medium onion, grated

Pinch ground cinnamon
Pinch ground cloves
CRANBERRY SAUCE:
    2 cups fresh *or* frozen cranberries
    1 small navel orange, peeled and diced
  1/2 cup sugar
    1 tablespoon red wine vinegar

1. Combine flour, garlic, salt and pepper; rub over the roast. In a Dutch oven, brown roast in oil. Add broth, onion, cinnamon and cloves. Cover and simmer for 2-1/2 hours or until the meat is tender.

2. Meanwhile, combine the cranberries, orange and sugar in a saucepan. Cover and cook over low heat for 5 minutes.

3. Uncover and simmer until the berries burst and the mixture is thickened, about 20 minutes. Remove roast and keep warm. Skim fat from pan juices, reserving 2 cups. Stir vinegar and reserved pan juices into the cranberry sauce. Slice roast; serve with the cranberry sauce. **Yield:** 8 servings.

♦♦♦
Microwave Tuna Casserole
(Pictured at right)

Laura Montoya, Williams Lake, British Columbia

My family digs into this moist, flavorful tuna casserole. Crisp celery along with zucchini and tomato give it a fresh twist.

- 1/2 cup sour cream
- 1/2 cup mayonnaise*
- 2 teaspoons prepared mustard
- 1/2 teaspoon salt
- 1/2 teaspoon dried thyme
- 1/4 teaspoon dill weed
- 5 cups cooked egg noodles
- 2 cans (6 ounces *each*) tuna, drained and flaked
- 1/2 cup chopped celery
- 1/3 cup sliced green onions
- 1 small zucchini, sliced
- 1 cup (4 ounces) shredded cheddar cheese
- 1 medium tomato, chopped

1. In a small bowl, combine the sour cream, mayonnaise, mustard, salt, thyme and dill. Mix well.

2. In a large bowl, combine noodles, tuna, celery and onions. Stir in the sour cream mixture. Spoon half into a greased 2-qt. microwave-safe dish; top with half of the zucchini. Repeat layers.

3. Microwave, uncovered, on high for 6-8 minutes or until heated through. Sprinkle with cheese and tomato. Microwave, uncovered, 2 minutes longer. Let stand for 3 minutes before serving. **Yield:** 6 servings.

*Editor's Note: Reduced-fat or fat-free mayonnaise may not be substituted for regular mayonnaise. This recipe was tested in an 850-watt microwave.

♦♦♦
Broccoli Fish Bundles
(Pictured below)

Frances Quinn, Farmingdale, New York

These bundles take a little time to assemble, but they're worth it! They're always popular at a shower or buffet. They're great for an everyday dinner, too. This flavorful dish goes nicely with rice pilaf or a saucy pasta.

- 18 fresh broccoli spears (about 1-1/2 pounds)
- 6 cubes Monterey Jack cheese (1-1/2 inches)
- 6 sole *or* flounder fillets (about 2 pounds)
- 1/8 teaspoon lemon-pepper seasoning, optional
- 1/3 cup butter, melted
- 2 teaspoons lemon juice
- 1 garlic clove, minced
- 1/4 teaspoon salt
- 1/8 teaspoon pepper

1. In a saucepan, place broccoli in a small amount of water. Bring to a boil. Reduce heat; cover and simmer for 2-3 minutes or until crisp-tender. Rinse in cold water; drain.

2. For each bundle, place a cheese cube on three broccoli spears. Wrap with a fish fillet and fasten with a toothpick if necessary. Place on a greased foil-lined baking sheet. Sprinkle with lemon-pepper if desired. Bake at 350° for 15-25 minutes or until fish flakes easily with a fork.

3. Meanwhile, combine the butter, lemon juice, garlic, salt and pepper. Transfer the fish bundles to a serving platter and remove toothpicks. Drizzle with butter mixture. **Yield:** 6 servings.

Marinated Catfish Fillets

(Pictured at right)

Pauletta Boese, Macon, Mississippi

When we hosted a group of people from Canada, we wanted to give them a taste of the South. They loved it.

- 6 catfish fillets (about 8 ounces *each*)
- 1 bottle (16 ounces) Italian salad dressing
- 1 can (10-3/4 ounces) condensed tomato soup, undiluted
- 3/4 cup vegetable oil
- 3/4 cup sugar
- 1/3 cup vinegar
- 3/4 teaspoon celery seed
- 3/4 teaspoon salt
- 3/4 teaspoon pepper
- 3/4 teaspoon ground mustard
- 1/2 teaspoon garlic powder

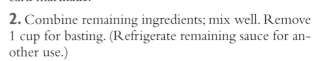

1. Place fillets in a large resealable plastic bag or shallow glass container; cover with salad dressing. Seal bag or cover container; refrigerate for 1 hour, turning occasionally. Drain and discard marinade.

2. Combine remaining ingredients; mix well. Remove 1 cup for basting. (Refrigerate remaining sauce for another use.)

3. Grill fillets, covered, over medium-hot heat for 3 minutes on each side. Brush with the basting sauce. Continue grilling for 6-8 minutes or until fish flakes easily with a fork, turning once and basting several times. **Yield:** 6 servings.

Editor's Note: Reserved sauce may be used to brush on grilled or broiled fish, chicken, turkey or pork.

Deep-Dish Sausage Pizza

(Pictured at right and on front cover)

Michele Madden, Washington Court House, Ohio

My grandma made the tastiest pizza for us when we stayed the night at her farm. Now I make it for my family.

- 1 package (1/4 ounce) active dry yeast
- 2/3 cup warm water (110° to 115°)
- 1-3/4 to 2 cups all-purpose flour
- 1/4 cup vegetable oil
- 1 teaspoon *each* dried oregano, basil and marjoram
- 1/2 teaspoon garlic salt
- 1/2 teaspoon onion salt

TOPPINGS:
- 4 cups (16 ounces) shredded mozzarella cheese, *divided*
- 1 large onion, chopped
- 2 medium green peppers, chopped
- 1/2 teaspoon *each* dried oregano, basil and marjoram
- 1 tablespoon olive oil
- 1 cup grated Parmesan cheese
- 1 pound bulk pork sausage, cooked and drained
- 1 can (28 ounces) diced tomatoes, well drained
- 2 ounces sliced pepperoni

1. In a mixing bowl, dissolve yeast in water. Add 1 cup flour, oil and seasonings; beat until smooth. Add enough remaining flour to form a soft dough. Turn onto a floured surface; knead until smooth and elastic, 6-8 minutes. Place in a greased bowl; turn once to grease top. Cover and let rise in a warm place until doubled, about 1 hour.

2. Punch dough down; roll out into a 15-in. circle. Transfer to a well-greased 12-in. heavy ovenproof skillet, letting dough drape over the edges. Sprinkle with 1 cup mozzarella.

3. In another skillet, saute onion, green peppers and seasonings in oil until tender; drain. Layer half of the mixture over crust. Layer with half of the Parmesan, sausage and tomatoes. Sprinkle with 2 cups mozzarella. Repeat layers. Fold crust over to form an edge.

4. Bake for 400° for 20 minutes. Sprinkle with pepperoni and remaining mozzarella. Bake 10-15 minutes longer or until crust is browned. Let stand 10 minutes before slicing. **Yield:** 8 slices.

🎗️ 🎗️ 🎗️

Spinach Beef Biscuit Bake

(Pictured above)

Bonnie Bootz, Scottsdale, Arizona

My family is from Greece, and I grew up on Greek food. I also like comfort food like casseroles, so I combined the two in this deliciously different main dish.

    2 tubes (7-1/2 ounces *each*) refrigerated buttermilk biscuits
1-1/2 pounds ground beef
  1/2 cup finely chopped onion
    2 eggs
    1 package (10 ounces) frozen chopped spinach, thawed and squeezed dry
    1 can (4 ounces) mushroom stems and pieces, drained
    4 ounces crumbled feta *or* shredded Monterey Jack cheese
  1/4 cup grated Parmesan cheese
1-1/2 teaspoons garlic powder
Salt and pepper to taste
    1 to 2 tablespoons butter, melted

1. Press and flatten biscuits onto the bottom and up the sides of a greased 11-in. x 7-in. x 2-in. baking dish; set aside.

2. In a skillet over medium heat, cook beef and onion until meat is no longer pink; drain.

3. In a bowl, beat eggs. Add spinach and mushrooms; mix well. Stir in the cheeses, garlic powder, salt, pepper and beef mixture; mix well. Spoon into prepared crust. Drizzle with butter.

4. Bake, uncovered, at 375° for 25-30 minutes or until crust is lightly browned. **Yield:** 6 servings.

🎗️ 🎗️ 🎗️

Peanutty Pork Kabobs

(Pictured at right)

Ellen Koch, St. Martinville, Louisiana

Cubes of pork tenderloin and green pepper chunks get a spicy treatment from a combination of peanut butter, brown sugar, ginger and red pepper flakes.

  1/2 cup soy sauce
  1/4 cup lime *or* lemon juice
  1/4 cup peanut butter
    2 tablespoons brown sugar
    2 garlic cloves, minced
    1 teaspoon crushed red pepper flakes
  1/4 teaspoon ground ginger
    1 pork tenderloin (about 1 pound), cut into 1-inch cubes
    2 medium green peppers, cut into 1-inch pieces

1. In a large bowl, combine the first seven ingredients; mix well. Set aside 1/2 cup for basting; cover and refrigerate. Pour remaining marinade into a large resealable plastic bag or shallow glass container; add pork and turn to coat. Seal or cover and refrigerate for 2-3 hours, turning occasionally.

2. Drain; discard marinade. On metal or soaked bamboo skewers, alternate pork and green peppers. Grill, uncovered, over medium heat for 6 minutes, turning once.

3. Baste with reserved marinade. Grill 8-10 minutes longer or until meat juices run clear, turning and basting frequently. **Yield:** 4 servings.

Reuben Meatballs

(Pictured at right)

Irlana Waggoner, Hays, Kansas

Those who like the taste of Reuben sandwiches and sauerkraut are sure to savor these distinctive meatballs. The recipe was given to me by a good friend from Germany.

1 egg
1 small onion, finely chopped
2/3 cup soft bread crumbs
1/4 cup minced fresh parsley
1/2 teaspoon salt
1/2 teaspoon pepper
1 cup cooked rice
1-1/2 pounds lean ground beef
2 cups sauerkraut, rinsed and well drained
1 to 2 teaspoons caraway seeds
1 can (10-3/4 ounces) condensed cream of mushroom soup, undiluted
1/2 cup Thousand Island salad dressing
1/4 cup shredded Swiss cheese
Rye bread, optional

1. In a bowl, combine the egg, onion, bread crumbs, parsley, salt and pepper. Stir in rice. Crumble beef over the mixture and mix well. Shape into 15 balls. Place in an ungreased 13-in. x 9-in. x 2-in. baking dish.

2. Bake, uncovered, at 350° for 15-20 minutes or until browned; drain. Arrange sauerkraut over meatballs; sprinkle with caraway seeds. Combine soup and salad dressing; spread over the top. Cover and bake for 35-45 minutes or until meat is no longer pink.

3. Uncover; sprinkle with Swiss cheese. Bake 10 minutes longer or until cheese is melted. Serve with rye bread if desired. **Yield:** 5 servings.

Corn Tortilla Pizzas

(Pictured on page 80)

Karen Housley-Raatz, Walworth, Wisconsin

These tasty individual pizzas have the zippy flavor of tacos. When I created this recipe and served these pizzas to my husband and day-care kids, they made them disappear. The recipe produces a big batch of the meat mixture, but leftovers can be frozen for up to three months.

1-1/4 pounds ground beef
1 small onion, chopped
1/2 cup chopped green pepper
3 cans (6 ounces *each*) tomato paste
1-1/4 cups water
1 cup salsa
2 cups fresh *or* frozen corn
1-1/2 cups chopped fresh tomatoes
3/4 cup chopped ripe olives
1 envelope taco seasoning
3 teaspoons garlic powder
1-1/2 teaspoons dried parsley flakes
1/2 teaspoon dried oregano
1/8 teaspoon salt
1/4 teaspoon pepper
32 corn *or* flour tortillas (6 inches)
8 cups (2 pounds) shredded mozzarella cheese

1. In a skillet over medium heat, cook beef, onion and green pepper until meat is no longer pink; drain.

2. In a bowl, combine tomato paste and water until blended; add salsa. Stir into meat mixture. Stir in the corn, tomatoes, olives and seasonings.

3. Place tortillas on ungreased baking sheets. Spread each with 1/4 cup meat mixture to within 1/2 in. of edge and sprinkle with 1/4 cup of cheese. Bake at 375° for 5-7 minutes or until the cheese is melted. **Yield:** 32 pizzas.

Chicken Fajita Pizza

(Pictured above)

Rosemary Miller, Lagrange, Indiana

Our family loves pizza, and this variation is one we enjoy often—the chicken is unexpected but delicious. On hectic days, I can make it in a snap using a prepared crust. Either way, it always disappears in a hurry.

✓ Uses less fat, sugar or salt. Includes Nutritional Analysis and Diabetic Exchanges.

   1 **package (1/4 ounce) active dry yeast**
   1 **cup warm water (110° to 115°)**
2-1/2 **cups all-purpose flour**
   4 **tablespoons vegetable oil,** *divided*
   2 **teaspoons salt,** *divided*
   1 **teaspoon sugar**
   1 **pound boneless skinless chicken breasts, cut into strips**

   2 **cups sliced onions**
   2 **cups sliced green peppers**
   2 **teaspoons chili powder**
   1 **teaspoon garlic powder**
   1 **cup salsa**
   2 **cups (8 ounces) shredded Monterey Jack** *or* **mozzarella cheese**

1. In a bowl, dissolve yeast in water. Add flour, 2 tablespoons oil, 1 teaspoon salt and sugar. Beat vigorously by hand 20 strokes. Cover and let rest about 15 minutes.

2. Divide dough in half; press each portion into a greased 12-in. pizza pan. Prick dough several times with a fork. Bake at 425° for 6-8 minutes.

3. In a skillet, saute chicken in remaining oil until juices run clear. Add onions, peppers, chili powder, garlic powder and remaining salt; cook until vegetables are tender. Spoon over crusts; top with salsa and cheese.

4. Bake for 14-18 minutes or until crust is golden and cheese is melted. **Yield:** 2 pizzas (8 slices each).

   Nutritional Analysis: One slice (prepared with reduced-fat cheese) equals 193 calories, 544 mg sodium, 23 mg cholesterol, 20 gm carbohydrate, 12 gm protein, 7 gm fat. **Diabetic Exchanges:** 1 starch, 1 meat, 1 vegetable, 1/2 fat.

French Country Casserole

(Pictured at right)

Kim Lowe, Coralville, Iowa

This delicious dish is great for busy nights when you don't have much time for dinner. It's a quick-to-fix version of a traditional French cassoulet that was an instant hit with my husband.

✓ Uses less fat, sugar or salt. Includes Nutritional Analysis and Diabetic Exchanges.

   1 **pound fully cooked kielbasa** *or* **Polish sausage, halved and cut into 1/4-inch slices**
   1 **can (16 ounces) kidney beans, rinsed and drained**
   1 **can (15-1/2 ounces) great northern beans, rinsed and drained**
   1 **can (15 ounces) black beans, rinsed and drained**
   1 **can (15 ounces) tomato sauce**
   3 **medium carrots, thinly sliced**
   2 **small onions, sliced into rings**
1/2 **cup red wine** *or* **beef broth**
   2 **tablespoons brown sugar**
   2 **garlic cloves, minced**
1-1/2 **teaspoons dried thyme**

1. Combine all ingredients in a bowl; transfer to an ungreased 3-qt. baking dish.

2. Cover and bake at 375° for 60-70 minutes or until the carrots are tender. **Yield:** 9 servings.

   Nutritional Analysis: One 1-cup serving (prepared with reduced-fat turkey kielbasa and reduced-sodium broth) equals 268 calories, 894 mg sodium, 33 mg cholesterol, 39 gm carbohydrate, 19 gm protein, 5 gm fat. **Diabetic Exchanges:** 2 starch, 2 vegetable, 1-1/2 lean meat.

1 cup soft bread crumbs
1 medium onion, chopped
1/2 cup tomato sauce
1 egg
1-1/2 teaspoons salt
1/4 teaspoon pepper
1-1/2 pounds lean ground beef
SAUCE:
1/2 cup ketchup
3 tablespoons brown sugar
3 tablespoons Worcestershire sauce
2 tablespoons vinegar
2 tablespoons prepared mustard

1. In a bowl, combine the first six ingredients. Crumble beef over mixture and mix well. Shape into two loaves; place each loaf in a disposable 8-in. x 4-in. x 2-in. loaf pan. Cover with foil. Grill, covered, over indirect medium heat for 30 minutes or until the meat is no longer pink and a meat thermometer reads 160°.

2. Meanwhile, in a saucepan, combine the sauce ingredients. Cook and stir over low heat until sugar is dissolved. Spoon over meat loaves before serving. **Yield:** 2 loaves (3 servings each).

🏅🏅🏅
Cool-Kitchen Meat Loaf
(Pictured above)

Susan Taul, Birmingham, Alabama

Juicy slices of this tender meat loaf are wonderful served with a homemade sweet-and-sour sauce. It's an easy way to fix supper.

🏅🏅🏅
Irish Lamb Stew
(Pictured at right)

Jeanne Dahling, Elgin, Minnesota

With our busy schedule, I cook lots of stews. This one—handed down to me by my mother-in-law—is nice because you can prepare it on the weekend and reheat it during the week. It's a great full-course meal; put out hard rolls and French bread, and you're set.

6 tablespoons all-purpose flour, *divided*
1 teaspoon salt
1/8 teaspoon pepper
1-1/2 pounds lamb stew meat, cut into 1-inch cubes
2 tablespoons vegetable oil
1/2 teaspoon dill weed
3 cups water
8 pearl onions
3 medium carrots, cut into 1-inch pieces
2 large potatoes, peeled and cubed
1/2 cup half-and-half cream
Hot biscuits

1. Combine 4 tablespoons flour, salt and pepper in a plastic bag. Add lamb; shake to coat.

2. In a 4-qt. Dutch oven, heat oil; brown the lamb on all sides. Add the dill and water; bring to a boil; Reduce heat; cover and simmer for 1-1/2 hours or until meat is almost tender.

3. Add onions, carrots and potatoes. Cover and simmer for 30 minutes or until the meat and vegetables are tender. Combine cream and remaining flour; stir into stew. Cook and stir until boiling and slightly thickened. Serve over biscuits. **Yield:** 6 servings.

Broccoli Ham Stroganoff

(Pictured above)

Amanda Denton, Barre, Vermont

This tasty main dish is a snap to prepare in the microwave and takes just minutes to make. It's a great way to use up extra ham and it works equally well with leftover chicken or turkey. The white sauce gets added creaminess from sour cream.

        2 cups frozen chopped broccoli
        1 tablespoon water
        1 tablespoon butter
    1/4 cup chopped onion
        3 tablespoons all-purpose flour
        1 can (10-1/2 ounces) chicken broth
        2 cups cubed fully cooked ham
        1 cup (8 ounces) sour cream
        1 jar (4-1/2 ounces) sliced mushrooms, drained
    Hot cooked noodles

1. Place broccoli and water in a 1-qt. microwave-safe bowl. Cover and microwave on high for 3-5 minutes or until the broccoli is tender, stirring once. Drain; set aside and keep warm.

2. In another microwave-safe bowl, heat butter, uncovered, on high for 20 seconds or until melted. Add onion; cover and microwave on high for 2 minutes or until tender. Stir in flour until blended. Gradually stir in broth; mix well. Microwave, uncovered, on high for 4-6 minutes or until thickened and bubbly, stirring once.

3. Add the ham, sour cream, mushrooms and reserved broccoli; mix well. Cook, uncovered, on high for 3-5 minutes or until heated through, stirring once. Serve over noodles. **Yield:** 4 servings.

Editor's Note: This recipe was tested in an 850-watt microwave.

🎀🎀🎀
Au Gratin Sausage Skillet

(Pictured at right)

Penny Greene, Lancaster, Ohio

Using frozen vegetables and a package of au gratin potatoes, I can get this satisfying stovetop supper on the table in no time. Even our oldest daughter, who can be a picky eater, loves it— and it gets her to eat her vegetables.

- 1 pound fully cooked kielbasa *or* Polish sausage, halved and sliced 1/2 inch thick
- 2 tablespoons vegetable oil
- 1 package (5-1/4 ounces) au gratin potatoes*
- 2-1/2 cups water
- 1 package (8 ounces) frozen California blend vegetables
- 1 to 2 cups (4 to 8 ounces) shredded cheddar cheese

1. In a skillet, cook sausage in oil until lightly browned; drain. Add potatoes with contents of sauce mix and water. Cover and cook over medium heat for 18-20 minutes or until the potatoes are almost tender, stirring occasionally.

2. Add vegetables; cover and cook for 8-10 minutes or until potatoes and vegetables are tender. Sprinkle with cheese.

3. Remove from the heat; cover and let stand for 2 minutes or until the cheese is melted. **Yield:** 4 servings.

*Editor's Note: The milk and butter listed on the potato package are not used in this recipe.

🎀🎀🎀
Firecracker Casserole

(Pictured above)

Teressa Eastman, El Dorado, Kansas

I loved this Southwestern-style casserole when my mother made it years ago. Now my husband enjoys it when I prepare it.

The flavor reminds us of enchiladas, but this handy recipe does not require the extra time to roll them up.

- 2 pounds ground beef
- 1 medium onion, chopped
- 1 can (15 ounces) black beans, rinsed and drained
- 1 to 2 tablespoons chili powder
- 2 to 3 teaspoons ground cumin
- 1/2 teaspoon salt
- 4 flour tortillas (7 inches)
- 1 can (10-3/4 ounces) condensed cream of mushroom soup, undiluted
- 1 can (10 ounces) diced tomatoes and green chilies, undrained
- 1 cup (4 ounces) shredded cheddar cheese

1. In a skillet, cook the beef and onion until the meat is no longer pink; drain. Add beans, chili powder, cumin and salt.

2. Transfer to a greased 13-in. x 9-in. x 2-in. baking dish. Arrange tortillas over the top. Combine soup and tomatoes; pour over the tortillas. Sprinkle with cheese.

3. Bake, uncovered, at 350° for 25-30 minutes or until heated through. **Yield:** 8 servings.

1/4 cup finely chopped onion
1/4 cup finely chopped celery
2-1/2 teaspoons garlic salt, *divided*
1/4 teaspoon pepper
1 pound ground beef
1 cup soft bread crumbs
1 tablespoon cornstarch
1 cup beef broth
1 can (14-1/2 ounces) stewed tomatoes
2 cups sliced zucchini
1 teaspoon dried oregano
1/2 teaspoon sugar
1/2 teaspoon dried basil

1. In a large bowl, combine the egg, Worcestershire sauce, onion, celery, 1-1/2 teaspoons garlic salt and pepper. Crumble beef over mixture and mix well. Sprinkle with bread crumbs; mix just until combined. Shape into 2-in. balls. Place in an ungreased 15-in. x 10-in. x 1-in. baking pan.

2. Bake, uncovered, at 375° for 20 minutes or until meat is no longer pink.

3. Meanwhile, in a saucepan, combine cornstarch and broth until smooth. Stir in the stewed tomatoes, zucchini, oregano, sugar, basil and remaining garlic salt. Bring to a boil; cook and stir for 2 minutes or until thickened.

4. Drain meatballs; top with the tomato mixture. Bake 10 minutes longer or until heated through. **Yield:** 4 servings.

🎀 🎀 🎀

Fiesta Meatballs

(Pictured above)

Patricia Archie, Glendo, Wyoming

My rancher husband is crazy about rice. When I serve these saucy meatballs over rice, he always comes back for more.

1 egg
1-1/2 teaspoons Worcestershire sauce

🎀 🎀 🎀

Chicken 'n' Chips

(Pictured at left)

Kendra Schneider, Grifton, North Carolina

My husband, Chad, is always ready to try a new recipe, so I surprised him with this creamy chicken casserole. He loves the flavor, and I like that it's the perfect size for our small family.

1 can (10-3/4 ounces) condensed cream of chicken soup, undiluted
1 cup (8 ounces) sour cream
2 tablespoons taco sauce
1/4 cup chopped green chilies
3 cups cubed cooked chicken
12 slices process American cheese
4 cups broken tortilla chips

1. In a bowl, combine the soup, sour cream, taco sauce and chilies. In an ungreased shallow 2-qt. baking dish, layer half of the chicken, soup mixture, cheese and tortilla chips. Repeat layers.

2. Bake, uncovered, at 350° for 25–30 minutes or until bubbly. **Yield:** 4-6 servings.

Marinated Flank Steak

(Pictured at right)

Ann Fox, Austin, Texas

I first grilled this appetizing flank steak for my father on a special occasion. We loved it so much that I now make it this way all the time. The steak marinates overnight, so there's little last-minute preparation to worry about.

- 2/3 cup olive oil
- 1/4 cup lemon juice
- 2 tablespoons red wine vinegar
- 1 tablespoon Worcestershire sauce
- 1 tablespoon soy sauce
- 1 tablespoon Dijon mustard
- 1 teaspoon dried basil
- 1/2 teaspoon dried oregano
- 1/4 teaspoon dried thyme
- 1 flank steak (about 1-1/2 pounds)

1. In a large resealable bag or shallow glass container, combine the first nine ingredients; mix well. Add steak and turn to coat. Seal or cover and refrigerate for 8 hours or overnight, turning occasionally.

2. Drain and discard marinade. Grill, covered, over medium-hot heat for 6-10 minutes on each side or until meat reaches desired doneness (for rare, a meat thermometer should read 140°; medium, 160°; well-done, 170°). **Yield:** 4-6 servings.

Four-Cheese Chicken Fettuccine

(Pictured above)

Rochelle Brownlee, Big Timber, Montana

As a cattle rancher, my husband's a big fan of beef. For him to comment on a poultry dish is rare. But he always tells me, "I love this casserole!"

- 8 ounces fettuccine
- 1 can (10-3/4 ounces) condensed cream of mushroom soup, undiluted
- 1 package (8 ounces) cream cheese, cubed
- 1 jar (4-1/2 ounces) sliced mushrooms, drained
- 1 cup heavy whipping cream
- 1/2 cup butter
- 1/4 teaspoon garlic powder
- 3/4 cup grated Parmesan cheese
- 1/2 cup shredded mozzarella cheese
- 1/2 cup shredded Swiss cheese
- 2-1/2 cups cubed cooked chicken

TOPPING:
- 1/3 cup seasoned bread crumbs
- 2 tablespoons butter, melted
- 1 to 2 tablespoons grated Parmesan cheese

1. Cook fettuccine according to package directions. Meanwhile, in a large kettle, combine soup, cream cheese, mushrooms, cream, butter and garlic powder. Stir in cheeses; cook and stir until melted. Add chicken; heat through. Drain fettuccine; add to the sauce.

2. Transfer to a shallow greased 2-1/2-qt. baking dish. Combine topping ingredients; sprinkle over chicken mixture.

3. Cover and bake at 350° for 25 minutes. Uncover; bake 5-10 minutes longer or until golden brown. **Yield:** 6-8 servings.

🎀🎀🎀

Garlic Beef Enchiladas

(Pictured above)

Jennifer Standridge, Dallas, Georgia

I use flour tortillas in this saucy casserole that has irresistible home-cooked flavor and a subtle kick we like.

- 1 **pound ground beef**
- 1 **medium onion, chopped**
- 2 **tablespoons all-purpose flour**
- 1 **tablespoon chili powder**
- 1 **teaspoon** *each* **salt and garlic powder**
- 1/2 **teaspoon ground cumin**
- 1/4 **teaspoon rubbed sage**
- 1 **can (14-1/2 ounces) stewed tomatoes**

SAUCE:
- 4 **to 6 garlic cloves, minced**
- 1/3 **cup butter**
- 1/2 **cup all-purpose flour**
- 1 **can (14-1/2 ounces) beef broth**
- 1 **can (15 ounces) tomato sauce**
- 1 **to 2 tablespoons chili powder**
- 1 **to 2 teaspoons ground cumin**
- 1 **to 2 teaspoons rubbed sage**
- 1/2 **teaspoon salt**
- 10 **flour tortillas (7 inches)**
- 2 **cups (8 ounces) shredded Colby-Monterey Jack cheese**

1. In a saucepan over medium heat, cook the beef and onion until meat is no longer pink; drain. Add flour and seasonings; mix well. Stir in tomatoes; bring to a boil. Reduce heat; cover and simmer for 15 minutes.

2. In another saucepan, saute garlic in butter until tender. Stir in flour until blended. Gradually stir in broth; bring to a boil. Cook and stir 2 minutes or until bubbly. Stir in tomato sauce and seasonings; heat through.

3. Pour about 1-1/2 cups sauce into an ungreased 13-in. x 9-in. x 2-in. baking dish. Spread about 1/4 cup beef mixture down the center of each tortilla; top with 1-2 tablespoons cheese. Roll up tightly; place seam side down over sauce. Top with remaining sauce. Cover; bake at 350° for 30-35 minutes. Sprinkle with remaining cheese. Bake, uncovered, 10-15 minutes longer or until cheese is melted. **Yield:** 4-6 servings.

🎀🎀🎀

Zucchini Con Carne

(Pictured at right)

Sharon Secrest, Tucson, Arizona

Living in the land of green chilies and hot peppers, my family has grown to love the flavors of the Southwest, as in this dish.

- 1-1/2 **pounds beef stew meat, cut into 1-inch cubes**
- 1/4 **cup all-purpose flour**
- 2 **tablespoons vegetable oil**
- 1-1/2 **cups water**
- 2 **garlic cloves, minced**
- 1 **teaspoon salt**
- 1/2 **teaspoon pepper**
- 4 **large zucchini, cut into chunks**
- 2 **cups whole kernel corn**
- 1 **medium onion, cut into wedges**
- 2 **cans (4 ounces** *each***) chopped green chilies**

Shredded Monterey Jack cheese
Warmed flour tortillas, optional

1. Toss beef with flour until coated. In a Dutch oven over medium heat, brown beef in oil.

2. Add water, garlic, salt and pepper; bring to a boil. Reduce heat; cover and simmer 1 hour and 15 minutes or until the meat is tender. Add zucchini, corn, onion and chilies with liquid; bring to a boil.

3. Reduce heat; cover and simmer 20-30 minutes, until vegetables are tender. Sprinkle with cheese; serve with tortillas if desired. **Yield:** 8-10 servings.

🎀 🎀 🎀

Chicken with Apple Cream Sauce

(Pictured above)

Victoria Casey, Coeur d'Alene, Idaho

Topping chicken with an apple cream sauce is a unique and delicious way to serve it. We think the sauce is wonderful.

4 boneless skinless chicken breast halves
1 tablespoon vegetable oil
1 cup apple juice
1 teaspoon lemon juice
1/4 to 1/2 teaspoon dried rosemary, crushed
1/2 teaspoon salt
1/8 teaspoon pepper
1 tablespoon cornstarch
1/2 cup heavy whipping cream
1 tablespoon minced fresh parsley *or* 1 teaspoon dried parsley flakes
Hot cooked rice

1. In a skillet over medium heat, cook the chicken in oil for 4 minutes on each side or until browned.

2. Combine the apple juice, lemon juice, rosemary, salt and pepper; pour over chicken. Reduce heat; cover and simmer for 10 minutes or until chicken juices run clear. Remove chicken and keep warm.

3. Combine cornstarch and cream until smooth; stir into cooking liquid in skillet. Bring to a boil; cook and stir for 2 minutes or until thickened. Add parsley. Return chicken to skillet and heat through. Serve over rice. **Yield:** 4 servings.

1 jar (6 ounces) sliced mushrooms, drained
4 teaspoons Worcestershire sauce
1 teaspoon dried basil
1 egg, beaten
1/2 cup soft bread crumbs
1 medium onion, finely chopped
1/2 to 1 teaspoon seasoned salt
1/4 teaspoon pepper, optional
1-1/2 pounds ground beef
Hot mashed potatoes *or* **cooked noodles**

1. In a bowl, combine cornstarch and consomme until smooth. Stir in mushrooms, Worcestershire sauce and basil; set aside.

2. In another bowl, combine egg, bread crumbs, onion, seasoned salt and pepper if desired. Crumble beef over mixture and mix well. Shape into six oval patties; place in a shallow 1-1/2-qt. microwave-safe dish.

3. Cover and microwave on high for 6 minutes; drain. Turn patties, moving the ones in the center to the outside of dish. Pour consomme mixture over patties. Cover and microwave on high for 8-10 minutes or until meat is no longer pink. Let stand for 5 minutes. Serve with potatoes or noodles. **Yield:** 6 servings.

Editor's Note: This recipe was tested in an 850-watt microwave.

🎗️🎗️🎗️
Mushroom Salisbury Steak
(Pictured above)

Louise Miller, Westminster, Maryland

My family looks forward to supper when these tasty beef patties with gravy are on the menu. I often bring it to covered-dish gatherings, and then hand out the recipe.

1/4 cup cornstarch
2 cans (10-1/2 ounces *each*) beef consomme, undiluted

🎗️🎗️🎗️
Creamy Chicken and Rice
(Pictured at right)

Jennifer Biggs Cassel, Mediapolis, Iowa

When my mom asked me to prepare a speedy supper to feed our family, I used leftover chicken to create this casserole. Cheese and sour cream make the chicken and rice so creamy and tasty.

4 cups cooked rice
1/2 cup butter, *divided*
1/4 cup all-purpose flour
2 cups milk
2 teaspoons chicken bouillon granules
1/2 to 1 teaspoon seasoned salt
1/2 teaspoon garlic powder
1/4 teaspoon pepper
4 to 5 cups cubed cooked chicken
12 ounces process American cheese, cubed
2 cups (16 ounces) sour cream
1-1/4 cups crushed butter-flavored crackers
(about 32 crackers)

1. Spread rice into a greased shallow 3-qt. or 13-in. x 9-in. x 2-in. baking dish; set aside.

2. In a saucepan, melt 1/4 cup butter; stir in flour until smooth. Gradually add milk, bouillon, seasoned salt, gar-

lic powder and pepper. Bring to a boil; cook and stir for 2 minutes or until thickened and bubbly. Reduce heat; add chicken, cheese and sour cream; stir until the cheese is melted. Pour over rice. Melt the remaining butter; toss with cracker crumbs. Sprinkle over casserole.

3. Bake, uncovered, at 425° for 10-15 minutes or until heated through. **Yield:** 6-8 servings.

Ham and Sweet Potato Cups

(Pictured at right)

Carleen Mullins, Wise, Virginia

This recipe is one of the very best sweet potato recipes I've ever tried. It makes a great light meal all by itself.

- 2 cups frozen California-blend vegetables
- 1 egg
- 2 tablespoons milk, *divided*
- 3 tablespoons dry bread crumbs
- 1/8 teaspoon pepper
- 3/4 pound fully cooked ham, ground
- 1 can (15 ounces) cut sweet potatoes, drained
- 1/2 cup condensed cheddar cheese soup, undiluted

1. Cook vegetables according to package directions; drain and set aside. In a bowl, beat egg and 1 tablespoon milk. Stir in bread crumbs and pepper. Add ham; mix well.

2. In another bowl, mash sweet potatoes until smooth; spread onto the bottom and up the sides of four 10-oz. baking cups. Place about 1/3 cup ham mixture in each cup. Top with vegetables. Combine the soup and remaining milk; spoon over vegetables.

3. Cover and bake at 350° for 40 minutes or until heated through. **Yield:** 4 servings.

Pizza with Stuffed Crust

(Pictured at right)

Sandy McKenzie, Braham, Minnesota

Cheese baked into the edge of the crust makes this extra-special pizza our favorite. It tastes like a restaurant-style pizza with mild ingredients. I sometimes substitute Canadian bacon for the pepperoni and green olives for the ripe ones.

- 2 teaspoons cornmeal
- 2 tubes (10 ounces *each*) refrigerated pizza crust
- 8 ounces string cheese*
- 1 tablespoon butter, melted
- 1-1/2 teaspoons minced fresh basil *or* 1/2 teaspoon dried basil
- 1 can (8 ounces) pizza sauce
- 1 package (3-1/2 ounces) sliced pepperoni
- 1 can (4 ounces) mushroom stems and pieces, drained
- 1 can (2-1/4 ounces) sliced ripe olives, drained
- 2 cups (8 ounces) shredded mozzarella cheese

1. Sprinkle cornmeal evenly over a greased 15-in. x 10-in. x 1-in. baking pan. Unroll pizza dough and place on pan, letting dough drape 1 in. over the edges. Pinch center seam to seal. Place pieces of string cheese around edges of pan. Fold dough over cheese; pinch to seal. Brush the crust with butter; sprinkle with basil.

2. Bake at 425° for 5 minutes. Spread sauce over crust. Place two-thirds of the pepperoni in a single layer over sauce. Sprinkle with mushrooms, olives and cheese. Top with remaining pepperoni.

3. Bake for 10-12 minutes or until crust and cheese are lightly browned. **Yield:** 8-10 slices.

*Editor's Note: 8 ounces of bulk mozzarella cheese, cut into 4-in. x 1/2-in. sticks, may be substituted for the string cheese.

🎗️ 🎗️ 🎗️

Quick Chicken Cordon Bleu

(Pictured above)

Shirley Jackson, Elkton, Virginia

I used this speedy microwave recipe the first time I made chicken cordon bleu. Although I've since tried other recipes that bake in the oven, this remains the quickest and the best.

    4 boneless skinless chicken breast halves
    2 teaspoons Dijon mustard
1/2 teaspoon paprika
    4 thin slices fully cooked ham
    1 cup soft bread crumbs
1/4 cup grated Parmesan cheese
1/4 teaspoon pepper
1/4 cup mayonnaise
SAUCE:
    1 tablespoon butter
    1 tablespoon all-purpose flour
    1 cup milk
1/4 teaspoon salt
1/2 cup shredded Swiss cheese
    2 tablespoons white wine *or* chicken broth

1. Flatten the chicken to 1/2-in. thickness. Spread mustard on one side; sprinkle with paprika. Top with a ham slice. Roll up tightly; secure with toothpicks.

2. In a bowl, combine the bread crumbs, Parmesan cheese and pepper. Brush chicken with mayonnaise; roll in crumb mixture.

3. Place in a shallow 2-qt. microwave-safe dish; cover loosely. Microwave on high for 7 minutes. Turn chicken; cook 7 minutes longer or until juices run clear. Remove toothpicks; set aside and keep warm.

4. In a 1-qt. microwave-safe dish, heat butter on high for 30 seconds; stir in flour until smooth. Cook, uncovered, on high for 30 seconds. Add milk and salt. Cook 3-4 minutes longer or until thickened. Stir in cheese until smooth. Add wine or broth. Serve over chicken. **Yield:** 4 servings.

🎗🎗🎗
Meatballs with Cream Sauce
(Pictured at right)
Michelle Thompson, Smithfield, Utah

I get raves from my husband and even our three fussy children when I serve these satisfying meatballs with mashed potatoes.

> 1 egg, lightly beaten
> 1/4 cup milk
> 2 tablespoons ketchup
> 1 teaspoon Worcestershire sauce
> 3/4 cup quick-cooking oats
> 1/4 cup finely chopped onion
> 1/4 cup minced fresh parsley
> 1 teaspoon salt
> 1/4 teaspoon pepper
> 1-1/2 pounds lean ground beef
> 3 tablespoons all-purpose flour

CREAM SAUCE:
> 2 tablespoons butter
> 2 tablespoons all-purpose flour
> 1/4 teaspoon dried thyme

Salt and pepper to taste
> 1 can (14-1/2 ounces) chicken broth
> 2/3 cup heavy whipping cream
> 2 tablespoons minced fresh parsley

1. In a bowl, combine the first nine ingredients. Crumble beef over mixture and mix well. Shape into 1-1/2-in. balls. Roll in flour, shaking off excess. Place 1 in. apart on greased 15-in. x 10-in. x 1-in. baking pans.

2. Bake, uncovered, at 400° for 10 minutes. Turn meatballs; bake 12-15 minutes longer or until meat is no longer pink.

3. Meanwhile, for sauce, melt butter in a saucepan over medium heat. Stir in flour, thyme, salt and pepper until smooth. Gradually add broth and cream; bring to a boil. Cook and stir for 2 minutes or until thickened and bubbly. Drain meatballs on paper towels; transfer to a serving dish. Top with sauce; sprinkle with parsley. **Yield:** 6 servings.

🎗🎗🎗
Salsa Beef Skillet
(Pictured at left)
Jeanne Bennett, North Richland Hills, Texas

Here's a main dish that's delicious, attractive and economical. It's great with a guacamole salad.

> 1 boneless chuck roast (2 to 2-1/2 pounds), cut into 3/4-inch cubes
> 2 tablespoons vegetable oil
> 1 jar (16 ounces) chunky salsa
> 1 can (8 ounces) tomato sauce
> 2 garlic cloves, minced
> 2 tablespoons brown sugar
> 1 tablespoon soy sauce
> 2 tablespoons minced fresh cilantro
> 2 tablespoons lime juice

Hot cooked rice

1. In a large skillet, brown beef in oil; drain. Add salsa, tomato sauce, garlic, brown sugar and soy sauce; bring to a boil.

2. Reduce heat; cover and simmer for 2 hours or until meat is tender. Stir in cilantro and lime juice; heat through. Serve over rice. **Yield:** 4-6 servings.

1 large onion, thinly sliced
1 garlic clove, minced
2 cans (14-1/2 ounces *each*) beef broth
1 teaspoon Italian seasoning
1 teaspoon salt
1/4 teaspoon pepper
1 bay leaf
1/3 cup all-purpose flour
1/2 cup water
1 package (10 ounces) frozen peas
DUMPLINGS:
1-1/2 cups biscuit/baking mix
2 tablespoons diced pimientos, drained
1 tablespoon minced chives
1/2 cup milk

1. In a Dutch oven, brown meat in oil. Add mushrooms, onion and garlic; cook until onion is tender, stirring occasionally. Stir in broth, Italian seasoning, salt, pepper and bay leaf; bring to a boil. Cover and simmer for 1-1/2 hours.

2. Discard bay leaf. Combine the flour and water until smooth; stir into stew. Bring to a boil; cook and stir for 1 minute. Reduce heat. Stir in peas.

3. For dumplings, combine biscuit mix, pimientos and chives in a bowl. Stir in enough milk to form a soft dough. Drop by tablespoonfuls onto the simmering stew. Cover and simmer for 10-12 minutes or until dumplings test done (do not lift lid while simmering). Serve immediately. **Yield:** 10-12 servings (about 3 quarts).

Stew with Confetti Dumplings

(Pictured above)

Lucile Cline, Wichita, Kansas

If you want a stew that will warm you up, try this. My family particularly likes the dumplings.

2 pounds boneless chuck roast, cut into 1-inch cubes
2 tablespoons vegetable oil
1/2 pound fresh mushrooms, halved

Southern Chicken Roll-Ups

(Pictured at right)

Catherine Darr, Charlotte, Arkansas

This is one of my favorite ways to cook chicken because it tastes so good and it doesn't take long to prepare. I like to serve these roll-ups over rice.

✓ Uses less fat, sugar or salt. Includes Nutritional Analysis and Diabetic Exchanges.

6 boneless skinless chicken breast halves (1-1/2 pounds)
6 slices Swiss cheese
3 tablespoons all-purpose flour
1/2 teaspoon pepper
2 tablespoons butter
3/4 cup chicken broth
1/2 teaspoon dried oregano

1. Flatten chicken to 1/4-in. thickness. Place a cheese slice on each; roll up jelly-roll style. In a shallow bowl, combine flour and pepper; add chicken and roll to coat.

2. In a skillet over medium heat, cook chicken in butter until browned, about 10 minutes, turning frequently. Add broth and oregano; bring to a boil. Reduce heat; simmer for 12-14 minutes or until chicken juices run clear. **Yield:** 6 servings.

Nutritional Analysis: One serving (prepared with reduced-fat cheese, margarine and reduced-sodium broth) equals 284 calories, 157 mg sodium, 94 mg cholesterol, 4 gm carbohydrate, 36 gm protein, 13 gm fat. **Diabetic Exchanges:** 4 lean meat, 1/2 starch, 1/2 fat.

🎖🎖🎖
Old-Fashioned Chicken Potpie

(Pictured at right)

Marilyn Hockey, Lisle, Ontario

Although this uses leftover chicken, I serve it sometimes as a special company dinner. My husband adores it!

- 1/3 **cup butter**
- 1/3 **cup all-purpose flour**
- 1 **garlic clove, minced**
- 1/2 **teaspoon salt**
- 1/4 **teaspoon pepper**
- 1-1/2 **cups water**
- 2/3 **cup milk**
- 2 **teaspoons chicken bouillon granules**
- 2 **cups cubed cooked chicken**
- 1 **cup frozen mixed vegetables**

PASTRY:
- 1-2/3 **cups all-purpose flour**
- 2 **teaspoons celery seed**
- 1 **package (8 ounces) cream cheese, cubed**
- 1/3 **cup cold butter**

1. In a saucepan, melt butter. Stir in flour, garlic, salt and pepper until blended. Gradually stir in water, milk and bouillon. Bring to a boil; boil and stir for 2 minutes.

Remove from the heat. Stir in chicken and vegetables; set aside.

2. For pastry, combine flour and celery seed in a bowl. Cut in cream cheese and butter until crumbly. Work mixture by hand until dough forms a ball. On a lightly floured surface, roll two-thirds of dough into a 12-in. square. Transfer to an 8-in. square baking dish. Pour filling into crust. Roll remaining dough into a 9-in. square; place over filling. Trim, seal and flute edges. Cut slits in pastry.

3. Bake at 425° for 30-35 minutes or until crust is golden brown and filling is bubbly. **Yield:** 6 servings.

🎖🎖🎖
Meaty Mac 'n' Cheese

(Pictured at right)

Charlotte Kremer, Pahrump, Nevada

My husband is disabled and requires constant care. This doesn't leave me a lot of time to cook, so I came up with this tasty way to beef up a box of macaroni and cheese. The hearty mixture gets extra flavor from corn, olives and salsa.

- 1 **package (7-1/4 ounces) macaroni and cheese***
- 1 **pound ground beef**
- 1/4 **cup chopped onion**
- 1-1/2 **cups salsa**
- 1/2 **cup fresh *or* frozen corn**
- 1 **can (2-1/4 ounces) sliced ripe olives, drained**
- 3 **tablespoons diced pimientos**

Shredded cheddar cheese
Chopped tomato

1. Set aside cheese sauce mix from macaroni and cheese; cook macaroni according to package directions.

2. Meanwhile, in a large saucepan, cook beef and onion until meat is no longer pink; drain. Add the salsa, corn, olives and pimientos; heat through.

3. Drain macaroni; add to beef mixture with contents of cheese sauce mix. Mix well; heat through. Garnish with cheese and tomato. **Yield:** 4-6 servings.

***Editor's Note:** The milk and butter listed on the macaroni and cheese package are not used in this recipe.

Sloppy Joe Under a Bun

(Pictured at left)

Trish Bloom, Romeo, Michigan

I usually keep a can of sloppy joe sauce in the pantry because our kids love sloppy joes. But sometimes I don't have buns on hand. With this fun casserole, we can still enjoy the flavor that they love in a flash. The bun-like top is made with biscuit mix.

1-1/2 pounds ground beef
    1 can (15-1/2 ounces) sloppy joe sauce
    2 cups (8 ounces) shredded cheddar cheese
    2 cups biscuit/baking mix
    2 eggs, beaten
    1 cup milk
    1 tablespoon sesame seeds

1. In a skillet, cook beef until no longer pink; drain. Stir in sloppy joe sauce; mix well. Transfer to a lightly greased 13-in. x 9-in. x 2-in. baking dish; sprinkle with cheese.

2. In a bowl, combine biscuit mix, eggs and milk just until blended. Pour over cheese; sprinkle with sesame seeds. Bake, uncovered, at 400° for 25 minutes or until golden brown. **Yield:** 8 servings.

Chicken Stroganoff

(Pictured at right)

Laura Schimanski, Coaldale, Alberta

I came up with this recipe, a variation on beef Stroganoff, as a way to use up roasted chicken. It was a hit. I'm usually the only one in my family who enjoys noodles, but even our son will have more when they're topped with this creamy chicken.

    4 bacon strips, diced
    1 pound boneless skinless chicken breasts, cut into 1/4-inch strips
    1 medium onion, chopped
    2 jars (4-1/2 ounces *each*) sliced mushrooms, drained
1-1/2 cups chicken broth
    2 garlic cloves, minced
1/2 teaspoon salt
1/8 teaspoon paprika
Pepper to taste
    2 tablespoons all-purpose flour
    1 cup (8 ounces) sour cream
Hot cooked noodles
Additional paprika, optional

1. In a skillet, cook bacon until crisp. Drain, reserving 2 tablespoons drippings; set bacon aside.

2. In the drippings, cook the chicken, onion and mushrooms until chicken is no longer pink. Add the broth, garlic, salt, paprika, pepper and bacon. Cover and simmer for 10 minutes.

3. Combine flour and sour cream until smooth; add to the skillet. Bring to a boil; cook and stir for 2 minutes or until thickened. Serve over noodles. Sprinkle with paprika if desired. **Yield:** 4 servings.

Turkey Dressing Pie

(Pictured above)

De De Boekelheide, Northville, South Dakota

People tell me this pie is almost better than the original dinner! I fix turkey all year long, and I purposely make too much just so we can have this later on. It's a complete meal in itself.

3-1/2 to 4 cups cooked turkey dressing
1/2 cup turkey *or* chicken broth
2 tablespoons butter, melted
1 egg, beaten
1/2 cup chopped onion
1 tablespoon vegetable oil
3 cups diced cooked turkey
1 cup turkey gravy
1 cup peas, optional
2 tablespoons dried parsley flakes
2 tablespoons diced pimientos
1 teaspoon Worcestershire sauce
1/2 teaspoon dried thyme
4 slices process American cheese, optional

1. In a large bowl, combine dressing, broth, butter and egg; mix well. Press into the bottom and up the sides of an ungreased 10-in. pie plate; set aside.

2. In a large skillet, saute onion in oil until tender. Stir in turkey, gravy, peas if desired, parsley, pimientos, Worcestershire sauce and thyme; heat through. Pour over crust.

3. Bake at 375° for 20 minutes or until golden. If desired, arrange the cheese slices on top of the pie and return to the oven for 5 minutes or until the cheese is melted. **Yield:** 6 servings.

🎖️🎖️🎖️

Great Pork Chop Bake

(Pictured above)

Rosie Glenn, Los Alamos, New Mexico

A friend brought this hearty meat-and-potatoes dish to our home when I returned from the hospital with our youngest child. Since then, we have enjoyed it many times. It's a snap to throw together on a busy day, then pop in the oven to bake. The tender chops, potato wedges and golden gravy are simple and satisfying.

- 6 bone-in pork chops (3/4 inch thick)
- 1 tablespoon vegetable oil
- 1 can (10-3/4 ounces) condensed cream of chicken soup, undiluted
- 3 tablespoons ketchup
- 2 tablespoons Worcestershire sauce
- 1/2 teaspoon salt
- 1/4 teaspoon pepper
- 4 medium potatoes, cut into 1/2-inch wedges
- 1 medium onion, sliced into rings

1. In a skillet, brown pork chops in oil. Transfer to a greased 13-in. x 9-in. x 2-in. baking dish.

2. In a bowl, combine the soup, ketchup, Worcestershire sauce, salt and pepper. Add potatoes and onion; toss to coat. Pour over the chops.

3. Cover and bake at 350° for 55-60 minutes or until the meat juices run clear and the potatoes are tender. **Yield:** 6 servings.

🎖️🎖️🎖️

Oven-Fried Chicken

(Pictured at right)

Dawn Supina, Edmonton, Alberta

My family tells me they'd like me to fix chicken with this coating mix all the time. I've had the delicious recipe for years.

- 2 cups all-purpose flour
- 2 tablespoons salt
- 2 tablespoons pepper
- 1 tablespoon dried thyme
- 1 tablespoon dried tarragon
- 1 tablespoon ground ginger
- 1 tablespoon ground mustard
- 1 teaspoon garlic salt
- 1 teaspoon dried oregano
- 2 eggs
- 1/2 cup milk
- 1 broiler/fryer chicken (2-1/2 to 3-1/2 pounds), cut up

Oil for frying

1. Combine the first nine ingredients; store in an air-tight container.

2. In a shallow bowl, beat eggs and milk. Place 3/4 cup coating mix in a large resealable plastic bag. Dip chicken into egg mixture, then add to the bag, a few pieces at a time; shake to coat. Heat 1/4 in. of oil in a skillet over medium-high heat. Brown chicken on all sides; transfer to an ungreased 15-in. x 10-in. x 1-in. baking pan.

3. Bake, uncovered, at 350° for 45-55 minutes or until juices run clear. **Yield:** 2-1/2 cups coating mix (enough for 3 batches, 4-6 servings per batch).

Tangy Beef Brisket

(Pictured at right)

Jacque Watkins, Green River, Wyoming

We like the sauce for my brisket over elk, moose and venison salami as well. We use it to spice grilled burgers and hot dogs.

- 1 large onion, diced
- 1/2 cup butter
- 1 bottle (28 ounces) ketchup
- 1-1/2 cups packed brown sugar
- 1/2 cup Worcestershire sauce
- 1/3 cup lemon juice
- 2 tablespoons chili powder
- 1-1/2 teaspoons hot pepper sauce
- 1 teaspoon prepared horseradish
- 1 teaspoon salt
- 1/2 teaspoon garlic powder
- 1 boneless beef brisket* (6 pounds)

1. In a saucepan, saute onion in butter until tender. Add the next nine ingredients; bring to a boil. Reduce heat; simmer, uncovered, for 30-40 minutes.

2. Place meat in a roasting pan. Add 3 cups of sauce.

3. Cover and bake at 350°for 4 hours, basting occasionally. Skim fat. Remove brisket; thinly slice the beef and return to pan. Add remaining sauce if desired. **Yield:** 12-14 servings (6 cups sauce).

*Editor's Note: This is a fresh beef brisket, not corned beef.

Colorful Stuffed Peppers

(Pictured at right)

Angie Dierikx, State Center, Iowa

You're sure to enjoy this tasty twist on traditional stuffed peppers. Crisp-tender pepper cups hold a colorful filling that gets south-of-the-border flavor from salsa and cumin.

- 1 pound ground beef
- 2 cups salsa
- 1 cup frozen corn
- 1/4 cup water
- 3/4 teaspoon ground cumin
- 3/4 teaspoon dried oregano
- 1 teaspoon salt
- 1/2 teaspoon pepper
- 1/2 cup uncooked instant rice
- 1 cup (4 ounces) shredded cheddar cheese, *divided*
- 4 medium green peppers, halved lengthwise

Sliced canned jalapeno peppers, optional

1. Crumble beef into a 2-qt. microwave-safe dish. Cover and microwave on high for 2 minutes; stir. Cook on high 1-2 minutes longer or until the meat is no longer pink; drain. Stir in the next seven ingredients.

2. Cover and microwave on high for 3 minutes or until mixture bubbles around the edges. Stir in rice and 1/2 cup cheese. Cover and let stand for 5 minutes; stir.

3. Spoon 1/2 cupful into each pepper half. Place on a 12-in. round microwave-safe plate. Cover loosely and cook on high for 8-10 minutes or until peppers are tender, rotating a half turn once. Cover and let stand for 4 minutes. Sprinkle with remaining cheese; top with jalapenos if desired. **Yield:** 4 servings.

Editor's Note: This recipe was tested in an 850-watt microwave.

🎖 🎖 🎖

Meatball Shish Kabobs

(Pictured above)

Shawn Solley, Lawton, Oklahoma

Convenience foods make this hearty entree a snap to prepare. Purchased meatballs are easy to thread onto skewers. And since they're precooked, you just need to grill the kabobs until the fresh veggies are tender. Bottled barbecue sauce adds fast flavor.

> **1** **package (16 ounces) frozen fully cooked meatballs, thawed (about 30 meatballs)**
> **2** **medium zucchini, cut into 1/2-inch slices**
> **2** **medium yellow summer squash, cut into 1/2-inch slices**
> **12** **cherry tomatoes**
> **12** **pearl onions**
> **1** **cup barbecue sauce**
> **Hot cooked rice**

1. On metal or soaked bamboo skewers, alternate meatballs, zucchini, summer squash, tomatoes and onions. Grill, uncovered, over medium heat for 6 minutes, turning once.

2. Baste with barbecue sauce. Grill 8–10 minutes longer or until meatballs are heated through and vegetables are tender, turning and basting frequently. Serve over rice. **Yield:** 5 servings.

Chicken with Pineapple Sauce

(Pictured at right)

Mary Ealey, Smithfield, Virginia

Here's a sweet thick glaze that really dresses up plain chicken. We think it tastes good over ham, too.

- **2 tablespoons brown sugar**
- **1 tablespoon cornstarch**
- **2 cans (8 ounces *each*) crushed pineapple, undrained**
- **1/4 cup soy sauce**
- **1/4 teaspoon garlic salt**
- **1/4 teaspoon ground ginger**
- **6 boneless skinless chicken breast halves**

Minced chives, optional

1. In a saucepan, combine brown sugar and cornstarch. Stir in pineapple, soy sauce, garlic salt and ginger. Cook and stir over low heat until thickened.

2. Place chicken in a greased 9-in. square baking dish. Pour half of the sauce over chicken. Bake, uncovered, at 350° for 15 minutes. Baste; bake 10 minutes longer or until chicken juices run clear, basting several times with the remaining sauce. Sprinkle with chives if desired. **Yield:** 6 servings.

Mashed Potato Beef Casserole

(Pictured below)

Helen McGeorge, Abbotsford, British Columbia

This recipe came out of my mother's cookbook. The smudges and splatters show that Mom used it extensively. Now I prepare it for our children and grandchildren.

- **2 bacon strips, diced**
- **1 pound ground beef**
- **1 large onion, finely chopped**
- **1/4 pound fresh mushrooms, sliced**
- **1 large carrot, finely chopped**
- **1 celery rib, finely chopped**
- **3 tablespoons all-purpose flour**
- **1 cup beef broth**
- **1 tablespoon Worcestershire sauce**
- **1 teaspoon dried tarragon**
- **1/4 teaspoon pepper**
- **3 cups hot mashed potatoes**
- **3/4 cup shredded cheddar cheese, *divided***

Paprika

1. In a skillet, cook bacon until crisp; drain, reserving 1 teaspoon drippings. Set bacon aside. Cook beef in drippings over medium heat until no longer pink; drain.

2. Toss onion, mushrooms, carrot and celery in flour; add to skillet with the broth, Worcestershire sauce, tarragon and pepper. Bring to a boil; reduce heat. Simmer, uncovered, for 15-20 minutes or until the vegetables are tender.

3. Add bacon; transfer to a greased 2-qt. baking dish. Combine potatoes and 1/2 cup of cheese; spread over beef mixture. Sprinkle with paprika and remaining cheese.

4. Bake, uncovered, at 350° for 20-25 minutes or until heated through. Broil 4 in. from the heat for 5 minutes or until bubbly. **Yield:** 4-6 servings.

CRUST:
- 1 package (1/4 ounce) active dry yeast
- 1-1/2 cups warm water (110° to 115°)
- 2 tablespoons vegetable oil
- 1-1/4 cups whole wheat flour
- 2 tablespoons sugar
- 1/2 teaspoon salt
- 1-3/4 to 2 cups all-purpose flour

TOPPINGS:
- 1 can (15 ounces) pizza sauce
- 1 teaspoon sugar
- 1/2 cup sliced mushrooms
- 1/4 cup chopped onion
- 1/4 cup sliced ripe olives
- 1/2 pound bulk Italian sausage, cooked and drained
- 4 ounces Canadian bacon, chopped
- 2 cups (8 ounces) shredded mozzarella cheese

🏵 🏵 🏵

Two-Meat Pizza with Wheat Crust

(Pictured above)

Kathy Mulville, Sterling Heights, Michigan

When our children were younger, I made this tasty, from-scratch pizza for their birthday parties. Everyone loved it so much there was never any left over.

1. In a bowl, dissolve yeast in water; add oil. Combine whole wheat flour, sugar and salt; add to yeast mixture and stir until smooth. Stir in enough all-purpose flour to form a soft dough. Turn onto a floured surface; knead until smooth and elastic, about 6-8 minutes. Place in a greased bowl; turn once to grease top. Cover and let rise in a warm place for 15-20 minutes.

2. Punch dough down. Pat dough onto the bottom and 1 in. up the sides of a greased 14-in. pizza pan.

3. Combine pizza sauce and sugar; spread over crust. Sprinkle with mushrooms, onion and olives. Layer with sausage, Canadian bacon and cheese. Bake at 350° for 25-30 minutes or until crust is golden and cheese is melted. **Yield:** 8 slices.

🏵 🏵 🏵

Pizza Tot Casserole

(Pictured at right)

Chris Stukel, Des Plaines, Illinois

You'll need just seven basic ingredients to make this effortless upside-down pizza casserole. Since I cook for two, I often divide it into two smaller casserole dishes—one for dinner and one to freeze. I take the frozen portion out of the freezer the night before to thaw in the fridge before baking as directed.

- 1 pound ground beef
- 1 medium green pepper, chopped
- 1 medium onion, chopped
- 1 can (10-3/4 ounces) condensed tomato with roasted garlic & herbs soup, undiluted
- 1 jar (4-1/2 ounces) sliced mushrooms, drained
- 2 cups (8 ounces) shredded mozzarella cheese
- 1 package (32 ounces) frozen Tater Tots

1. In a skillet, cook the beef, pepper and onion until meat is no longer pink; drain. Add soup and mushrooms.

2. Transfer to a greased 13-in. x 9-in. x 2-in. baking dish. Top with cheese and potatoes. Bake, uncovered, at 400° for 30-35 minutes or until golden brown. **Yield:** 6-8 servings.

✿✿✿
Western-Style Beef 'n' Beans

(Pictured at right)

Jolene Lopez, Wichita, Kansas

This hearty, crowd-pleasing dish is a comforting meal on a chilly night with bread and a salad. It's also an easy and delicious side dish that tastes like you really worked at it.

- 3 pounds ground beef
- 2 medium onions, chopped
- 2 celery ribs, chopped
- 2 teaspoons beef bouillon granules
- 2/3 cup boiling water
- 2 cans (28 ounces *each*) baked beans with molasses
- 1-1/2 cups ketchup
- 1/4 cup prepared mustard
- 3 garlic cloves, minced
- 1-1/2 teaspoons salt
- 1/2 teaspoon pepper
- 1/2 pound sliced bacon, cooked and crumbled

1. In a Dutch oven over medium heat, cook beef, onions and celery until meat is no longer pink and vegetables are tender; drain.

2. Dissolve bouillon in water; stir into beef mixture. Add beans, ketchup, mustard, garlic, salt and pepper; mix well.

3. Cover and bake at 375° for 60-70 minutes or until bubbly; stir. Top with bacon. **Yield:** 12 servings.

- -

✿✿✿
No-Fuss Pork Chops

(Pictured at right)

Sally Jones, Lancaster, New Hampshire

These tender, mouth-watering chops taste a bit like sweet-and-sour pork but require little attention or time. I prepare them when I'm on a tight schedule but still want something tasty.

- 4 boneless pork loin chops (3/4 inch thick)
- 2 tablespoons olive oil
- 2 medium onions, chopped
- 1/2 cup pineapple juice
- 2 tablespoons brown sugar
- 2 tablespoons cider vinegar
- 1/2 teaspoon salt

Hot cooked noodles, optional

1. In a skillet, cook pork chops in oil until browned on both sides, about 8 minutes. Add the onions; cook until tender. Combine pineapple juice, brown sugar, vinegar and salt; pour over pork chops.

2. Cover and simmer until the meat is tender, about 15 minutes. Serve over noodles if desired. **Yield:** 4 servings.

I work full time as a nurse, so I like meals that are quick and easy. This comforting all-in-one pie is filled with ground beef and tender vegetables. At my sister's suggestion, I replaced the prepared gravy I had been using with canned soups for better flavor. Now my husband and son ask for seconds and thirds.

- 1 pound ground beef
- 1 small onion, chopped
- 1 can (11 ounces) condensed beef with vegetables and barley soup, undiluted
- 1 can (10-3/4 ounces) condensed golden mushroom soup, undiluted
- 3 medium uncooked potatoes, cut into 1/2-inch cubes
- 4 medium carrots, sliced 1/8 inch thick
- 1/4 teaspoon salt
- 1/8 teaspoon pepper
Pastry for double-crust pie (9 inches)

1. In a skillet, cook beef and onion until meat is no longer pink; drain. Add the soups, potatoes, carrots, salt and pepper; mix well. Divide between two ungreased 9-in. pie plates.

2. On a floured surface, roll pastry to fit the top of each pie; place over filling. Seal and flute edges; cut slits in top.

3. Bake at 350° for 45-50 minutes or until golden brown. Let stand on a wire rack for 15 minutes before serving. **Yield:** 2 pies (6 servings each).

🎖️🎖️🎖️

Tasty Meat Pie

(Pictured above)

Cheryl Cattane, Lapeer, Michigan

. . . .

🎖️🎖️🎖️

Cajun Cabbage

(Pictured at right)

Bobbie Soileau, Opelousas, Louisiana

Looking for a different treatment for cabbage? Try this spicy cheese-topped dish that I adapted from a friend's recipe. I added a little of this and that until it tasted the way I wanted. I get rave reviews when I make it for company or church functions.

- 1 pound ground beef
- 1 medium green pepper, chopped
- 1 medium onion, chopped
- 2 garlic cloves, minced
- 1 can (10 ounces) diced tomatoes and green chilies
- 1 can (8 ounces) tomato sauce
- 1/2 cup uncooked long grain rice
- 1 teaspoon salt
- 1/2 teaspoon dried basil
- 1/2 teaspoon dried oregano
- 1/4 to 1/2 teaspoon *each* white, black and cayenne pepper
- 4 to 6 drops hot pepper sauce

- 1 small head cabbage, chopped
- 1 cup (4 ounces) shredded Colby cheese

1. In a skillet, cook the beef, green pepper, onion and garlic until meat is no longer pink; drain. Stir in the tomatoes, tomato sauce, rice and seasonings.

2. Spread into an ungreased 13-in. x 9-in. x 2-in. baking dish. Top with the cabbage and cheese. Cover and bake at 350° for 65-75 minutes or until the rice is tender. **Yield:** 6-8 servings.

🎀🎀🎀

Spaghetti 'n' Meatballs

(Pictured above)

Ann Rath, Mankato, Minnesota

Always a favorite with my family and friends, these delectable meatballs take little time to prepare because they don't need to be browned before being added to the sauce. The meatballs taste best if they are mixed just until all the ingredients are blended.

    1 cup chopped onion
    1 tablespoon vegetable oil
    1 can (28 ounces) stewed tomatoes
    2 cans (6 ounces *each*) tomato paste
    1 tablespoon sugar
    1 teaspoon salt
  1/2 teaspoon dried basil
  1/4 teaspoon dried oregano
  1/8 teaspoon dried marjoram
  1/8 teaspoon paprika
Dash pepper
    2 eggs
    1 garlic clove, minced
    2 teaspoons dried parsley flakes
    1 pound lean ground beef
    1 cup grated Parmesan cheese
  1/2 cup dry bread crumbs
Hot cooked spaghetti

1. In a soup kettle or Dutch oven, saute onion in oil until tender. Stir in the tomatoes, tomato paste, sugar and seasonings. Bring to a boil.

2. Meanwhile, in a large bowl, beat the eggs, garlic and parsley. Crumble the beef over mixture and mix well. Sprinkle with the cheese and bread crumbs; mix gently. Shape into 1-1/2-in. balls. Add to the sauce; reduce heat. Cover and simmer for 30 minutes or until the meat is no longer pink. Serve the meatballs and sauce over spaghetti. **Yield:** 4 servings.

While this special dish is perfect for a company dinner, it's also just too good not to make often for everyday family meals.

1 small onion, chopped
1/3 cup butter
1/3 cup all-purpose flour
1-1/2 teaspoons salt
1/2 teaspoon pepper
1 can (14-1/2 ounces) chicken broth
1 cup half-and-half cream
4 cups cubed cooked chicken
4 cups cooked wild rice
2 jars (4-1/2 ounces *each*) sliced mushrooms, drained
1 jar (4 ounces) diced pimientos, drained
1 tablespoon minced fresh parsley
1/3 cup slivered almonds

1. In a large saucepan, saute onion in butter until tender. Stir in flour, salt and pepper until blended. Gradually stir in broth; bring to a boil. Boil and stir for 2 minutes or until thickened and bubbly. Stir in the cream, chicken, rice, mushrooms, pimientos and parsley; heat through.

2. Transfer to a greased 2-1/2-qt. baking dish. Sprinkle with almonds. Bake, uncovered, at 350° for 30-35 minutes or until bubbly. **Yield:** 6-8 servings.

Chicken Wild Rice Casserole

(Pictured above)

Elizabeth Tokariuk, Lethbridge, Alberta

Sesame Chicken with Mustard Sauce

(Pictured at right)

Wanda White, Antioch, Tennessee

For variety, you can substitute turkey for the chicken or grill it instead of baking it. It's delicious either way.

1-1/2 cups buttermilk
2 tablespoons lemon juice
2 teaspoons Worcestershire sauce
1 teaspoon *each* salt, pepper and paprika
1 teaspoon soy sauce
1/2 teaspoon dried oregano
2 garlic cloves, minced
6 boneless skinless chicken breast halves (about 1-1/2 pounds)
2 cups dry bread crumbs
1/2 cup sesame seeds
1/4 cup butter, melted
1/4 cup shortening, melted
SAUCE:
1-1/2 cups prepared mustard
1-1/2 cups plum jam
4-1/2 teaspoons prepared horseradish
1-1/2 teaspoons lemon juice

1. In a large resealable plastic bag or shallow glass container, combine the first nine ingredients; mix well. Add chicken and turn to coat. Seal or cover and refrigerate for 8 hours or overnight, turning occasionally.

2. Drain and discard marinade. In a shallow dish, combine bread crumbs and sesame seeds. Dredge chicken in the crumb mixture. Place in a greased 13-in. x 9-in. x 2-in. baking dish. Combine butter and shortening; drizzle over chicken.

3. Bake, uncovered, at 350° for 35-40 minutes or until juices run clear. Combine sauce ingredients in a saucepan; heat through. Serve with the chicken. **Yield:** 6 servings.

🎀🎀🎀
Tenderloin with Creamy Garlic Sauce

(Pictured above)

Beth Taylor, Chapin, South Carolina

This is the main course at my family's annual Christmas gathering. Everyone always comments on its tenderness and flavor. Since garlic goes well with everything, the sauce would be good with pork or poultry, too.

1 jar (8 ounces) Dijon mustard, *divided*
10 garlic cloves, *divided*
2 tablespoons whole black peppercorns, coarsely crushed, *divided*
3 tablespoons vegetable oil, *divided*
1 beef tenderloin (4 to 5 pounds), halved
2 cups heavy whipping cream
1 cup (8 ounces) sour cream

1. In a blender, combine half of the mustard, eight garlic cloves and 1 tablespoon peppercorns. Cover and process for 1 minute, scraping sides occasionally. Add 1 tablespoon oil; process until a paste forms. Spread over the tenderloin.

2. In a large skillet, heat the remaining oil over medium-high heat. Brown beef on all sides. Transfer to an ungreased 13-in. x 9-in. x 2-in. baking dish. Cover and bake at 375° for 40-50 minutes or until meat reaches desired doneness (for rare, a meat thermometer should read 140°; medium, 160°; well-done, 170°).

3. Remove to a warm serving platter. Let stand for 10-15 minutes. Meanwhile, mince remaining garlic.

4. In a saucepan, combine garlic, whipping cream, sour cream and remaining mustard and peppercorns. Cook and stir over low heat until heated through. Slice beef; serve with the sauce. **Yield:** 12-15 servings.

🎀🎀🎀
Green Chili Pork Stew

(Pictured at right)

Pat Henderson, Deer Park, Texas

Green chilies are a big favorite here in the Southwest—my family likes anything with them in it, especially this stew.

2 pounds lean boneless pork, cut into 1-1/2-inch cubes
1 tablespoon vegetable oil
4 cups chicken broth, *divided*
3 cans (11 ounces *each*) whole kernel corn, drained
2 celery ribs, diced
2 medium potatoes, peeled and diced
2 medium tomatoes, diced
3 cans (4 ounces *each*) chopped green chilies
2 teaspoons ground cumin
1 teaspoon dried oregano
1 teaspoon salt
3 tablespoons all-purpose flour
Corn bread *or* warmed flour tortillas, optional

1. In a 5-qt. Dutch oven over medium-high heat, brown pork in oil. Add 3-1/2 cups broth, corn, celery, potatoes, tomatoes, chilies, cumin, oregano and salt; bring to a boil. Reduce heat; cover and simmer for 1 hour or until meat and vegetables are tender.

2. Combine flour and remaining broth; stir into stew. Bring to a boil; cook, stirring constantly, until thickened. Serve with corn bread or tortillas if desired. **Yield:** 8 servings.

🏵 🏵 🏵

Apple Beef Stew
(Pictured above)

Paula Pelis, Rocky Point, New York

Just about everyone has a recipe they know by heart. Well, this is mine. It's easy because all the ingredients (except the salt) are in measurements of two.

- 2 **pounds boneless chuck roast, cut into 1-1/2-inch cubes**
- 2 **tablespoons butter**
- 2 **medium onions, cut into wedges**
- 2 **tablespoons all-purpose flour**
- 1/8 **teaspoon salt**
- 2 **cups water**
- 2 **tablespoons apple juice**
- 2 **bay leaves**
- 2 **whole allspice**
- 2 **whole cloves**
- 2 **medium carrots, sliced**
- 2 **medium apples, peeled and cut into wedges**

1. In a large skillet or Dutch oven over medium heat, brown beef in butter. Add onions; cook until lightly browned. Sprinkle with flour and salt. Gradually add water and apple juice. Bring to a boil; cook and stir for 2 minutes.

2. Place bay leaves, allspice and cloves in a double thickness of cheesecloth; bring up corners of cloth and tie with string to form a bag. Add to pan.

3. Reduce heat; cover and simmer for 1-1/2 hours or until meat is almost tender. Add carrots and apples; cover and simmer 15 minutes longer or until meat, carrots and apples are tender. Discard spice bag. Thicken if desired. **Yield:** 4 servings.

Chili Nacho Supper

(Pictured at right)

Laurie Withers, Wildomar, California

The recipe for this creamy, chili-like dish was passed down through our church years ago. It's so warm and filling that we often prepare it when we take skiing trips to Colorado. It can be served over corn chips and eaten with a fork…or kept warm in a slow cooker and served as a hearty dip at parties.

- 2-1/2 **pounds ground beef**
- 3 **cans (15 ounces *each*) tomato sauce**
- 2 **cans (16 ounces *each*) pinto beans, rinsed and drained**
- 1 **can (10 ounces) diced tomatoes and green chilies, undrained**
- 2 **envelopes chili mix**
- 2 **pounds process American cheese, cubed**
- 1 **cup heavy whipping cream**
- 2 **packages (16 ounces *each*) corn chips**

Sour cream

1. In a Dutch oven, cook the beef until no longer pink; drain. Add tomato sauce, beans, tomatoes and chili mix; heat through.

2. Add cheese and cream; cook until the cheese is melted. Serve over chips. Top with sour cream. **Yield:** 14-16 servings.

Southwestern Veggie Bake

(Pictured below)

Julie Zeager, Kent, Ohio

Refrigerated corn bread twists create an appealing lattice top on this zippy main dish. The original recipe contained cooked chicken instead of kidney beans and celery, but my family prefers my meatless version, which is spicier, too. It's such a time-saver that I make it a lot!

- 3 **medium carrots, sliced**
- 2 **celery ribs, chopped**
- 1 **small onion, chopped**
- 2 **to 3 teaspoons chili powder**
- 1 **teaspoon ground cumin**
- 1/4 **teaspoon cayenne pepper**
- 2 **tablespoons butter**
- 3 **tablespoons all-purpose flour**
- 1/2 **cup milk**
- 1 **can (16 ounces) kidney beans, rinsed and drained**
- 1 **can (15 ounces) black beans, rinsed and drained**
- 1 **can (15-1/4 ounces) whole kernel corn, drained**
- 1 **can (14-1/2 ounces) diced tomatoes, undrained**
- 1 **can (4 ounces) chopped green chilies**
- 1 **tube (11-1/2 ounces) refrigerated corn bread twists**

1. In a large skillet, saute the carrots, celery, onion and seasonings in butter until vegetables are crisp-tender. Stir in flour until blended. Gradually add the milk. Bring to a boil; cook and stir for 2 minutes or until thickened and bubbly.

2. Remove from the heat; add beans, corn, tomatoes and chilies. Spoon into an ungreased 13-in. x 9-in. x 2-in. baking dish. Separate corn bread twists; weave a lattice crust over filling.

3. Bake, uncovered, at 350° for 20-25 minutes or until corn bread is done. **Yield:** 8 servings.

A friend and I discovered this recipe together and both consider it a staple menu item. I fix the moist, mild-tasting patties often for family and friends. We love them with the mushroom gravy poured over mashed potatoes, rice or noodles.

1 egg
2 green onions with tops, sliced
1/4 cup seasoned bread crumbs
1 tablespoon prepared mustard
1-1/2 pounds ground beef
1 jar (12 ounces) beef gravy
1/2 cup water
2 to 3 teaspoons prepared horseradish
1/2 pound fresh mushrooms, sliced

1. In a bowl, beat the egg; stir in onions, bread crumbs and mustard. Crumble beef over mixture and mix well. Shape into four 1/2-in.-thick patties.

2. In an ungreased skillet, cook patties for 4-5 minutes on each side or until meat is no longer pink; drain.

3. In a small bowl, combine gravy, water and horseradish; add mushrooms. Pour over patties. Cook, uncovered, for 5 minutes or until mushrooms are tender and heated through. **Yield:** 4 servings.

🎗️🎗️🎗️

Blue Plate Beef Patties

(Pictured above)

Phyllis Miller, Danville, Indiana

🎗️🎗️🎗️

Pork and Apple Supper

(Pictured at right)

Sharon Root, Wynantskill, New York

Our part of upstate New York was settled by the Dutch, and this recipe originated there. This is also apple country.

1-1/2 pounds boneless pork, cubed
1 tablespoon vegetable oil
4 cups water
1 tablespoon chicken bouillon granules
1 teaspoon dried thyme
1/4 teaspoon pepper
1 bay leaf
10 to 12 small red potatoes (about 2 pounds), quartered
4 medium tart apples, peeled and cut into wedges
2 tablespoons cornstarch
2 tablespoons cold water

1. In a Dutch oven, brown pork in oil. Add water, bouillon, thyme, pepper and bay leaf; bring to a boil. Reduce heat; cover and simmer for 1-1/2 to 2 hours or until pork is almost tender.

2. Add potatoes; cover and cook for 15 minutes. Add apples; cover and cook for 10-12 minutes or until crisp-tender. Discard bay leaf.

3. Combine cornstarch and cold water until smooth; stir into pork mixture. Bring to a boil; cook and stir for 2 minutes or until thickened. **Yield:** 6-8 servings.

🏅 🏅 🏅

Beef Stroganoff Meatballs

(Pictured above)

Chris Duncan, Ellensburg, Washington

A rich sour cream and mushroom sauce gives this dish an elegant flavor. It's so easy to prepare for a special occasion. The meatballs can be made ahead and frozen to save time.

    1   egg
    1/4 cup milk
    1/4 cup finely chopped onion
    2   teaspoons Worcestershire sauce
    1-1/2 cups soft bread crumbs
    1   teaspoon salt
    1/4 teaspoon pepper
    1-1/2 pounds ground beef
SAUCE:
    1-1/2 cups sliced fresh mushrooms
    1/2 cup chopped onion
    1/4 cup butter

    4   tablespoons all-purpose flour, *divided*
    1/4 teaspoon salt
    1-1/2 cups beef broth
    1   cup (8 ounces) sour cream
Hot cooked noodles
Paprika, optional

1. In a bowl, combine the egg, milk, onion and Worcestershire sauce. Stir in bread crumbs, salt and pepper. Crumble beef over mixture; mix well. Shape into 1-1/4-in. balls. Place in a lightly greased 15-in. x 10-in. x 1-in. baking pan. Bake, uncovered, at 350° for 15-20 minutes or until meat is no longer pink.

2. In a saucepan, saute mushrooms and onion in butter until tender. Stir in 3 tablespoons flour and salt until blended. Gradually add broth. Bring to a boil over medium heat. Cook and stir for 2 minutes; reduce heat.

3. Combine sour cream and remaining flour until smooth; stir into mushroom mixture. Add meatballs. Simmer, uncovered, for 4-5 minutes or until heated through, stirring occasionally. Serve over noodles. Sprinkle with paprika if desired. **Yield:** 6 servings.

Crab-Stuffed Chicken Breasts

(Pictured above)

Therese Bechtel, Montgomery Village, Maryland

Busy as a member of the Coast Guard and a mother, I prepare this elegant dish for special occasions. The sauce is so versatile, I've used it on pork chops and baked potatoes, too.

- **4 tablespoons butter, *divided***
- **1/4 cup all-purpose flour**
- **1 cup chicken broth**
- **3/4 cup milk**
- **1/4 cup chopped onion**
- **1 can (6 ounces) crabmeat, drained, flaked and cartilage removed**
- **1 can (4 ounces) mushroom stems and pieces, drained**
- **1/3 cup crushed saltines (about 10 crackers)**
- **2 tablespoons minced fresh parsley**
- **1/2 teaspoon salt**
- **Dash pepper**
- **4 boneless skinless chicken breast halves (about 1 pound)**
- **1 cup (4 ounces) shredded Swiss cheese**
- **1/2 teaspoon paprika**
- **Hot cooked rice, optional**

1. In a saucepan, melt 3 tablespoons butter. Stir in flour until smooth. Gradually stir in broth and milk. Bring to a boil; boil and stir for 2 minutes. Remove from the heat; set aside.

2. In a skillet, saute onion in remaining butter until tender. Add the crab, mushrooms, cracker crumbs, parsley, salt, pepper and 2 tablespoons of the white sauce; heat through.

3. Flatten chicken to 1/4-in. thickness. Spoon about 1/2 cup of the crab mixture on each chicken breast. Roll up and secure with a toothpick. Place in a greased 9-in. square baking dish. Top with remaining white sauce.

4. Cover and bake at 350° for 30 minutes or until chicken juices run clear. Sprinkle with cheese and paprika. Bake, uncovered, 5 minutes longer or until cheese is melted. Remove toothpicks. Serve with rice if desired. **Yield:** 4 servings.

🎀🎀🎀
Pepperoni Pan Pizza

(Pictured at right)

Susan Lindahl, Alford, Florida

I've spent years trying to come up with the perfect pizza crust and sauce, and they're paired up in this recipe.

2-3/4 to 3 cups all-purpose flour
    1 package (1/4 ounce) active dry yeast
  1/4 teaspoon salt
    1 cup warm water (120° to 130°)
    1 tablespoon vegetable oil
SAUCE:
    1 can (14-1/2 ounces) diced tomatoes, undrained
    1 can (6 ounces) tomato paste
    1 tablespoon vegetable oil
    1 teaspoon salt
  1/2 teaspoon *each* dried basil, oregano, marjoram
     and thyme
  1/4 teaspoon garlic powder
  1/4 teaspoon pepper
    1 package (3-1/2 ounces) sliced pepperoni
    5 cups (20 ounces) shredded mozzarella cheese
  1/4 cup grated Parmesan cheese
  1/4 cup grated Romano cheese

1. In a mixing bowl, combine 2 cups flour, yeast and salt. Add water and oil; beat until smooth. Add enough re-maining flour to form a soft dough. Turn onto a floured surface; knead until smooth and elastic, about 5-7 minutes. Cover and let stand for 10 minutes.

2. Meanwhile, in a bowl, combine tomatoes, tomato paste, oil and seasonings. Divide dough in half; press each portion into a 15-in. x 10-in. x 1-in. baking pan coated with nonstick cooking spray. Prick dough generously with a fork. Bake at 425° for 12-16 minutes or until crust is lightly browned.

3. Spread sauce over each crust; top with pepperoni and cheeses. Bake 8-10 minutes longer or until cheese is melted. Cut into squares. **Yield:** 2 pizzas (9 slices each).

🎀🎀🎀
Lemon-Batter Fish

(Pictured below)

Jackie Hannahs, Muskegon, Michigan

My husband ranks this recipe as one of his favorites. A lot of fishing takes place in our area, which makes this a good choice for a regional recipe.

1-1/2 cups all-purpose flour, *divided*
    1 teaspoon baking powder
  3/4 teaspoon salt
  1/2 teaspoon sugar
    1 egg, beaten
  2/3 cup water
  2/3 cup lemon juice, *divided*
    2 pounds perch *or* walleye fillets, cut into
     serving-size pieces
Vegetable oil
Lemon wedges, optional

1. In a bowl, combine 1 cup flour, baking powder, salt and sugar; set aside. Combine egg, water and 1/3 cup lemon juice; add to the dry ingredients and mix until smooth.

2. Dip fillets in remaining lemon juice and flour, then coat with the batter. Heat 1 in. of oil in a skillet.

3. Fry fish, a few fillets at a time, over medium-high heat for 2-3 minutes on each side or until the fish flakes easily with a fork. Drain on paper towels. Garnish with lemon if desired. **Yield:** 6-8 servings.

🎀🎀🎀
Glazed Country Ribs

(Pictured above)

Tamrah Bird, Gaines, Michigan

When I take these mouth-watering ribs to our frequent potlucks at work, they're always a hit. I like them basted only with the mildly sweet glaze, but you can serve your favorite barbecue sauce on the side, too. We think they taste as good reheated as they do right off the grill.

- **3 pounds boneless country-style ribs**
- **3/4 cup pineapple juice**
- **1/2 cup vegetable oil**
- **1/2 cup white wine *or* chicken broth**
- **1/4 cup packed brown sugar**
- **1 tablespoon Worcestershire sauce**
- **6 garlic cloves, minced**
- **1 teaspoon salt**
- **1 teaspoon pepper**
- **1 teaspoon dried rosemary, crushed**

1. Place ribs in a large shallow glass container. Pierce several times with a fork.

2. In a bowl, combine the remaining ingredients; set aside 1/2 cup for basting. Pour the remaining marinade over ribs. Cover and refrigerate for 8 hours or overnight, turning once.

3. Drain and discard marinade. Grill ribs, covered, over indirect medium heat for 10 minutes on each side. Baste with some of the reserved marinade. Grill 20-25 minutes longer or until juices run clear and meat is tender, turning and basting occasionally. **Yield:** 6 servings.

🎗🎗🎗
Li'l Cheddar Meat Loaves

(Pictured at right)

Katy Bowron, Cocolalla, Idaho

I got this recipe from my aunt when I was a teen and have made these lip-smacking miniature meat loaves many times.

 1 egg
3/4 cup milk
 1 cup (4 ounces) shredded cheddar cheese
1/2 cup quick-cooking oats
1/2 cup chopped onion
 1 teaspoon salt
 1 pound lean ground beef
2/3 cup ketchup
1/2 cup packed brown sugar
1-1/2 teaspoons prepared mustard

1. In a bowl, beat the egg and milk. Stir in cheese, oats, onion and salt. Crumble beef over mixture and mix well.

2. Shape into eight loaves; place in a greased 13-in. x 9-in. x 2-in. baking dish. Combine ketchup, brown sugar and mustard; spoon over loaves.

3. Bake, uncovered, at 350° for 45 minutes or until the meat is no longer pink and a meat thermometer reads 160°. **Yield:** 8 servings.

🎗🎗🎗
Meatball Sub Casserole

(Pictured at right)

Gina Harris, Seneca, South Carolina

If you like meatball subs, you'll love this tangy casserole—it has all the rich flavor of the popular sandwiches with none of the mess. Served with a green salad, it's a hearty meal.

1/3 cup chopped green onions
1/4 cup seasoned bread crumbs
 3 tablespoons grated Parmesan cheese
 1 pound ground beef
 1 loaf (1 pound) Italian bread, cut into 1-inch slices
 1 package (8 ounces) cream cheese, softened
1/2 cup mayonnaise*
 1 teaspoon Italian seasoning
1/4 teaspoon pepper
 2 cups (8 ounces) shredded mozzarella cheese, *divided*
 1 jar (28 ounces) spaghetti sauce
 1 cup water
 2 garlic cloves, minced

1. In a bowl, combine onions, bread crumbs and Parmesan cheese. Crumble beef over mixture and mix well. Shape into 1-in. balls; place on a rack in a shallow baking pan. Bake at 400° for 15-20 minutes or until no longer pink.

2. Meanwhile, arrange bread in a single layer in an ungreased 13-in. x 9-in. x 2-in. baking dish (all of the bread might not be used). Combine cream cheese, mayonnaise, Italian seasoning and pepper; spread over the bread. Sprinkle with 1/2 cup mozzarella.

3. Combine sauce, water and garlic; add meatballs. Pour over cheese mixture; sprinkle with remaining mozzarella. Bake, uncovered, at 350° for 30 minutes or until heated through. **Yield:** 6-8 servings.

*Editor's Note: Reduced-fat or fat-free mayonnaise may not be substituted for regular mayonnaise in this recipe.

Three-Rice Pilaf, p. 145

Blackberry Apple Jelly, p. 136

Artichoke Spinach Casserole, p. 140

Texas Two-Step Corn Medley, p. 143

Side Dishes & Condiments

When you want to round out a meal, turn to this handy chapter. You'll find a tempting variety of hearty recipes putting vegetables—and even some fruits—to good use.

Cheddar-Mushroom Stuffed Potatoes, p. 133

Vegetables Mornay 132

Salsa Corn Cakes 132

Festive Green Bean Casserole 133

Cheddar-Mushroom Stuffed Potatoes..133

Corn Stuffing Balls 134

Spinach Artichoke Pie 134

Grilled Three-Cheese Potatoes 135

Cheesy Corn Spoon Bread.................136

Blackberry Apple Jelly......................136

Mushroom Corn Casserole.................137

Colorful Oven Vegetables 137

Picante Biscuit Bake.........................138

Creamy Carrot Casserole....................138

Scalloped Apples.............................139

Cherry Almond Preserves 139

Root Vegetable Medley 140

Artichoke Spinach Casserole..............140

Sweet Potatoes with Apples 141

Calico Chowchow 141

Microwave Mac 'n' Cheese 142

Crabby Potatoes..............................142

Texas Two-Step Corn Medley..............143

Wild Rice Floret Bake 143

Company Mac and Cheese.................144

Three Bean Casserole........................144

Three-Rice Pilaf...............................145

Cranberry Chutney...........................145

Savory Cauliflower Pie......................146

Squash Stuffing Casserole 146

Grilled Potato Fans...........................147

Swiss Potato Squares.........................147

Grandma's Sweet-Sour Veggies 148

Church Supper Potatoes.....................149

Apple-a-Day Casserole.......................149

Golden Mashed Potatoes....................150

Herbed Garlic Potatoes......................150

Red Cabbage Casserole......................151

End-of-Summer Vegetable Bake 151

🎀🎀🎀

Vegetables Mornay

(Pictured above)

Jo Anne Remmele, Echo, Minnesota

These saucy vegetables are a colorful, satisfying side dish we enjoy often. Our daughter, a 4-H member, earned the Reserve Grand Champion ribbon at our local county fair with the recipe.

6 to 8 medium carrots, sliced 1/4 inch thick
1/4 cup water
1 package (10 ounces) frozen broccoli florets
1 package (10 ounces) frozen cauliflowerets
2 jars (4-1/2 ounces *each*) whole mushrooms, drained
2 tablespoons cornstarch
1 teaspoon salt
1/4 teaspoon pepper
1-1/2 cups milk
8 tablespoons butter, melted, *divided*
1 cup (4 ounces) shredded Swiss cheese
2 tablespoons Parmesan cheese
1/2 cup seasoned croutons

1. Place the carrots and water in a 3-qt. microwave-safe dish. Cover and microwave on high for 2 minutes. Add broccoli and cauliflower. Cover and microwave for 8-12 minutes or until vegetables are tender; drain. Add mushrooms; cover and set aside.

2. In another microwave-safe dish, combine cornstarch, salt, pepper, milk and 6 tablespoons butter until smooth. Cover and microwave on high for 4-6 minutes or until thickened and smooth. Add cheeses and stir until melted. Pour over the vegetables.

3. Cover and microwave for 3-5 minutes or until heated through. Combine croutons and remaining butter; stir into vegetables. **Yield:** 8-10 servings.

Editor's Note: This recipe was tested in an 850-watt microwave.

🎀🎀🎀

Salsa Corn Cakes

(Pictured at right)

Lisa Boettcher, Rosebush, Michigan

This recipe is super with fresh or canned corn. I whip up these patties to serve alongside nachos or tacos on hot summer evenings. The salsa is subtle but adds flavor.

1-1/2 cups all-purpose flour
1/2 cup cornmeal
1 teaspoon baking powder
1 teaspoon salt
2 packages (3 ounces *each*) cream cheese, softened
6 eggs
1 cup milk
1/4 cup butter, melted
1 can (15-1/4 ounces) whole kernel corn, drained
1/2 cup salsa, drained
1/4 cup minced green onions
Sour cream and additional salsa

1. Combine the flour, cornmeal, baking powder and salt; set aside.

2. In a mixing bowl, beat cream cheese and eggs; add milk and butter. Add the dry ingredients just until moistened. Fold in the corn, salsa and onions.

3. Pour batter by 1/4 cupfuls onto a greased hot griddle. Turn when bubbles form on top; cook until the second side is golden brown. Serve with sour cream and salsa. **Yield:** 6-8 servings.

Festive Green Bean Casserole

(Pictured at right)

June Mullins, Livonia, Missouri

This recipe came from a cookbook my son gave to me over 20 years ago. It's a tasty dish that I make often for family get-togethers and potluck suppers.

- 1 cup chopped sweet red pepper
- 1 small onion, finely chopped
- 1 tablespoon butter
- 1 can (10-3/4 ounces) condensed cream of celery soup, undiluted
- 1/2 cup milk
- 1 teaspoon Worcestershire sauce
- 1/8 teaspoon hot pepper sauce
- 2 packages (16 ounces *each*) frozen French-style green beans, thawed and drained
- 1 can (8 ounces) sliced water chestnuts, drained
- 1 cup (4 ounces) shredded cheddar cheese

1. In a skillet, saute red pepper and onion in butter until tender. Add soup, milk, Worcestershire sauce and hot pepper sauce; stir until smooth. Stir in beans and water chestnuts.

2. Transfer to an ungreased 1-1/2-qt. baking dish.

Sprinkle with cheese. Bake, uncovered, at 350° for 15 minutes or until heated through. **Yield:** 6-8 servings.

Cheddar-Mushroom Stuffed Potatoes

(Pictured on page 131)

Jenean Schuetz, Longmont, Colorado

To come up with this recipe, I just put together three of my family's favorite ingredients—potatoes, mushrooms and bacon. I prepare it as a quick-and-easy party dish. It's also a natural contribution to a potluck. And I serve it as an entree at times with a side vegetable.

- 6 large russet potatoes
- 2/3 cup heavy whipping cream
- 1 cup (4 ounces) shredded cheddar cheese, *divided*
- 1/4 cup chopped fresh mushrooms
- 1/2 to 1 teaspoon garlic salt
- 1/2 teaspoon dried basil
- 1/2 teaspoon dried oregano
- 4 bacon strips, cooked and crumbled, *divided*

1. Bake potatoes at 375° for 1 hour or until tender. When cool enough to handle, cut a thin slice off the top of each potato and discard. Scoop out pulp, leaving a 1/4-in. shell; set shells aside.

2. Place pulp in a mixing bowl; add cream and mash. Blend in 3/4 cup cheese, mushrooms, garlic salt, basil and oregano. Reserve 2 tablespoons bacon; stir the remaining bacon into potato mixture. Spoon into potato shells. Top with remaining cheese and bacon.

3. Microwave on high for 5-8 minutes or bake, uncovered, at 375° for 25-30 minutes or until potatoes are heated through. **Yield:** 6 servings.

Editor's Note: This recipe was tested in an 850-watt microwave.

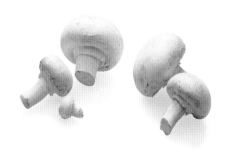

🎀🎀🎀

Corn Stuffing Balls

(Pictured above)

Audrey Groe, Lake Mills, Iowa

My mom had many "winning" recipes, and this was one of our family's favorites. I can still picture these stuffing balls encircling a large meat platter piled high with one of her tasty entrees.

  6 **cups herb-seasoned stuffing croutons**
  1 **cup chopped celery**
1/2 **cup chopped onion**
3/4 **cup butter,** *divided*
  1 **can (14-3/4 ounces) cream-style corn**
  1 **cup water**
1-1/2 **teaspoons poultry seasoning**
3/4 **teaspoon salt**
1/4 **teaspoon pepper**
  3 **egg yolks, beaten**

1. Place croutons in a large bowl and set aside. In a skillet, saute celery and onion in 1/2 cup butter. Add corn, water, poultry seasoning, salt and pepper; bring to a boil.

2. Remove from the heat; cool for 5 minutes. Pour over croutons. Add egg yolks and mix gently. Shape 1/2 cupfuls into balls; flatten slightly. Place in a greased 15-in. x 10-in. x 1-in. baking pan. Melt remaining butter; drizzle over stuffing balls.

3. Bake, uncovered, at 375° for 30 minutes or until lightly browned. **Yield:** 12 servings.

🎀🎀🎀

Spinach Artichoke Pie

(Pictured at right)

Lori Coleman, Glassboro, New Jersey

Spinach is an abundant vegetable grown here in our state. I make this side dish often when spinach is in season.

  3 **tablespoons vegetable oil,** *divided*
1/4 **cup dry bread crumbs**
1/2 **pound fresh mushrooms, sliced**
  1 **pound fresh spinach, chopped and cooked**
  1 **jar (6-1/2 ounces) marinated artichoke hearts, drained and quartered**
  1 **cup day-old bread cubes**
1-1/4 **cups shredded cheddar cheese,** *divided*
  1 **jar (4 ounces) diced pimientos, drained**
  2 **eggs, beaten**
1/4 **to 1/2 teaspoon garlic powder**

1. Brush the bottom and sides of a 9-in. pie plate with 2 tablespoons oil; sprinkle with bread crumbs. Set aside.

2. In a skillet, saute mushrooms in remaining oil; drain. Remove from the heat. Squeeze spinach dry; add to mushrooms. Stir in artichokes, bread cubes, 1 cup of cheese, pimientos, eggs and garlic powder; stir well.

3. Spoon into the prepared pie plate. Bake, uncovered, at 350° for 30 minutes. Sprinkle with remaining cheese. Bake 5-10 minutes longer or until the cheese is melted. Let stand for 10 minutes before cutting. **Yield:** 6-8 servings.

Grilled Three-Cheese Potatoes

(Pictured above)

Margaret Hanson-Maddox, Montpelier, Indiana

While this is delicious grilled, I've also cooked it in the oven at 350° for an hour. Add cubed ham and you have a main dish. I learned cooking basics in 4-H. But mostly my education came after I was married…through trial and error!

- **6 large potatoes, sliced 1/4 inch thick**
- **2 medium onions, chopped**
- **1/3 cup grated Parmesan cheese**
- **1 cup (4 ounces) shredded sharp cheddar cheese, *divided***
- **1 cup (4 ounces) shredded mozzarella cheese, *divided***
- **1 pound sliced bacon, cooked and crumbled**
- **1/4 cup butter, cubed**
- **1 tablespoon minced fresh *or* dried chives**
- **1 to 2 teaspoons seasoned salt**
- **1/2 teaspoon pepper**

1. Divide the potatoes and onions equally between two pieces of heavy-duty foil (about 18-in. square) that have been coated with nonstick cooking spray.

2. Combine Parmesan cheese and 3/4 cup each cheddar and mozzarella; sprinkle over potatoes and onions. Top with bacon, butter, chives, seasoned salt and pepper. Bring opposite ends of foil together over filling and fold down several times. Fold unsealed ends toward filling and crimp tightly.

3. Grill, covered, over medium heat for 35-40 minutes or until potatoes are tender. Remove from the grill. Open foil carefully and sprinkle with remaining cheeses. **Yield:** 6-8 servings.

Homey and comforting, this custard-like side dish is a much-requested recipe at potlucks and holiday dinners. The jalapeno pepper adds just the right "bite". Second helpings of this tasty casserole are common—leftovers aren't.

    1 **medium onion, chopped**
1/4 **cup butter**
    2 **eggs**
    2 **cups (16 ounces) sour cream**
    1 **can (15-1/4 ounces) whole kernel corn, drained**
    1 **can (14-3/4 ounces) cream-style corn**
1/4 **teaspoon salt**
1/4 **teaspoon pepper**
    1 **package (8-1/2 ounces) corn bread/muffin mix**
    1 **medium jalapeno pepper, minced***
    2 **cups (8 ounces) shredded cheddar cheese, *divided***

1. In a skillet, saute onion in butter until tender and set aside.

2. In a bowl, beat the eggs; add sour cream, both cans of corn, salt and pepper. Stir in corn bread mix just until blended. Fold in sauteed onion, jalapeno and 1-1/2 cups of cheese. Transfer to a greased shallow 3-qt. baking dish. Sprinkle with the remaining cheese.

3. Bake, uncovered, at 375° for 35-40 minutes or until a toothpick inserted near the center comes out clean; cool slightly. **Yield:** 12-15 servings.

    ***Editor's Note:** When cutting or seeding hot peppers, use rubber or plastic gloves to protect your hands. Avoid touching your face.

🎗🎗🎗

Cheesy Corn Spoon Bread

(Pictured above)

Katherine Franklin, Carbondale, Illinois

- -

🎗🎗🎗

Blackberry Apple Jelly

(Pictured on page 130)

Liz Endacott, Matsqui, British Columbia

August is the busiest month of the year on our small farm—that's when we're harvesting sweet corn, pumpkins and pickling cucumbers for our stand. But I always make time to put up this jelly, which is usually gone by January!

    3 **pounds blackberries (about 2-1/2 quarts)**
1-1/4 **cups water**
    7 **to 8 medium apples**
Additional water
Bottled apple juice, optional
1/4 **cup lemon juice**
    8 **cups sugar**
    2 **pouches (3 ounces *each*) liquid fruit pectin**

1. In a large kettle, combine the blackberries and water; simmer for 5 minutes. Strain through a jelly bag, reserving juice and discarding pulp.

2. Remove and discard stems and blossom ends from apples (do not pare or core); cut into small pieces. Place in kettle; add just enough water to cover. Simmer until apples are soft, about 20 minutes. Strain through a jelly bag, reserving juice but not pulp.

3. Measure the reserved blackberry and apple juices; return to the kettle. If necessary, add water or bottled apple juice to equal 4 cups. Stir in lemon juice and sugar. Bring to a full rolling boil, stirring constantly. Add pectin, stirring until mixture boils. Boil for 1 minute. Remove from the heat; skim off foam.

4. Pour hot into hot jars, leaving 1/4-in. headspace. Adjust caps. Process for 15 minutes in a boiling-water bath. **Yield:** about 9 half-pints.

Mushroom Corn Casserole

(Pictured at right)

Mary Jones, Cumberland, Maine

Corn brightens up any meal with its sunny color and sweet crispness. I decided to create a casserole that combined corn, mushrooms and a rich cheesy sauce. I succeeded with this recipe.

- 1/3 cup chopped green pepper
- 1/3 cup finely chopped onion
- 3 tablespoons butter, *divided*
- 1/4 cup all-purpose flour
- 1 can (14-3/4 ounces) cream-style corn
- 1/2 teaspoon salt
- 1/8 teaspoon pepper
- 1 package (3 ounces) cream cheese, cubed
- 1 can (15-1/4 ounces) whole kernel corn, drained
- 1 can (4 ounces) mushroom stems and pieces, drained
- 1/2 cup shredded Swiss cheese
- 1-1/2 cups soft bread crumbs

1. In a saucepan, saute green pepper and onion in 1 tablespoon butter until tender. Stir in flour, cream corn, salt and pepper until blended. Add cream cheese; stir until melted. Stir in the whole kernel corn, mushrooms and Swiss cheese.

2. Transfer to a greased 1-1/2-qt. baking dish. Melt remaining butter; toss with bread crumbs. Sprinkle over the corn mixture.

3. Bake, uncovered, at 400° for 20-25 minutes or until heated through. **Yield:** 4-6 servings.

Colorful Oven Vegetables

(Pictured at left)

Grace Ammann, Richfield, Minnesota

As a party planner for a catering company, I often serve this attractive side dish with a steak dinner or at a brunch. Our two grown sons and their families frequently request it, too.

- 1/3 cup butter
- 1/2 teaspoon dried thyme
- 1/4 to 1/2 teaspoon salt
- 1/4 teaspoon pepper
- 3 cups cauliflowerets
- 2 cups broccoli florets
- 6 medium carrots,* julienned
- 3 small onions, quartered

1. Place butter in a shallow 3-qt. baking dish; place in a 400° oven for 5 minutes or until melted. Stir in thyme, salt and pepper. Add the vegetables and toss to coat.

2. Cover and bake for 25-30 minutes or until the vegetables are crisp-tender. **Yield:** 10-12 servings.

*Editor's Note: 2 cups baby carrots may be substituted; cut into julienne strips.

Picante Biscuit Bake

(Pictured at right)

Lanita Anderson, Jacksonville, North Carolina

This tasty Mexican-flavored side dish calls for just six convenient ingredients, so it's a breeze to put together. To make it into a main dish, add a pound of cooked ground beef. Or try a pizza variation using pizza sauce, pepperoni and mozzarella cheese. It's sure to be a hit with all ages.

- 2 tubes (12 ounces *each*) refrigerated buttermilk biscuits
- 1 jar (16 ounces) picante sauce *or* salsa
- 1 medium green pepper, chopped
- 1 medium onion, chopped
- 1 can (2-1/4 ounces) sliced ripe olives, drained
- 2 cups (8 ounces) shredded Monterey Jack cheese

1. Quarter the biscuits; place in a greased 13-in. x 9-in. x 2-in. baking dish. Top with picante sauce, green pepper, onion and olives.

2. Bake, uncovered, at 350° for 20 minutes. Sprinkle with cheese. Bake 10 minutes longer or until the cheese is melted. **Yield:** 6 servings.

Creamy Carrot Casserole

(Pictured at left)

Laurie Heward, Fillmore, Utah

My mom and I developed this recipe to see if there was a carrot dish that even people who don't care for carrots would enjoy. So far, I haven't met anyone who hasn't liked our casserole—especially when the carrots are garden-fresh.

- 1-1/2 pounds carrots, peeled and sliced *or* 1 bag (20 ounces) frozen sliced carrots, thawed
- 1 cup mayonnaise
- 1 tablespoon grated onion
- 1 tablespoon prepared horseradish
- 1/4 cup shredded cheddar cheese
- 2 tablespoons buttered bread crumbs

1. In a saucepan, cook carrots just until crisp-tender; drain, reserving 1/4 cup cooking liquid.

2. Place carrots in a 1-1/2-qt. baking dish. Combine mayonnaise, onion, horseradish and reserved cooking liquid; spread evenly over carrots. Sprinkle with cheese; top with bread crumbs.

3. Bake, uncovered, at 350° for 30 minutes. **Yield:** 8-10 servings.

Scalloped Apples

(Pictured at right)

Sandy Daniels, Grandville, Michigan

When I was a child, I loved eating at my grandma's house, especially when she baked this comforting side dish. As a busy mother of seven, I'm often short on time, so I use the microwave to fix it quickly. My family enjoys its "apple pie" flavor with a meal or topped with ice cream for dessert.

✓ Uses less fat, sugar or salt. Includes Nutritional Analysis and Diabetic Exchanges.

- 10 **cups sliced peeled tart apples (about 8 medium)**
- 1/3 **cup sugar**
- 2 **tablespoons cornstarch**
- 1/2 to 1 **teaspoon ground cinnamon**
- 1/4 **teaspoon ground nutmeg**
- 2 **tablespoons butter, cubed**

1. Place apples in a 2-1/2-qt. microwave-safe bowl. Combine the sugar, cornstarch, cinnamon and nutmeg; sprinkle over apples and toss to coat. Dot with butter.

2. Cover; microwave on high 15 minutes or until apples are tender, stirring every 5 minutes. **Yield:** 8 servings.

Nutritional Analysis: One 1/2-cup serving (prepared with artificial sweetener equivalent to 1/3 cup sugar and reduced-fat margarine) equals 116 calories, 33 mg sodium, 0 cholesterol, 30 gm carbohydrate, trace protein, 2 gm fat. **Diabetic Exchange:** 2 fruit.

Editor's Note: This recipe was tested in an 850-watt microwave.

Cherry Almond Preserves

(Pictured at right)

Connie Lawrence, Hamilton, Montana

This recipe came from my mother-in-law. It's very old-fashioned—in fact, the friend who gave it to her used to cook it up on an old wood stove. With all the cherry orchards here in the Bitterroot Valley, I make two batches of these preserves each summer. My family likes them on fresh bread, muffins, pancakes and even ice cream—the consistency's similar to a topping. I have to be careful, though, and ration the jars out or they'd be the first thing to disappear from the root cellar!

- 8 **cups pitted sour cherries (about 4 pounds)**
- 1-1/2 **cups water**
- 10 **cups sugar**
- 2 **pouches (3 ounces *each*) liquid fruit pectin**
- 1 **teaspoon almond extract**

1. In a large kettle, bring the cherries and water to a boil; boil for 15 minutes.

2. Add sugar and bring to a full rolling boil, stirring constantly. Boil for 4 minutes. Stir in pectin; return to a full rolling boil. Boil for 1 minute, stirring constantly. Remove from the heat; stir in extract. Skim off foam.

3. Pour hot into hot jars, leaving 1/4-in. headspace. Adjust caps. Process 15 minutes in a boiling-water bath. **Yield:** 11 half-pints.

6 small red potatoes, quartered
1 medium rutabaga, peeled, cut into 1-inch cubes
1/2 teaspoon salt, optional
3 medium carrots, cut into 1/2-inch slices
1 medium turnip, peeled, cut into 1-inch cubes
1 to 2 medium parsnips, peeled and cut into 1/2-inch slices
1 medium onion, cut into eighths

GLAZE:
1 tablespoon butter
3 tablespoons brown sugar
1 teaspoon cornstarch
1/4 cup water
3 tablespoons lemon juice
1/2 teaspoon dill weed
1/8 teaspoon pepper
1/2 teaspoon salt, optional

🎗️🎗️🎗️
Root Vegetable Medley
(Pictured above)

Marilyn Smudzinski, Peru, Illinois

Equally good with pork or beef roast—or with a Thanksgiving turkey—this dish is one my husband of 40 years requests at least once a month. Our four grown children and their families enjoy it, too.

✓ Uses less fat, sugar or salt. Includes Nutritional Analysis and Diabetic Exchanges.

1. Place potatoes and rutabaga in a large saucepan; cover with water. Add salt if desired. Bring to a boil. Reduce heat; cover and simmer for 8 minutes. Add remaining vegetables; return to a boil. Reduce heat; cover and simmer for 10 minutes or until vegetables are tender; drain.

2. For glaze, melt butter in a saucepan; stir in brown sugar and cornstarch. Stir in water, lemon juice, dill, pepper and salt if desired; bring to a boil. Cook and stir 2 minutes. Pour over vegetables; toss to coat. **Yield:** 8 servings.
   Nutritional Analysis: One 1-cup serving (prepared with margarine and without salt) equals 85 calories, 41 mg sodium, 0 cholesterol, 17 gm carbohydrate, 1 gm protein, 2 gm fat. **Diabetic Exchange:** 1 starch.

🎗️🎗️🎗️
Artichoke Spinach Casserole
(Pictured on page 130)

Judy Johnson, Missoula, Montana

Although he isn't a fan of spinach, my husband loves this dish. The combination of ingredients may sound unusual, but the flavors meld well. It's an excellent side dish for a formal dinner.

1 pound fresh mushrooms, sliced
1/3 cup chicken broth
1 tablespoon all-purpose flour
1/2 cup evaporated milk
4 packages (10 ounces *each*) frozen chopped spinach, thawed and well drained
2 cans (14-1/2 ounces *each*) diced tomatoes, drained
2 cans (14 ounces *each*) water-packed artichoke hearts, drained and thinly sliced
1 cup (8 ounces) sour cream
1/2 cup mayonnaise
3 tablespoons lemon juice
1/2 teaspoon garlic powder
1/4 teaspoon salt
1/4 teaspoon pepper
Paprika, optional

1. In a large skillet, cook mushrooms and broth over medium heat until tender, about 3 minutes. Remove mushrooms with a slotted spoon and set aside.

2. Whisk flour and milk until smooth; add to skillet. Bring to a boil; cook and stir for 2 minutes. Remove from the heat; stir in spinach, tomatoes and mushrooms.

3. Place half of the artichokes in an ungreased 13-in. x 9-in. x 2-in. baking dish. Top with half of the spinach mixture. Repeat layers. Combine sour cream, mayonnaise, lemon juice, garlic powder, salt and pepper; dollop over casserole. Sprinkle with paprika if desired.

4. Bake, uncovered, at 350° for 25-30 minutes or until bubbly. **Yield:** 12-14 servings.

🎀🎀🎀
Sweet Potatoes with Apples

(Pictured at right)

Jean Winfree, Merrill, Wisconsin

This satisfying dish is very welcome at any meal at our house, especially on holidays. The tart apple slices taste so good baked on top of the mild sweet potatoes.

- **3 to 3-1/2 pounds sweet potatoes**
- **2 tart apples, peeled, cored and cut into 1/4-inch rings**
- **1/2 cup orange juice**
- **1/4 cup packed brown sugar**
- **1/4 teaspoon ground ginger**
- **1/4 teaspoon ground cinnamon**
- **2 tablespoons butter**

1. In a large saucepan, cover sweet potatoes with water; bring to a boil. Reduce heat; cover and simmer for 30 minutes or until just tender. Drain and cool slightly. Peel and cut into 1/4-in. slices.

2. Alternate layers of potatoes and apples in a greased 13-in. x 9-in. x 2-in. baking dish. Pour orange juice over. Mix brown sugar, ginger and cinnamon; sprinkle over potatoes and apples. Dot with butter.

3. Bake, uncovered, at 350° for 35-45 minutes or until apples have reached desired doneness. **Yield:** 8 servings.

🎀🎀🎀
Calico Chowchow

(Pictured below)

Doris Haycroft, Westbank, British Columbia

I make this special relish each fall when fresh vegetables are at their peak. I usually prepare several batches so I can give away jars to friends as gifts. It's a saucy relish that goes well with both hot and cold meats.

- **7 cups shredded cabbage (about 1 small head)**
- **4 cups fresh corn (about 5 ears)**
- **4 cups cauliflowerets (about 1 small head)**
- **2 cups diced sweet red pepper**
- **1 cup diced green pepper**
- **1 cup chopped onion**
- **1/4 cup canning salt**
- **7 cups water, *divided***
- **3-1/2 cups packed brown sugar**
- **1/2 cup all-purpose flour**
- **1/4 cup ground mustard**
- **1 tablespoon celery seed**
- **2 teaspoons ground turmeric**
- **1-1/2 teaspoons salt**
- **5 cups vinegar**

1. In a large bowl, combine the first six ingredients; sprinkle with canning salt. Add 6 cups water; cover and refrigerate for 4 hours. Drain and rinse well.

2. In a large heavy saucepan or Dutch oven, combine the brown sugar, flour, mustard, celery seed, turmeric and salt. Stir in vinegar and remaining water until smooth. Bring to a boil; cook and stir for 5 minutes or until thickened. Add vegetables; bring to a boil. Simmer, uncovered, for 8-10 minutes or until crisp-tender.

3. Pack the hot mixture into hot jars, leaving 1/4-in. headspace. Adjust caps. Process for 15 minutes in a boiling-water bath. **Yield:** 7 pints.

✿✿✿ Microwave Mac 'n' Cheese

(Pictured at right)

Linda Gingrich, Freeburg, Pennsylvania

My family prefers homemade macaroni and cheese over the kind you get out of a box. This recipe is an easy way to keep them happy. Whenever we have a family get-together, I bring this comforting dish. Its from-scratch taste can't be beat.

- 2 cups uncooked elbow macaroni
- 2 cups hot water
- 1/3 cup butter
- 1/4 cup chopped onion
- 3/4 teaspoon salt
- 1/4 teaspoon pepper
- 1/4 teaspoon ground mustard
- 1/3 cup all-purpose flour
- 1-1/4 cups milk
- 8 ounces process American cheese, cubed

1. In a 2-qt. microwave-safe dish, combine first seven ingredients. Cover and microwave on high for 3-1/2 minutes; stir. Cover; cook at 50% power for 4 minutes or until mixture comes to a boil, rotating a half turn once.

2. Combine flour and milk until smooth; stir into macaroni mixture. Add cheese. Cover and cook on high for 6-8 minutes or until the macaroni is tender and sauce is bubbly, rotating a half turn once and stirring every 3 minutes. **Yield:** 4 servings.

Editor's Note: This recipe was tested in an 850-watt microwave.

✿✿✿ Crabby Potatoes

(Pictured at left)

Suzanne Rawlings, Jacksonville, Florida

We have potato and crab festivals near our home. I combined the two ingredients to give potatoes a surprise taste.

- 3 large baking potatoes
- 1/2 cup butter, melted
- 2 tablespoons milk
- 1 tablespoon mayonnaise

Salt and pepper to taste
- 2 cans (6 ounces *each*) crabmeat, drained, flaked and cartilage removed
- 3/4 cup shredded cheddar cheese, optional

1. Bake potatoes at 375° for 1 hour or until tender. Cool. Cut potatoes in half lengthwise. Scoop out the pulp and place in a mixing bowl; set shells aside.

2. Add butter to pulp and mash. Beat in milk, mayonnaise, salt and pepper until smooth. Fold in crab. Spoon into potato shells. Place in an ungreased 11-in. x 7-in. x 2-in. baking dish. Sprinkle with cheese if desired.

3. Bake, uncovered, at 350° for 30 minutes or until heated through. **Yield:** 6 servings.

🎖🎖🎖
Texas Two-Step Corn Medley

(Pictured on page 130)

Pauline Howard, Lago Vista, Texas

I came up with this pleasing pairing of corn and summer squash as a side dish for a Mexican buffet. Family and friends who have tried it are generous with their compliments and recipe requests. This delicious dish is a regular menu item when my husband, Bob, and I entertain.

- 1 medium onion, chopped
- 1/4 cup butter
- 2 medium yellow summer squash, sliced
- 2 garlic cloves, minced
- 2 tablespoons canned chopped green chilies
- 1/4 teaspoon salt
- 1/8 teaspoon pepper
- 2 cans (11 ounces *each*) Mexicorn, drained
- 3/4 cup shredded Colby-Monterey Jack cheese

1. In a skillet, saute onion in butter until tender. Add the squash, garlic, chilies, salt and pepper. Saute until squash is crisp-tender, about 5 minutes. Add corn; cook and stir for 2 minutes.

2. Sprinkle with cheese; cover and let stand until the cheese is melted. **Yield:** 4 servings.

🎖🎖🎖
Wild Rice Floret Bake

(Pictured at right)

Donna Torgerson, Park Rapids, Minnesota

My mom used to make this hearty dish for family get-togethers. Now I do the same when our five grown children and their families come to visit.

- 1 medium onion, chopped
- 3 tablespoons butter
- 2 tablespoons all-purpose flour
- 1/2 teaspoon salt

Dash pepper

- 2 cups milk
- 1 cup (8 ounces) sour cream
- 1 cup (4 ounces) shredded cheddar cheese, *divided*
- 4 cups cooked wild rice, *divided*
- 6 cups chopped cooked broccoli (about 1 large bunch)
- 5 cups chopped cooked cauliflower (about 1 small head)
- 6 bacon strips, cooked and crumbled

1. In a saucepan, saute the onion in butter until tender. Stir in flour, salt and pepper until blended. Gradually add milk. Bring to a boil; cook and stir for 2 minutes or until thickened and bubbly.

2. Remove from the heat; stir in sour cream and 1/2 cup

cheese until smooth.

3. Place 2 cups of wild rice in a greased 13-in. x 9-in. x 2-in. baking dish. Top with broccoli and cauliflower. Place remaining wild rice lengthwise down the center of dish. Pour the sauce over all. Sprinkle with remaining cheese.

4. Cover and bake at 350° for 20 minutes. Uncover; sprinkle with bacon. Bake 10-15 minutes longer or until bubbly. **Yield:** 8-10 servings.

★★★
Company Mac and Cheese
(Pictured at right)

Catherine Odgen, Middlegrove, New York

This is by far the creamiest, tastiest and most special macaroni and cheese I have ever tried. Since it's so little fuss and well received, it's a terrific potluck dish.

- 1 package (7 ounces) elbow macaroni
- 6 tablespoons butter, *divided*
- 3 tablespoons all-purpose flour
- 2 cups milk
- 1 package (8 ounces) cream cheese, cubed
- 2 cups (8 ounces) shredded cheddar cheese
- 2 teaspoons spicy brown mustard
- 1/2 teaspoon salt
- 1/4 teaspoon pepper
- 3/4 cup dry bread crumbs
- 2 tablespoons minced fresh parsley

1. Cook macaroni according to package directions. Meanwhile, melt 4 tablespoons butter in a large saucepan. Stir in flour until smooth. Gradually add milk. Bring to a boil; cook and stir for 2 minutes.

2. Reduce heat; add cheeses, mustard, salt and pepper. Stir until cheese is melted and sauce is smooth. Drain macaroni; add to the cheese sauce and stir to coat.

3. Transfer to a greased shallow 3-qt. baking dish. Melt the remaining butter; toss with bread crumbs and parsley. Sprinkle over macaroni. Bake, uncovered, at 400° for 15-20 minutes or until golden brown. **Yield:** 6-8 servings.

★★★
Three Bean Casserole
(Pictured above)

Georgia Hennings, Alliance, Nebraska

When our church cookbook was revised a few years ago, this recipe was included among the favorites. My family feels the same way about it.

- 1 can (16 ounces) red kidney beans, rinsed and drained
- 1 can (15 ounces) garbanzo beans, rinsed and drained
- 1 can (16 ounces) lima beans, rinsed and drained
- 1 pound lean ground beef
- 1 large onion, chopped
- 1 garlic clove, minced
- 1/4 cup packed brown sugar
- 1/2 teaspoon salt
- Dash pepper
- 2 tablespoons prepared mustard
- 1/2 cup ketchup
- 1 teaspoon ground cumin
- 1/4 cup water
- 1 tablespoon vinegar

1. In a 2-1/2-qt. casserole, combine beans; set aside. In a skillet, cook beef, onion and garlic until beef is no longer pink. Remove from the heat; drain. Add remaining ingredients to skillet; mix well. Stir beef mixture into beans.

2. Bake at 350° for about 45 minutes or until heated through. **Yield:** 6-8 servings.

🎗🎗🎗 Three-Rice Pilaf

(Pictured on page 130)

Ricki Bingham, Ogden, Utah

My family's favorite rice dish is this tempting medley of white, brown and wild rice. I prepare it as a side dish or a stuffing. In fall I add chopped dried apricots, and for the holidays I mix in dried cranberries. My guests always ask for seconds.

1/2 cup uncooked brown rice
1/2 cup finely chopped carrots
1/2 cup chopped onion
1/2 cup sliced fresh mushrooms
  2 tablespoons vegetable oil
1/2 cup uncooked wild rice
  3 cups chicken broth
1/4 teaspoon dried thyme
1/4 teaspoon dried rosemary, crushed
1/2 cup uncooked long grain rice
1/3 cup chopped dried apricots
  2 tablespoons minced green onions
1/4 teaspoon salt
1/8 teaspoon pepper
1/2 cup chopped pecans, toasted

1. In a large saucepan, saute brown rice, carrots, onion and mushrooms in oil for 10 minutes or until rice is golden.

2. Add wild rice, broth, thyme and rosemary; bring to a boil. Reduce heat; cover and simmer for 25 minutes. Stir in long grain rice; cover and simmer for 25 minutes or until liquid is absorbed and wild rice is tender.

3. Remove from the heat; stir in apricots, green onions, salt and pepper. Cover and let stand for 5 minutes. Sprinkle with pecans just before serving. **Yield:** 8-10 servings.

🎗🎗🎗 Cranberry Chutney

(Pictured at right)

Joyce Vivian, Mitchell, Ontario

I discovered this recipe years ago and revised it to suit our tastes. It's a hit with poultry or pork, plus I've given it as gifts.

  3 cups fresh *or* frozen cranberries
  1 cup chopped dried apricots
1/2 cup chopped dates
1/2 cup chopped onion
1/2 cup cider vinegar
1/2 cup light corn syrup
3/4 cup packed brown sugar
  1 tablespoon grated orange peel
3/4 cup orange juice
1/2 teaspoon ground mustard
1/2 teaspoon salt
1/4 teaspoon ground ginger

1. In a large heavy saucepan, combine all ingredients. Bring to a boil. Reduce heat and simmer, uncovered, for 15-20 minutes or until mixture has thickened and cranberries have popped.

2. Chill. Serve as an accompaniment to turkey or pork. **Yield:** about 3-1/2 cups.

🎗️ 🎗️ 🎗️

Savory Cauliflower Pie

(Pictured above)

Debbie Hart, Ft. Wayne, Indiana

If you're looking for a meatless main dish or a hearty side to take to a church potluck or family gathering, this pie is the perfect choice. It's a family favorite.

> 3 cups seasoned croutons, crushed
> 1/2 cup butter, melted, *divided*
> 1 cup chopped onion

> 1 small head cauliflower, cut into small florets (about 5 cups)
> 1/2 cup thinly sliced carrot
> 1 garlic clove, minced
> 1/2 teaspoon salt
> 1/4 to 1/2 teaspoon dried oregano
> 1 cup (4 ounces) shredded cheddar cheese, *divided*
> 2 eggs
> 1/4 cup milk

1. In a bowl, combine croutons and 1/4 cup butter. Press onto the bottom and up the sides of an ungreased 9-in. pie plate. Bake at 375° for 8 minutes or until lightly browned; set aside.

2. In a large skillet, saute the onion, cauliflower, carrot, garlic, salt and oregano in remaining butter over medium heat for 10 minutes, stirring frequently.

3. Sprinkle 1/2 cup cheese into prepared crust. Top with the cauliflower mixture and remaining cheese. In a bowl, beat the eggs and milk. Pour over pie.

4. Bake, uncovered, at 375° for 30 minutes or until a knife inserted near the center comes out clean and the cauliflower is tender. **Yield:** 6-8 servings.

🎗️ 🎗️ 🎗️

Squash Stuffing Casserole

(Pictured at right)

Tara Kay Cottingham, Munday, Texas

The recipe for this zippy side dish was given to me by my husband's grandmother. Convenient corn bread stuffing mix and a can of green chilies give fast flavor to sliced summer squash.

> 3/4 cup water
> 1/4 teaspoon salt
> 6 cups sliced yellow summer squash (1/4 inch thick)
> 1 small onion, halved and sliced
> 1 can (10-3/4 ounces) condensed cream of mushroom soup, undiluted
> 1 cup (8 ounces) sour cream
> 1 package (6 ounces) instant corn bread stuffing mix
> 1 can (4 ounces) chopped green chilies
> Salt and pepper to taste
> 1 cup (4 ounces) shredded cheddar cheese

1. In a large saucepan, bring the water and salt to a boil. Add the squash and onion. Reduce heat; cover and cook until the squash is crisp-tender, about 6 minutes. Drain well; set aside.

2. In a bowl, combine soup, sour cream, stuffing and the contents of seasoning packet, chilies, salt and pepper; mix well. Fold in squash mixture. Pour into a greased shallow 2-qt. baking dish. Sprinkle with cheese.

3. Bake, uncovered, at 350° for 25-30 minutes or until heated through. **Yield:** 8-10 servings.

🎗🎗🎗
Grilled Potato Fans
(Pictured at right)

Jennifer Black-Ortiz, San Jose, California

If you're looking for a change from plain baked potatoes, try these buttery potato fans seasoned with oregano, garlic powder, celery and onion. To cut down on grilling time, I sometimes microwave the potatoes for 5-6 minutes before slicing them.

  6 **medium baking potatoes**
  2 **medium onions, halved and thinly sliced**
  6 **tablespoons butter, cubed**
1/4 **cup finely chopped celery**
  1 **teaspoon** *each* **salt and dried oregano**
1/4 **teaspoon garlic powder**
1/4 **teaspoon pepper**

1. With a sharp knife, make cuts 1/2 in. apart in each potato, leaving slices attached at the bottom. Fan the potatoes slightly. Place each on a piece of heavy-duty foil (about 12 in. square).

2. Insert onions and butter between potato slices. Sprinkle with celery, salt, oregano, garlic powder and pepper. Fold foil around potatoes and seal tightly.

3. Grill, covered, over medium-hot heat for 40-45 minutes or until tender. **Yield:** 6 servings.

🎗🎗🎗
Swiss Potato Squares
(Pictured at right)

Nancy Foust, Stoneboro, Pennsylvania

To vary these squares, you can substitute cheddar cheese for the Swiss or try Canadian bacon in place of the ham. However you make them, they taste wonderful.

    8 **medium russet potatoes (about 3 pounds),**
      peeled and cubed
 1/3 **cup butter, melted**
    1 **tablespoon minced fresh parsley**
1-1/2 **teaspoons salt**
 1/4 **teaspoon pepper**
1-1/2 **cups cubed Swiss cheese**
    1 **cup cubed fully cooked ham**
    1 **small onion, grated**
    1 **teaspoon garlic powder**
    3 **eggs**
 1/2 **cup milk**
Paprika

1. Place potatoes in a saucepan and cover with water. Cover and bring to a boil; cook for 20-25 minutes or until very tender. Drain well. Mash with butter, parsley, salt and pepper.

2. Spread about 4 cups of the potato mixture onto the bottom and up the sides of a greased 8-in. square baking dish. Combine cheese, ham, onion and garlic powder; spoon into potato shell. Combine eggs and milk; pour over all. Top with remaining potato mixture. Sprinkle with paprika.

3. Bake, uncovered, at 400° for 45-50 minutes or until top is golden brown. Let stand 5 minutes before cutting. **Yield:** 8-9 servings.

🎀🎀🎀

Grandma's Sweet-Sour Veggies

(Pictured above)

Jeanne Schuyler, Wauwatosa, Wisconsin

Every summer, we look forward to a bonanza of fresh vegetables. There's nothing like a large bowl to perk up a meal.

✓ Uses less fat, sugar or salt. Includes Nutritional Analysis and Diabetic Exchanges.

3 cups cauliflowerets
3 cups broccoli florets
2 medium carrots, thinly sliced
1 medium zucchini, quartered and thinly sliced
1 small red onion, julienned
3/4 cup cider vinegar
1/4 cup sugar
1/2 teaspoon salt, optional
2 tablespoons vegetable oil
Sunflower kernels, optional

1. In a bowl, combine the cauliflower, broccoli, carrots, zucchini and onion; set aside.

2. In a saucepan over medium heat, bring vinegar, sugar and salt if desired to a boil. Remove from the heat; stir in oil. Pour over vegetables and toss to coat.

3. Cover and refrigerate overnight. Just before serving, sprinkle with sunflower kernels if desired. **Yield:** 12-14 servings.

Nutritional Analysis: One 3/4-cup serving (prepared without salt and sunflower kernels) equals 60 calories, 17 mg sodium, 0 cholesterol, 10 gm carbohydrate, 1 gm protein, 2 gm fat. **Diabetic Exchanges:** 1-1/2 vegetable, 1/2 fat.

🎀🎀🎀
Church Supper Potatoes
(Pictured at right)

Michelle Grigsby, Beavercreek, Ohio

As a pastor's wife, I cook for crowds often. This dish is always a hit. My own family thinks the potatoes are a must with London broil or marinated grilled chicken breasts.

- **3 pounds russet potatoes (about 9 medium), peeled and cut into 1/2-inch cubes**
- **2 garlic cloves, peeled**
- **2 packages (3 ounces *each*) cream cheese, softened**
- **2 tablespoons butter**
- **1/2 cup sour cream**
- **2 cups (8 ounces) shredded cheddar cheese, *divided***
- **1 teaspoon garlic salt**
- **1 teaspoon onion salt**
- **1 package (10 ounces) frozen chopped spinach, thawed and squeezed dry**

1. Place the potatoes and garlic in a large saucepan; cover with water. Cover and bring to a boil; cook for 20-25 minutes or until very tender. Drain well.

2. In a mixing bowl, mash potatoes and garlic with the cream cheese and butter. Add the sour cream, 1 cup of cheddar cheese, garlic salt, onion salt and spinach. Stir just until mixed. Spread into a greased 2-qt. baking dish.

3. Bake, uncovered, at 350° for 30-35 minutes or until heated through. Top with remaining cheese; bake 5 minutes longer or until the cheese is melted. **Yield:** 10-12 servings.

🎀🎀🎀
Apple-a-Day Casserole
(Pictured at right)

Elizabeth Erwin, Syracuse, New York

This sweet-tart casserole is a fun change of pace from traditional vegetable side dishes. It's super-quick to prepare if you use a food processor to slice the apples and carrots.

- **6 medium tart apples, peeled and sliced**
- **6 medium carrots, thinly sliced**
- **1/2 cup orange juice**
- **1/3 cup all-purpose flour**
- **1/3 cup sugar**
- **1/2 teaspoon ground nutmeg**
- **2 tablespoons cold butter**

1. Combine apples and carrots; place in a greased shallow 2-qt. baking dish. Drizzle with orange juice. Cover and bake at 350° for 40-45 minutes or until carrots are crisp-tender.

2. In a bowl, combine the flour, sugar and nutmeg; cut in butter until crumbly. Sprinkle over apple mixture. Bake, uncovered, 10-15 minutes longer or until the carrots are tender. **Yield:** 6-8 servings.

🎀🎀🎀
Golden Mashed Potatoes

(Pictured at right)

Cindy Stith, Wickliffe, Kentucky

When there's no gravy with the meat, this is great to serve in place of regular mashed potatoes. I make it to take to picnics and church socials. My husband even made it for his family's reunion one year!

- **9 large potatoes (about 4 pounds), peeled and cubed**
- **1 pound carrots, cut into 1/2-inch chunks**
- **8 green onions, thinly sliced**
- **1/2 cup butter**
- **1 cup (8 ounces) sour cream**
- **1-1/2 teaspoons salt**
- **1/8 teaspoon pepper**
- **3/4 cup shredded cheddar cheese**

1. In a soup kettle or Dutch oven, cook the potatoes and carrots in boiling salted water until tender; drain. Place in a mixing bowl; mash and set aside.

2. In a skillet, saute onions in butter until tender. Add to potato mixture. Add sour cream, salt and pepper; mix until blended.

3. Transfer mixture to a greased 13-in. x 9-in. x 2-in. baking dish. Sprinkle with cheese. Bake, uncovered, at 350° for 30-40 minutes or until heated through. **Yield:** 10-12 servings.

🎀🎀🎀
Herbed Garlic Potatoes

(Pictured above)

Sherry DesJardin, Fairbanks, Alaska

My dad invented this dish. The potatoes fit any kind of meal—fancy or burgers—and everyone asks for the recipe.

- **15 small red potatoes (about 2 pounds)**
- **1/3 cup butter**
- **1/4 cup minced fresh parsley**
- **2 tablespoons minced fresh *or* dried chives**
- **1-1/2 teaspoons minced fresh tarragon *or* 1/2 teaspoon dried tarragon**
- **2 to 3 garlic cloves, minced**
- **1/2 to 1 teaspoon salt**
- **1/4 teaspoon pepper**
- **3 bacon strips, cooked and crumbled, optional**

1. Cut the potatoes in half and place in a saucepan; cover with water. Cover and bring to a boil; cook until tender, about 15 minutes. Drain well.

2. In a large skillet, melt butter. Add the parsley, chives, tarragon and garlic; cook and stir over low heat for 1-2 minutes. Add the potatoes, salt, pepper and bacon if desired; toss to coat. Cook until heated through, about 5 minutes. **Yield:** 6-8 servings.

🎗🎗🎗
Red Cabbage Casserole

(Pictured at right)

Julie Murray, Sunderland, Ontario

With its color and eye appeal, this dish is a hit on special days like Christmas or Easter, when I'm cooking for a crowd.

   1 tablespoon shortening
   8 cups shredded red cabbage
   1 medium onion, chopped
 1/2 cup lemon juice *or* vinegar
 1/4 cup sugar
   1 teaspoon salt
   1 to 2 medium apples, chopped
 1/4 cup red currant jelly
Lemon slices, optional

1. In a Dutch oven, melt shortening. Add the cabbage, onion, lemon juice or vinegar, sugar and salt; mix well. Cover and cook over medium heat for 10-15 minutes or until cabbage is crisp-tender, stirring occasionally.

2. Add apples; cook 10-15 minutes more or until cabbage and apples are tender. Stir in jelly until melted. Garnish with lemon slices if desired. **Yield:** 8-10 servings.

🎗🎗🎗
End-of-Summer Vegetable Bake

(Pictured at right)

Judy Williams, Hayden, Idaho

When my husband was a deputy agriculture commissioner, he'd bring me bushels of vegetables from area farms. This pretty side dish is the result—it's easy to fix yet impressive.

   1 small head cauliflower, broken into small
     florets (about 5 cups)
   1 medium bunch broccoli, cut into small florets
     (about 4 cups)
   1 medium onion, chopped
   2 garlic cloves, minced
   1 tablespoon butter
   2 medium tomatoes, chopped
 3/4 teaspoon *each* dried basil, dried oregano and salt
 1/4 teaspoon pepper
 1/4 teaspoon hot pepper sauce
   4 eggs
 1/3 cup half-and-half cream
1-1/2 cups (6 ounces) shredded Swiss cheese, *divided*
 1/4 cup shredded Parmesan cheese

1. Place the cauliflower and broccoli in a saucepan with a small amount of water. Bring to a boil. Reduce heat; cover and simmer for 5-10 minutes or until crisp-tender. Drain and set aside.

2. In a large skillet, saute onion and garlic in butter until tender. Stir in tomatoes, seasonings, cauliflower and broccoli. Cook, uncovered, until heated through, about 4 minutes, stirring occasionally. Remove from heat; set aside.

3. In a large bowl, beat eggs and cream; stir in 1 cup Swiss cheese, Parmesan cheese and the vegetable mixture. Transfer to a greased shallow 2-qt. baking dish. Sprinkle with remaining Swiss cheese.

4. Bake, uncovered, at 375° for 25-30 minutes or until a knife inserted near the center comes out clean. Let stand 10 minutes before serving. **Yield:** 12 servings.

Strawberries 'n' Cream Bread, p. 162

Cinnamon-Raisin Soft Pretzels, p. 161

Italian Cheese Bread, p. 157

Breads

You'll find just the right bread to accompany your family meals, whether you're looking for a zippy corn bread, flaky biscuits, fresh-from-the-oven rolls or a sweet quick bread.

Sesame Wheat Braids, p. 155

Golden Potato Rolls...........................154

Sesame Wheat Braids...........................155

Savory Chicken Vegetable Strudel........155

Triple-Chocolate Quick Bread...........156

Sweet Onion Muffins........................156

Caraway Cloverleaf Rolls 157

Italian Cheese Bread 157

Bacon Swiss Bread 158

Savory Italian Rounds........................158

Poppy Seed Lemon Scones.................159

Aloha Quick Bread...........................160

Tex-Mex Biscuits 160

Cinnamon-Raisin Soft Pretzels............161

Chive-Cheese Corn Bread...................161

Poppy Seed Rolls...............................162

Strawberries 'n' Cream Bread..............162

Green Chili Corn Muffins...................163

Citrus Streusel Quick Bread...............163

Three-Cheese Twists...........................164

Gingerbread Loaf 165

Broccoli Corn Bread..........................165

Flaky Dill Biscuits.............................166

Onion Sandwich Rolls.......................166

Tomato Pizza Bread 167

Golden Potato Rolls

(Pictured above)

Noni Ruegner, Salt Lake City, Utah

My mother got me started in cooking. Dad has also always been a ready coach in the kitchen. I'll never forget some of the first food advice he gave me— "If you just put onions in everything you make, it will come out tasting better!"

     1 package (1/4 ounce) active dry yeast
   1/2 cup warm water (110° to 115°)
     1 cup milk
   3/4 cup shortening
 1-1/4 cups mashed potatoes
   1/2 cup sugar
     2 teaspoons salt
     8 to 8-1/2 cups all-purpose flour, *divided*
     2 eggs, beaten

1. Dissolve yeast in water; set aside. In a saucepan, combine milk, shortening and potatoes; cook and stir over low heat just until shortening is melted. Remove from the heat and place in a large bowl with sugar, salt, 2 cups of flour and the yeast mixture. Add eggs; mix well. Cover loosely and allow to stand for 2 hours (the dough will be like a sponge).

2. Stir in enough of the remaining flour to form a soft dough. Turn out onto a floured surface and knead until smooth and elastic, about 6 minutes. Place in a greased bowl, turning once to grease top. Cover and let rise in a warm place until doubled, about 1 hour.

3. Punch dough down and divide into thirds. On a floured surface, roll each portion into a 12-in. circle. Cut each circle into 12 pie-shaped wedges. Beginning at the wide end, roll up each wedge.

4. Place rolls, point side down, 2 in. apart on greased baking sheets. Cover and let rise 30 minutes or until nearly doubled. Bake at 400° for 15 minutes or until golden. **Yield:** 3 dozen.

Sesame Wheat Braids

(Pictured on page 153)

Nancy Montgomery, Hartville, Ohio

I was thrilled when the judges at our county fair gave these braids both a blue ribbon and best of show award!

    2 packages (1/4 ounce *each*) active dry yeast
2-1/4 cups warm water (110° to 115°)
    1/3 cup sugar
      1 tablespoon vegetable oil
      1 cup whole wheat flour
      2 eggs
      1 tablespoon water
      1 tablespoon salt
      5 to 6 cups all-purpose flour
      2 teaspoons sesame seeds

1. In a large mixing bowl, dissolve yeast in water. Add sugar and oil; mix well. Stir in whole wheat flour; let stand until the mixture bubbles, about 5 minutes.

2. In a small bowl, beat eggs and water. Remove 2 tablespoons to a small bowl; cover and refrigerate. Add remaining egg mixture and salt to batter; mix until smooth. Add 4 cups all-purpose flour and beat until smooth. Add enough remaining flour to form a soft dough.

3. Turn onto a floured surface and knead until smooth and elastic, about 6-8 minutes. Place in a greased bowl, turning once to grease top. Cover and let rise in a warm place until doubled, about 1 hour. Punch dough down and divide in half. Divide each half into thirds.

4. Shape each into a rope about 15 in. long. Place three ropes on a greased baking sheet; braid. Pinch ends firmly and tuck under. Repeat, placing second braid on another baking sheet. Let rise until doubled, about 45 minutes.

5. Brush with the reserved egg mixture; sprinkle with sesame seeds. Bake at 350° for 20-25 minutes. Remove from pans cool on wire racks. **Yield:** 2 loaves.

Savory Chicken Vegetable Strudel

(Pictured at right)

Michele Barneson, Washburn, Wisconsin

If you're looking for a way to "sneak" vegetables into a dish, try this one that looks fancy without the fuss. I make it for my husband and me as well as for company.

      2 cups diced cooked chicken
    1/2 cup shredded carrots
    1/2 cup finely chopped fresh broccoli
    1/3 cup finely chopped sweet red pepper
      1 cup (4 ounces) shredded sharp cheddar cheese
    1/2 cup mayonnaise
      2 garlic cloves, minced
    1/2 teaspoon dill weed
    1/4 teaspoon salt
    1/4 teaspoon pepper
      2 tubes (8 ounces *each*) refrigerated crescent rolls
      1 egg white, beaten
      2 tablespoons slivered almonds

1. In a bowl, combine the first 10 ingredients; mix well. Unroll crescent dough and place in a greased 15-in. x 10-in. x 1-in. baking pan; press seams and perforations together, forming a 15-in. x 12-in. rectangle (dough will hang over edges of pan).

2. Spread filling lengthwise down the center of dough. On each long side, cut 1-1/2-in.-wide strips 3-1/2 in. into center. Starting at one end, alternate strips, twisting twice and laying at an angle across filling. Seal ends.

3. Brush dough with egg white; sprinkle with almonds. Bake at 375° for 30-35 minutes or until golden brown. Cut into slices; serve warm. **Yield:** 12 servings.

Triple-Chocolate Quick Bread

(Pictured above)

Karen Grimes, Stephens City, Virginia

Every year around Christmastime, I make this bread for my family. I've also given it as a gift wrapped in colored foil.

- **1/2 cup butter, softened**
- **2/3 cup packed brown sugar**
- **2 eggs**
- **1 cup (6 ounces) miniature semisweet chocolate chips, melted**
- **1-1/2 cups applesauce**
- **2 teaspoons vanilla extract**
- **2-1/2 cups all-purpose flour**
- **1 teaspoon *each* baking powder, baking soda and salt**
- **1/2 cup miniature semisweet chocolate chips**
- **GLAZE:**
- **1/2 cup miniature semisweet chocolate chips**
- **1 tablespoon butter**
- **2 to 3 tablespoons half-and-half cream**
- **1/2 cup confectioners' sugar**
- **1/4 teaspoon vanilla extract**
- **Pinch salt**

1. In a mixing bowl, cream butter and sugar. Add eggs and melted chocolate; mix well. Add applesauce and vanilla. Set aside.

2. Combine the flour, baking powder, baking soda and salt; add to creamed mixture and mix well. Stir in chocolate chips.

3. Spoon the batter into four greased 5-1/2-in. x 3-in. x 2-in. loaf pans. Bake at 350° for 35-40 minutes or until done. Cool in pans 10 minutes before removing to wire racks to cool completely.

4. For the glaze, melt chocolate chips and butter in a saucepan; stir in cream. Remove from the heat; stir in sugar, vanilla and salt. Drizzle over warm bread. **Yield:** 4 mini loaves.

Sweet Onion Muffins

(Pictured at right)

Mildred Spinn, Cameron, Texas

These savory muffins are wonderful alongside any main dish and make a great snack. It's hard to stop eating them.

- **1-1/2 cups all-purpose flour**
- **1/2 cup sugar**
- **1-1/2 teaspoons baking powder**
- **1/2 teaspoon salt**
- **2 eggs**
- **1 cup finely chopped onion**
- **1/2 cup butter, melted**
- **1-1/2 cups chopped walnuts**

1. In a bowl, combine flour, sugar, baking powder and salt. In another bowl, beat the eggs, onion and butter until blended; stir into the dry ingredients just until moistened. Fold in walnuts.

2. Fill greased or paper-lined miniature muffin cups three-fourths full. Bake at 400° for 10-12 minutes or until a

toothpick inserted near center comes out clean. Cool for 5 minutes before removing from pans to wire racks. **Yield:** 3 dozen mini muffins or 1 dozen regular muffins.

    Editor's Note: If using regular-size muffin cups, bake for 20-25 minutes.

🎗🎗🎗
Caraway Cloverleaf Rolls

(Pictured at right)

Ruth Reid, Jackson, Minnesota

I've taken these rolls to numerous get-togethers and have received many compliments. Folks around here love to bake, so there's always good eating at our socials.

> 2 packages (1/4 ounce *each*) active dry yeast
> 1-1/2 cups warm water (110° to 115°)
> 1 cup whole wheat flour
> 1/2 cup sugar
> 1/2 cup vegetable oil
> 2 teaspoons caraway seeds
> 1-1/2 teaspoons salt
> 3-1/2 to 4 cups all-purpose flour

1. In a mixing bowl, dissolve yeast in water. Add whole wheat flour, sugar, oil, caraway, salt and 2 cups all-purpose flour; beat until smooth. Add enough of the remaining all-purpose flour to form a soft dough.

2. Turn onto a floured surface; knead until smooth and elastic, about 6-8 minutes. Place in a greased bowl, turning once to grease top. Cover and let rise in a warm place until doubled, about 1 hour.

3. Punch dough down. Divide in half, then divide each half into 36 pieces. Shape into balls; place three

balls each in greased muffin cups. Cover and let rise until doubled, about 30 minutes.

4. Bake at 375° for 15-18 minutes or until golden brown. **Yield:** 2 dozen.

🎗🎗🎗
Italian Cheese Bread

(Pictured on page 152)

Sandra Wingert, Star City, Saskatchewan

People are astounded to learn I make this savory Italian bread from scratch in under an hour. With this recipe from my brother-in-law, warm slices are a delicious, easy alternative to garlic toast. I sometimes serve them as a snack or appetizer.

> 2-1/2 cups all-purpose flour
> 1 teaspoon salt
> 1 teaspoon sugar
> 1 tablespoon quick-rise yeast
> 1 cup warm water (120° to 130°)
> 1 tablespoon vegetable oil
> TOPPING:
> 1/4 to 1/3 cup prepared Italian salad dressing
> 1/4 teaspoon *each* salt, garlic powder, dried oregano and dried thyme
> Dash pepper
> 1 tablespoon grated Parmesan cheese
> 1/2 cup shredded mozzarella cheese

1. In a bowl, combine the first four ingredients. Combine water and oil; add to flour mixture. Add additional flour if needed to form a soft dough. Turn onto a floured surface; knead for 1-2 minutes or until smooth and elastic.

2. Place in a greased bowl, turning once to grease top. Cover and let rise in a warm place for 20 minutes. Punch the dough down; place on a greased 12-in. pizza pan and pat into a 12-in. circle. Brush with salad dressing. Combine the seasonings; sprinkle over top. Sprinkle with cheeses.

3. Bake at 450° for 15 minutes or until golden brown. Serve warm. **Yield:** 1 loaf.

🎀🎀🎀

Bacon Swiss Bread

(Pictured above)

Shirley Mills, Tulsa, Oklahoma

I'm a busy mom, so I'm always looking for fast and easy recipes. These savory slices of jazzed-up French bread are great with soup and salad. My daughter and her friends like to snack on them instead of pizza.

> 1 loaf (1 pound) French bread (20 inches)
> 2/3 cup butter, softened
> 1/3 cup chopped green onions
> 4 teaspoons prepared mustard
> 5 slices process Swiss cheese
> 5 bacon strips

1. Cut bread into 1-in.-thick slices, leaving the slices attached at bottom.

2. In a bowl, combine butter, onions and mustard; spread on both sides of each slice of bread. Cut each cheese slice diagonally into four triangles; place between the slices of bread. Cut bacon in half widthwise and then lengthwise; drape a piece over each slice.

3. Place the loaf on a double thickness of heavy-duty foil. Bake at 400° for 20-25 minutes or until bacon is crisp. Serve warm. **Yield:** 10 servings.

🎀🎀🎀

Savory Italian Rounds

(Pictured at right)

Donna Ebert, Jackson, Wisconsin

A friend gave me the recipe for these cheesy golden rounds years ago. Her dad used to make them for her when she was little. Because they're a snap to put together, I often fix them for my family during the week and for company on weekends.

> 2/3 cup grated Parmesan cheese
> 1/2 cup mayonnaise*
> 1/4 teaspoon dried basil
> 1/8 teaspoon garlic powder
> 1/8 teaspoon garlic salt
> 1/8 teaspoon dried oregano
> Dash onion salt
> 1 tube (12 ounces) refrigerated buttermilk biscuits

1. In a small bowl, combine the first seven ingredients. Separate biscuits and place on two ungreased baking sheets. Let stand for 5 minutes.

2. Flatten biscuits into 4-in. circles. Spread about 1 tablespoon mayonnaise mixture over each circle to within 1/2 in. of edge.

3. Bake at 400° for 10-13 minutes or until golden brown. Serve immediately. **Yield:** 10 servings.

*Editor's Note: Reduced-fat or fat-free mayonnaise may not be substituted for regular mayonnaise.

Poppy Seed Lemon Scones

(Pictured above)

Linda Murray, Allenstown, New Hampshire

You'll love the appealing look and delicate texture of these lightly sweet scones. For the best results, work quickly to mix and cut them. The less you handle the dough, the more tender the scones are. They're delightful served warm with the home-made lemon curd for breakfast or with a salad for lunch.

LEMON CURD:
    2 eggs
    1 cup sugar
    6 tablespoons butter, melted
1/4 cup lemon juice
    2 tablespoons grated lemon peel
SCONES:
    2 cups all-purpose flour
1/4 cup sugar
    1 tablespoon baking powder
    1 tablespoon poppy seeds
1/4 teaspoon salt

1/3 cup cold butter
3/4 cup milk
    2 tablespoons lemon juice
Additional sugar

1. In the top of a double boiler, beat eggs and sugar. Stir in butter, lemon juice and peel. Cook and stir over simmering water 15 minutes or until mixture reaches 160° and is thickened. Cover; refrigerate until chilled (may be stored in the refrigerator for up to 1 week).

2. For scones, combine the first five ingredients in a bowl. Cut in butter until mixture resembles fine crumbs. Combine milk and lemon juice; stir into crumb mixture just until blended (dough will be soft).

3. Turn onto a floured surface; knead gently six times. Shape into a ball. Pat dough into an 8-in. circle. Using a sharp knife, cut into eight wedges. Separate wedges and transfer to a greased baking sheet. Sprinkle with additional sugar.

4. Bake at 425° for 12-15 minutes or until lightly browned. Serve with the lemon curd. **Yield:** 8 scones (1-1/2 cups lemon curd).

✿✿✿
Aloha Quick Bread

(Pictured at right)

Lanita Anderson, Chesapeake, Virginia

The addition of coconut, orange peel, pineapple and nuts gives a new twist to a loaf of banana bread. It's so good I sometimes serve slices of it for dessert.

- 1/2 cup butter, softened
- 1 cup sugar
- 2 eggs
- 1 cup mashed ripe bananas (about 2 medium)
- 1/4 cup milk
- 1 tablespoon grated orange peel
- 1 teaspoon vanilla extract
- 1/2 teaspoon almond extract
- 2 cups all-purpose flour
- 1 teaspoon baking soda
- 1/2 teaspoon salt
- 1 cup flaked coconut
- 1/2 cup chopped nuts
- 1/2 cup crushed pineapple

1. In a mixing bowl, cream butter and sugar. Add the eggs, one at a time, beating well after each addition. Beat in banana, milk, orange peel and extracts.

2. Combine flour, baking soda and salt; add to the creamed mixture just until moistened. Fold in the co- conut, nuts and pineapple. Transfer to a greased 9-in. x 5-in. x 3-in. loaf pan.

3. Bake at 350° for 1 hour and 20 minutes or until a toothpick inserted near the center comes out clean. Cool for 10 minutes before removing from pan to a wire rack. **Yield:** 1 loaf.

✿✿✿
Tex-Mex Biscuits

(Pictured at left)

Angie Trolz, Jackson, Michigan

I love cooking with green chilies because they add so much flavor to ordinary dishes. Once while making a pot of chili, I had some green chilies left over and mixed them into my biscuit dough, creating this recipe. The fresh-from-the-oven treats are a wonderful accompaniment to soup or chili.

- 2 cups biscuit/baking mix
- 2/3 cup milk
- 1 cup (4 ounces) finely shredded cheddar cheese
- 1 can (4 ounces) chopped green chilies, drained

1. In a bowl, combine biscuit mix and milk until a soft dough forms. Stir in cheese and chilies. Turn onto a floured surface; knead 10 times. Roll out to 1/2-in. thickness; cut with a 2-1/2-in. biscuit cutter.

2. Place on an ungreased baking sheet. Bake at 450° for 8-10 minutes or until golden brown. Serve warm. **Yield:** about 1 dozen.

Cinnamon-Raisin Soft Pretzels

(Pictured on page 152)

Susie King, Quarryville, Pennsylvania

I came up with this recipe after sampling pretzels at a Pennsylvania Dutch farmer's market. They're a nice morning treat— quicker than cinnamon rolls and easy for kids to eat.

    1 package (1/4 ounce) active dry yeast
1-1/2 cups warm water (110° to 115°)
    2 tablespoons brown sugar
    1 teaspoon salt
    2 cups cake flour
    2 to 2-1/4 cups all-purpose flour
  3/4 cup raisins
    2 tablespoons baking soda
    2 cups hot water (120° to 130°)
    3 tablespoons butter, melted
  3/4 cup sugar
    1 teaspoon ground cinnamon

1. In a large bowl, dissolve the yeast in warm water. Stir in brown sugar and salt. Add the cake flour; stir well. Add enough all-purpose flour to form a soft dough.

2. Stir in the raisins. Turn onto a floured surface; knead until smooth and elastic, about 6-8 minutes. Place in a greased bowl, turning once to grease top. Cover and let rise in a warm place until dough has risen slightly, about 30 minutes. Punch dough down; divide into 14 balls. Roll each ball into a 15-in. rope.

3. In a bowl, dissolve baking soda in hot water. Dip each rope in baking soda mixture; drain on paper towels. Form into pretzel shapes and place on greased baking sheets. Bake at 400° for 15 minutes or until golden brown.

4. Combine sugar and cinnamon in a small bowl. Brush pretzels with butter, then dip in cinnamon-sugar. Serve warm. **Yield:** 14 pretzels.

Chive-Cheese Corn Bread

(Pictured at right)

Sybil Eades, Gainesville, Georgia

This corn bread goes well with any main dish. The chives and sharp cheddar cheese give it a special flavor.

    1 cup cornmeal
    1 cup all-purpose flour
  1/4 cup sugar
    4 teaspoons baking powder
    2 eggs
    1 cup milk
  1/4 cup butter, melted
    1 cup (4 ounces) shredded sharp cheddar cheese
    3 tablespoons minced chives

1. In a large bowl, combine cornmeal, flour, sugar and baking powder. In another bowl, whisk the eggs, milk and butter. Stir into dry ingredients just until moistened. Gently fold in cheese and chives.

2. Pour into a greased 13-in. x 9-in. x 2-in. baking pan. Bake at 400° for 18 minutes or until golden brown. Cut into strips; serve warm. **Yield:** 12-15 servings.

1/2 cup shortening
1-1/2 teaspoons salt
1 egg, beaten
3-3/4 to 4 cups all-purpose flour
Butter, melted
Poppy seeds

1. In a mixing bowl, dissolve yeast in water. Add 1 teaspoon of sugar; let stand for 5 minutes. Beat in milk, shortening, salt, egg and remaining sugar. Add enough flour to form a soft dough.

2. Turn onto a floured surface; knead until smooth and elastic, about 6-8 minutes. Place in a greased bowl, turning once to grease top. Cover and let rise in a warm place until doubled, about 1 hour.

3. Punch the dough down. Divide into 18 portions; shape into balls. Place in greased muffin cups. Cover and let rise until doubled, about 30 minutes.

4. Brush tops with butter; sprinkle with poppy seeds. Bake at 375° for 11-13 minutes or until golden brown. Remove from pans to wire racks. **Yield:** 1-1/2 dozen.

🎀 🎀 🎀

Poppy Seed Rolls

(Pictured above)

Dottie Miller, Jonesborough, Tennessee

I've made these often for Sunday dinner, and they are delicious! There's nothing like homemade rolls to top off a meal.

1 package (1/4 ounce) active dry yeast
1/4 cup warm water (110° to 115°)
1/4 cup plus 1 teaspoon sugar, *divided*
1 cup warm milk (110° to 115°)

🎀 🎀 🎀

Strawberries 'n' Cream Bread

(Pictured on page 152)

Suzanne Randall, Dexter, Maine

Once strawberry-picking time arrives here each summer, my husband and I look forward to this bread. Since only fresh strawberries will do, I have been thinking of trying a different kind of berry so we can enjoy it more often.

1/2 cup butter, softened
3/4 cup sugar
2 eggs
1/2 cup sour cream
1 teaspoon vanilla extract
1-3/4 cups all-purpose flour
1/4 teaspoon ground cinnamon

1/2 teaspoon *each* baking powder, baking soda and salt
3/4 cup chopped fresh strawberries
3/4 cup chopped walnuts, toasted, *divided*

1. In a mixing bowl, cream butter and sugar until fluffy. Beat in eggs, one at a time. Add sour cream and vanilla; mix well.

2. Combine the flour, cinnamon, baking powder, baking soda and salt; stir into creamed mixture just until moistened. Fold in strawberries and 1/2 cup nuts.

3. Pour into a greased 8-in. x 4-in. x 2-in. loaf pan. Sprinkle with remaining nuts. Bake at 350° for 65-70 minutes or until a toothpick inserted near the center comes out clean. Cool for 10 minutes; remove from pan to a wire rack to cool completely. **Yield:** 1 loaf.

🎗️🎗️🎗️
Green Chili Corn Muffins

(Pictured at right)

Melissa Cook, Chico, California

While visiting a local restaurant, I sampled a spicy corn muffin with a surprising sweetness. This recipe is the result of numerous attempts to re-create that treat using convenient mixes. These moist muffins are tasty with Mexican dishes, chili and soup.

> 1 package (8-1/2 ounces) corn bread/muffin mix
> 1 package (9 ounces) yellow cake mix
> 2 eggs
> 1/2 cup milk
> 1/3 cup water
> 2 tablespoons vegetable oil
> 1 can (4 ounces) chopped green chilies, drained
> 1 cup (4 ounces) shredded cheddar cheese, *divided*

1. In a bowl, combine the dry corn bread and cake mixes. In another bowl, combine the eggs, milk, water and oil. Stir into the dry ingredients just until moistened. Add chilies and 3/4 cup cheese.

2. Fill greased or paper-lined muffin cups two-thirds full. Bake at 350° for 20-22 minutes or until a toothpick inserted near the center comes out clean. Immediately sprinkle with remaining cheese. Cool for 5 minutes before removing from pans to wire racks. Serve warm. **Yield:** 16 servings.

🎗️🎗️🎗️
Citrus Streusel Quick Bread

(Pictured below)

Debra White, Williamson, West Virginia

As a minister's wife, I do a lot of baking and cooking for church. Often, I'll find myself copying down recipes to share. This one's generally in demand.

> 1 package (18-1/4 ounces) lemon *or* orange cake mix, *divided*
> 2 tablespoons brown sugar
> 1 teaspoon ground cinnamon
> 1 tablespoon cold butter
> 1/2 cup chopped pecans
> 1 package (3.4 ounces) instant vanilla pudding mix
> 4 eggs
> 1 cup (8 ounces) sour cream
> 1/3 cup vegetable oil
> **GLAZE:**
> 1 cup confectioners' sugar
> 2 to 3 tablespoons milk

1. In a small bowl, combine 2 tablespoons cake mix, brown sugar and cinnamon; cut in butter until crumbly. Stir in pecans; set aside.

2. In a mixing bowl, combine the pudding mix, eggs, sour cream, oil and remaining cake mix; beat on medium speed for 2 minutes. Pour into two greased 8-in. x 4-in. x 2-in. loaf pans. Sprinkle with pecan mixture.

3. Bake at 350° for 45-50 minutes or until a toothpick inserted near the center comes out clean. Cool in pans for 10 minutes before removing to wire racks. Combine the glaze ingredients and drizzle over warm bread. **Yield:** 2 loaves.

Three-Cheese Twists

(Pictured above)

June Poepping, Quincy, Illinois

My daughter has given me many great recipes, but this is one of my favorites. Although these tasty twists look like you fussed, convenient frozen dinner rolls hurry along the preparation. I usually serve them with chili. They're great with a salad, too.

1/2 cup butter, melted
1/4 teaspoon garlic salt
1-1/2 cups (6 ounces) finely shredded mozzarella cheese
1-1/2 cups (6 ounces) finely shredded cheddar cheese
3/4 cup grated Parmesan cheese
1 tablespoon dried parsley flakes
24 frozen dinner rolls, thawed

1. In a shallow bowl, combine butter and garlic salt. In another shallow bowl, combine cheeses and parsley.

2. On a lightly floured surface, roll each dinner roll into a 10-in. rope. Dip in butter mixture, then in cheese mixture. Fold each rope in half and twist twice; pinch ends together to seal. Place 2 in. apart on greased baking sheets. Cover and let rise in a warm place until almost doubled, about 30 minutes.

3. Bake at 350° for 15 minutes or until golden brown. **Yield:** 2 dozen.

Gingerbread Loaf

(Pictured at right)

Martina Biemond, Rosedale, British Columbia

Enjoy the old-fashioned appeal of gingerbread with this recipe, which originated in Holland. This moist spicy bread smells delicious while it's baking and slices are wonderful spread with cream cheese. The recipe makes two big loaves, so we have one to eat and one to freeze for later or to give away.

       4 cups all-purpose flour
       2 cups sugar
       4 teaspoons baking powder
       2 teaspoons ground cinnamon
 1-1/4 teaspoons ground cloves
 1-1/4 teaspoons ground nutmeg
       1 teaspoon baking soda
       1 teaspoon ground ginger
       2 eggs
       2 cups milk
       1 cup maple syrup
       2 tablespoons vegetable oil

1. In a large bowl, combine dry ingredients. In another bowl, combine the eggs, milk, syrup and oil. Stir into the dry ingredients just until moistened (batter will be thin).

2. Pour into two greased 9-in. x 5-in. x 3-in. loaf pans. Bake at 325° for 60-70 minutes or until a toothpick inserted near the center comes out clean. Cool 10 minutes remove from pans to wire racks. **Yield:** 2 loaves.

Broccoli Corn Bread

(Pictured below)

Lois Triplet, Springhill, Louisiana

This recipe was inspired by my husband's love of corn bread. It's so good, he and folks who dine with us eat it plain.

       1 cup plus 1 tablespoon cornmeal, *divided*
     1/3 cup all-purpose flour
 1-1/2 teaspoons baking powder
     3/4 teaspoon salt
     1/4 teaspoon baking soda
       5 eggs, beaten
       1 package (10 ounces) frozen chopped broccoli, thawed and drained
 1-1/2 cups (6 ounces) shredded cheddar cheese
 1-1/2 cups (12 ounces) small-curd cottage cheese
       1 medium onion, chopped
     3/4 cup butter, melted

1. In a bowl, combine 1 cup of cornmeal, flour, baking powder, salt and baking soda. In another bowl, combine the eggs, broccoli, cheeses, onion and butter. Add to cornmeal mixture; mix just until moistened.

2. Sprinkle remaining cornmeal in a greased 13-in. x 9-in. x 2-in baking pan. Pour batter into pan.

3. Bake at 350° for 30-40 minutes or until a toothpick inserted near the center comes out clean. Serve warm. **Yield:** 12-15 servings.

The dill weed in these lovely golden biscuits really comes through. My friends like them because they're fluffy, tender and delicious. I like them because they don't take as much time to make as yeast rolls.

- 2 **cups all-purpose flour**
- 3 **teaspoons baking powder**
- 2 **to 3 teaspoons dill weed**
- 3/4 **teaspoon salt**
- 1/4 **teaspoon pepper**
- 1/2 **cup cold butter**
- 2 **eggs, lightly beaten**
- 1/2 **cup plus 1 tablespoon half-and-half cream,** *divided*

1. In a bowl, combine the flour, baking powder, dill, salt and pepper. Cut in butter until the mixture resembles coarse crumbs. With a fork, stir in eggs and 1/2 cup cream just until moistened.

2. Drop by 1/4 cupfuls onto an ungreased baking sheet. Brush tops with remaining cream. Bake at 450° for 10-12 minutes, until golden brown. **Yield:** 9 servings.

🎀 🎀 🎀

Flaky Dill Biscuits

(Pictured above)

Audrey Lockau, Kitchener, Ontario

🎀 🎀 🎀

Onion Sandwich Rolls

(Pictured at right)

Josie-Lynn Belmont, Woodbine, Georgia

These tempting rolls have a mild onion flavor from dry soup mix. They are great with Italian meals or as sandwich rolls or hamburger buns. I freeze them and take rolls out as needed.

✓ Uses less fat, sugar or salt. Includes Nutritional Analysis and Diabetic Exchanges.

- 1 **envelope onion soup mix**
- 1/2 **cup boiling water**
- 1 **tablespoon butter**
- 3-1/2 **to 4 cups all-purpose flour,** *divided*
- 2 **packages (1/4 ounce** *each***) quick-rise yeast**
- 1 **tablespoon sugar**
- 1 **cup warm water (120° to 130°)**

1. In a bowl, combine soup mix, boiling water and butter; cool to 120°-130°. In a mixing bowl, combine 1 cup flour, yeast and sugar. Add warm water; beat until smooth. Stir in 1 cup flour. Beat in onion soup mixture and enough remaining flour to form a soft dough.

2. Turn onto a floured surface; knead until smooth and elastic, about 6 minutes. Cover and let stand for 10 min-utes. Divide dough into 12 portions and shape each into a ball. Place on greased baking sheets; flatten slightly.

3. Place two large shallow pans on the work surface; fill half full with boiling water. Place baking pans with rolls over water-filled pans. Cover; let rise 15 minutes.

4. Bake at 375° for 16-19 minutes or until golden brown. Remove from pans to a wire rack. **Yield:** 1 dozen.

Nutritional Analysis: One roll (prepared with margarine and reduced-sodium soup mix) equals 160 calories, 168 mg sodium, 0 cholesterol, 32 gm carbohydrate, 5 gm protein, 1 gm fat. **Diabetic Exchange:** 2 starch.

Tomato Pizza Bread

(Pictured above)

Kimberly McFarland, Broken Arrow, Oklahoma

Refrigerated pizza crust dough gets a tasty treatment from pleasant seasonings and easy cheese and tomato toppings. This basic recipe can be modified to suit individual tastes. My husband loves to add sliced ripe olives just before baking.

- 1 tube (10 ounces) refrigerated pizza crust
- 2 garlic cloves, minced
- 1/2 teaspoon dried oregano
- 1 cup (4 ounces) shredded mozzarella cheese, *divided*
- 1 plum tomato, halved lengthwise and thinly sliced
- 1/2 teaspoon Italian seasoning, optional

1. On a greased baking sheet, roll pizza crust into a 12-in. x 8-in. rectangle. Bake at 425° for 6-8 minutes or until the edges are lightly browned.

2. Sprinkle with garlic, oregano and half of the cheese. Arrange tomato slices in a single layer over cheese. Top with remaining cheese and Italian seasoning if desired.

3. Bake 6-8 minutes longer or until cheese is melted and crust is lightly browned. **Yield:** 8 servings.

Raspberry Truffle Brownies, p. 171

Rainbow Cookies, p. 172

Caramel-Chocolate Oat Squares, p. 174

Brownies, Bars & Cookies

This will become one of your favorite chapters on those days when your sweet tooth starts acting up. You'll find an impressive array of mouth-watering brownies and cookies.

Black-Bottom Banana Bars, p. 176

Molasses Spice Cutouts 170

Raspberry Truffle Brownies.................171

Chocolate Cream Cheese Brownies......171

Cinnamon Brownies...........................172

Rainbow Cookies...............................172

Shortbread Squares............................173

Chocolate Crunch Brownies...............173

Vanilla-Butter Sugar Cookies 174

Caramel-Chocolate Oat Squares..........174

Best Cake Brownies 175

German Chocolate Brownies 175

White Chocolate Cookies...................176

Black-Bottom Banana Bars.................176

Chocolate Mint Brownies...................177

Chocolate Buttermilk Squares.............178

Fruitcake Cookies...............................179

Maple Butterscotch Brownies.............179

Chocolate Peanut Butter Brownies......180

Swiss Chocolate Brownies...................180

Frosted Cashew Cookies.....................181

Fudge Puddles 181

Black Forest Brownies........................182

Frosted Banana Bars 182

Apricot Angel Brownies 183

Frosted Cashew Cookies, p. 181

Molasses Spice Cutouts

(Pictured above)

Doris Heinen, St. Cloud, Minnesota

It hardly ever fails—when I send these cookies to school with our youngsters, I'm almost always asked for the recipe by their teachers! I'm happy to share it.

    1 cup butter, softened
1-1/2 cups sugar
    1 cup light molasses
    1/2 cup cold coffee
    6 cups all-purpose flour
    2 teaspoons baking soda
    1 teaspoon salt
    1/2 teaspoon ground nutmeg
    1/4 teaspoon ground cloves
ICING (optional):
    1 envelope unflavored gelatin
    3/4 cup cold water
    3/4 cup sugar
    3/4 cup confectioners' sugar
    3/4 teaspoon baking powder

    1/2 teaspoon vanilla extract
Colored sugar *or* nonpareils
Decorator icing, optional

1. In a mixing bowl, cream butter and sugar; beat in molasses and coffee. Stir together flour, baking soda, salt and spices; add to molasses mixture and mix well. Chill the dough 1-2 hours or until easy to handle.

2. If needed, add a little additional flour before rolling. On a lightly floured surface, roll dough to a 1/4-in. thickness. Cut with holiday cutters dipped in flour. Place on ungreased baking sheets. Bake at 350° for 12-15 minutes. Cool on wire racks.

3. For icing, if desired, combine gelatin and water in a small saucepan. Let stand for 5 minutes to soften. Add sugar. Heat and stir over very low heat until the gelatin and sugar dissolve. Transfer to a mixing bowl. Add confectioners' sugar; beat until foamy. Add baking powder and vanilla; beat until very thick, about 10 minutes.

4. Frost cookies by inverting them and quickly swirling the tops in the icing; decorate with colored sugar or nonpareils. For traditional gingerbread men, use decorator icing to add features as desired. **Yield:** about 7-8 dozen (2-1/2-in. cookies).

Raspberry Truffle Brownies

(Pictured on page 168)

Leslie Knicl, Mahomet, Illinois

On the outside, these look like traditional brownies. When people bite in, though, are they surprised! It's almost like eating a rich, filled chocolate candy.

- 1/2 cup butter
- 1-1/4 cups semisweet chocolate chips
- 2 eggs
- 3/4 cup packed brown sugar
- 1 teaspoon instant coffee granules
- 2 tablespoons water
- 1/2 teaspoon baking powder
- 3/4 cup all-purpose flour

FILLING:
- 1 cup (6 ounces) semisweet chocolate chips
- 1 package (8 ounces) cream cheese, softened
- 1/4 cup confectioners' sugar

- 1/3 cup seedless red raspberry jam

GLAZE:
- 1/4 cup semisweet chocolate chips
- 1 teaspoon shortening

1. In a heavy saucepan, melt butter and chocolate chips over low heat. Cool slightly. In a large bowl, beat eggs and brown sugar. Dissolve coffee granules in water; add to egg mixture with melted chocolate. Mix well. Combine baking powder and flour; stir into chocolate mixture.

2. Spread in a greased 9-in. square baking pan. Bake at 350° for 30-35 minutes or until a toothpick inserted near the center comes out clean. Cool.

3. For filling, melt chocolate chips; cool. In a mixing bowl, beat cream cheese until fluffy; add confectioners' sugar and jam. Stir in melted chocolate; spread over cooled brownies.

4. For glaze, melt chocolate chips and shortening. Drizzle over filling. Chill before cutting. Store in the refrigerator. **Yield:** about 5 dozen.

Chocolate Cream Cheese Brownies

(Pictured at right)

Lisa Godfrey, Temple, Georgia

Whenever I take these to a gathering, someone will announce, "Lisa brought those brownies"—and everyone knows exactly which ones they are!

- 1 package (4 ounces) German sweet chocolate
- 3 tablespoons butter
- 2 eggs
- 3/4 cup sugar
- 1/2 cup all-purpose flour
- 1/2 teaspoon baking powder
- 1/4 teaspoon salt
- 1 teaspoon vanilla extract
- 1/4 teaspoon almond extract
- 1/2 cup chopped nuts

FILLING:
- 2 tablespoons butter
- 1 package (3 ounces) cream cheese, softened
- 1/4 cup sugar
- 1 egg
- 1 tablespoon all-purpose flour
- 1/2 teaspoon vanilla extract

1. In a saucepan, melt chocolate and butter over low heat, stirring frequently. Set aside.

2. In a bowl, beat the eggs. Gradually add sugar, beating until thick. Combine flour, baking powder and salt; add to egg mixture. Stir in melted chocolate, extracts and nuts. Pour half of the batter into a greased 8-in. square baking pan; set aside.

3. For filling, beat butter and cream cheese in a mixing bowl until light. Gradually add sugar, beating until fluffy. Blend in egg, flour and vanilla; mix well. Spread over batter in pan. Dollop remaining batter over filling. With a knife, cut through batter to create a marbled effect.

4. Bake at 350° for 35-40 minutes or until a toothpick comes out clean. Cool. Store in the refrigerator. **Yield:** about 2 dozen.

2/3 cup butter, melted, *divided*
1/2 cup boiling water
2 cups sugar
2 eggs, beaten
1 teaspoon vanilla extract
1-1/3 cups all-purpose flour
1-1/2 to 2 teaspoons ground cinnamon
1/4 teaspoon salt
1 cup (6 ounces) semisweet chocolate chips
FROSTING:
6 tablespoons butter, softened
1/2 cup baking cocoa
2-2/3 cups confectioners' sugar
1 to 1-1/2 teaspoons ground cinnamon
1/3 cup evaporated milk
1 teaspoon vanilla extract

1. In a mixing bowl, combine cocoa and baking soda; blend in 1/3 cup melted butter. Add boiling water, stirring until thickened. Stir in sugar, eggs, vanilla and remaining butter. Add flour, cinnamon and salt. Fold in the chocolate chips.

2. Pour into a greased 13-in. x 9-in. x 2-in. baking pan. Bake at 350° for 40 minutes or until a toothpick inserted near the center comes out clean. Cool.

3. For frosting, cream butter in a mixing bowl. Combine cocoa, sugar and cinnamon; add alternately with the milk. Beat to a spreading consistency; add vanilla. Add more milk if necessary. Spread over the brownies. **Yield:** 3 dozen.

Cinnamon Brownies

(Pictured above)

Gail Mehle, Rock Springs, Wyoming

For Christmas one year, a friend gave us a pan of these delicious brownies. Before I figured out their secret was cinnamon, half the pan was already gone!

3/4 cup baking cocoa
1/2 teaspoon baking soda

Rainbow Cookies

(Pictured on page 168)

Mary Ann Lee, Marco Island, Florida

I always bake these cookies 2 weeks ahead to allow them to "mellow", leaving them moist and full of almond flavor!

1 can (8 ounces) almond paste
1 cup butter, softened
1 cup sugar
4 eggs, *separated*
2 cups all-purpose flour
6 to 8 drops red food coloring
6 to 8 drops green food coloring
1/4 cup seedless red raspberry jam
1/4 cup apricot jam
1 cup (6 ounces) semisweet chocolate chips

1. Grease bottoms of three 13-in. x 9-in. x 2-in. baking pans (or reuse one pan). Line pans with waxed paper; grease paper. Place almond paste in a large mixing bowl; break up with a fork. Cream with butter, sugar and egg yolks until light, fluffy and smooth. Stir in flour.

2. In another mixing bowl, beat egg whites until soft peaks form. Fold into dough, mixing until thoroughly blended. Divide dough into three portions (about 1-1/3 cups each). Color one portion with red food coloring and one with green; leave the remaining portion uncolored.

3. Spread each portion into the prepared pans. Bake at 350° for 10-12 minutes or until edges are light golden brown. Invert onto wire racks; remove waxed paper. Place another wire rack on top and turn over. Cool completely.

4. Place green layer on a large piece of plastic wrap. Spread evenly with raspberry jam. Top with uncolored layer and spread with apricot jam. Top with pink layer. Bring plastic wrap over layers. Slide onto a cookie sheet and set a cutting board or heavy, flat pan on top to compress layers. Refrigerate overnight.

5. The next day, melt chocolate in a double boiler. Spread over top layer; allow to harden. With a sharp knife, trim edges. Cut into 1/2-in. strips across the width; then cut each strip into 4-5 pieces. Store in airtight containers. **Yield:** about 8 dozen.

Shortbread Squares

(Pictured at right)

Mrs. G.C. Mayhew, Grass Valley, California

Here's a traditional shortbread recipe that's perfect with a cup of hot tea or coffee. It's a favorite during the holidays.

1 pound butter, softened
1 cup sifted confectioners' sugar
3-1/2 cups all-purpose flour
1/2 cup cornstarch

1. In a mixing bowl, cream butter and sugar. Combine flour and cornstarch; gradually add to creamed mixture.

2. Pat into an ungreased 15-in. x 10-in. x 1-in. baking pan. Pierce several times with a fork. Bake at 325° for 40-45 minutes or until lightly browned. Cut while warm. **Yield:** about 6 dozen.

Chocolate Crunch Brownies

(Pictured above)

Pat Mueller, Mitchell, South Dakota

The first time I took these to work, I knew I'd better start making copies of the recipe—they disappeared fast!

1 cup butter, softened
2 cups sugar
4 eggs
6 tablespoons baking cocoa
1 cup all-purpose flour
2 teaspoons vanilla extract
1/2 teaspoon salt
1 jar (7 ounces) marshmallow creme
1 cup creamy peanut butter
2 cups (12 ounces) semisweet chocolate chips
3 cups crisp rice cereal

1. In a mixing bowl, cream butter and sugar; add eggs. Stir in cocoa, flour, vanilla and salt. Spread into a greased 13-in. x 9-in. x 2-in. baking pan.

2. Bake at 350° for 25 minutes or until a toothpick inserted near the center comes out clean. Cool. Spread marshmallow creme over cooled brownies.

3. In a small saucepan, melt peanut butter and chocolate chips over low heat, stirring constantly. Remove from the heat; stir in the cereal. Spread over marshmallow layer. Chill before cutting. Store in the refrigerator. **Yield:** 3 dozen.

1-1/2 cups butter, softened
1-1/2 cups sugar
2 eggs
2 tablespoons vanilla extract
4 cups all-purpose flour
1 teaspoon salt
1 teaspoon baking soda
1 teaspoon cream of tartar

FROSTING:
1-1/2 cups confectioners' sugar
3 tablespoons butter, softened
1 tablespoon vanilla extract
1 tablespoon milk

Food coloring, optional
Colored sugar

1. In a mixing bowl, cream butter and sugar. Add eggs and vanilla; beat well. Stir together dry ingredients; gradually add to creamed mixture until completely blended. Chill for 30 minutes.

2. On a lightly floured surface, roll dough to a 1/4-in. thickness. Cut with holiday cutters dipped in flour. Using a floured spatula, transfer cookies to ungreased baking sheets. Bake at 350° for 10-12 minutes. Cool on wire racks.

3. For frosting, combine sugar, butter, vanilla and milk; beat until creamy. Thin with additional milk to desired spreading consistency if necessary. Add a few drops of food coloring if desired. Spread frosting over cookies and decorate with colored sugar. **Yield:** 7 dozen (2-1/2-in. cookies).

Vanilla-Butter Sugar Cookies

(Pictured above)

Cindy Ettel, Hutchinson, Minnesota

I bake these cookies for Christmas, at Valentine's Day (in the shape of hearts, with messages written in frosting), at Thanksgiving (shaped like turkeys) and at Halloween (pumpkins).

Caramel-Chocolate Oat Squares

(Pictured on page 168)

Kellie Ochsner, Newton, Iowa

In the summer, we often have weekend guests who go boating with us. These sweet, chewy bars are the perfect treat to take along. I use my microwave and don't heat up the kitchen.

3/4 cup butter
1-1/4 cups all-purpose flour
1-1/4 cups quick-cooking oats
3/4 cup packed brown sugar
1/2 teaspoon baking soda
1/4 teaspoon salt
24 caramels
1/4 cup milk
1 cup (6 ounces) semisweet chocolate chips
1/2 cup chopped walnuts, optional

1. In a microwave-safe bowl, heat butter, uncovered, on high for 30-45 seconds or until softened. Combine flour, oats, brown sugar, baking soda and salt; stir into butter until blended.

2. Set a third of the mixture aside for topping. Press remaining mixture into an 8-in. square microwave-safe dish. Cook, uncovered, on high for 2-3 minutes or until crust is raised and set (crust will be uneven), rotating a half turn after each minute.

3. In a 1-qt. microwave-safe dish, heat the caramels and milk, uncovered, on high for 3-4 minutes or until melted and smooth, stirring every minute. Sprinkle chips and nuts if desired over crust. Pour caramel mixture over all. Sprinkle with reserved oat mixture; press down lightly.

4. Microwave, uncovered, on high for 3-4 minutes or until the caramel is bubbly, rotating a quarter turn every minute. Cool before cutting. **Yield:** 16 servings.

Editor's Note: This recipe was tested with Hershey caramels and in an 850-watt microwave.

❦❦❦
Best Cake Brownies

(Pictured at right)

Jean Kennedy, Springfield, Oregon

This recipe caught my eye because it uses a whole can of chocolate syrup! I had searched for years for a brownie everyone likes, and this is it. We often dig in before they're cooled.

- 1/2 **cup butter, softened**
- 1 **cup sugar**
- 4 **eggs**
- 1 **can (16 ounces) chocolate syrup**
- 1 **teaspoon vanilla extract**
- 1 **cup all-purpose flour**
- 1/2 **teaspoon salt**

GLAZE:
- 1 **cup sugar**
- 1/3 **cup butter**
- 1/3 **cup milk**
- 2/3 **cup semisweet chocolate chips**
- 2/3 **cup miniature marshmallows**

1. In a mixing bowl, cream butter and sugar. Add eggs, one at a time, beating well after each. Beat in chocolate syrup and vanilla. Add flour and salt until blended.

2. Pour into a greased 15-in. x 10-in. x 1-in. baking pan. Bake at 350° for 20-25 minutes or until a toothpick inserted near the center comes out clean (top of brownies will still appear wet). Cool on a wire rack for 15-20 minutes.

3. In a small saucepan, combine sugar, butter and milk. Bring to a boil; boil until the sugar is dissolved. Remove from the heat; stir in chocolate chips and marshmallows until melted. Pour over the brownies and spread evenly. Refrigerate for 5 minutes before cutting. **Yield:** about 3 dozen.

❦❦❦
German Chocolate Brownies

(Pictured below)

Karen Grimes, Stephens City, Virginia

Even as a young girl, I was always going through recipe books in search of something new to make. That's how I came across these brownies, a favorite for our family reunions and church dinners.

- 1/2 **cup butter**
- 1 **package (4 ounces) German sweet chocolate, broken into squares**
- 1/2 **cup sugar**
- 1 **teaspoon vanilla extract**
- 2 **eggs, lightly beaten**
- 1 **cup all-purpose flour**
- 1/2 **teaspoon baking powder**
- 1/4 **teaspoon salt**

TOPPING:
- 2 **tablespoons butter, melted**
- 1/2 **cup packed brown sugar**
- 1 **cup flaked coconut**
- 1/2 **cup chopped pecans**
- 2 **tablespoons corn syrup**
- 2 **tablespoons milk**

1. In a saucepan, melt butter and chocolate, stirring until smooth. Cool slightly. Add sugar and vanilla; mix. Beat in the eggs. Mix in flour, baking powder and salt.

2. Pour into a greased 9-in. square baking pan. Bake at 350° for 18-22 minutes or until a toothpick inserted near the center comes out clean.

3. For topping, combine butter and brown sugar in a bowl. Add coconut, pecans, corn syrup and milk; mix well. Drop by teaspoonfuls onto warm brownies; spread evenly. Broil several inches from the heat for 2-4 minutes or until top is browned and bubbly. **Yield:** 16 brownies.

I often make these cookies for Christmas. Their pale-white color adds a special touch to all the seasonal reds and greens.

- 1/2 cup butter
- 1/2 cup shortening
- 3/4 cup sugar
- 1/2 cup packed brown sugar
- 1 egg
- 1-3/4 cups all-purpose flour
- 1 teaspoon baking soda
- 1/2 teaspoon salt
- 2 teaspoons vanilla extract
- 10 ounces white chocolate, coarsely chopped
- 1/2 cup coarsely chopped macadamia nuts, lightly toasted

1. In a large mixing bowl, cream butter and shortening. Gradually add sugars, beating until light and fluffy. Add egg; mix well. Combine flour, baking soda and salt; add to creamed mixture. Blend in vanilla. Stir in chocolate and nuts. Cover and chill dough for 1 hour.

2. Drop by heaping tablespoonful about 3 in. apart on ungreased baking sheets.

3. Bake at 350° for 12-14 minutes or until lightly browned. Let stand a few minutes before removing to a wire rack to cool. **Yield:** about 2-1/2 dozen.

🎀🎀🎀

White Chocolate Cookies

(Pictured above)

Shana Bounds, Magee, Mississippi

- - -

🎀🎀🎀

Black-Bottom Banana Bars

(Pictured on page 169)

Renee Wright, Ferryville, Wisconsin

These bars stay very moist, and their rich banana and chocolate flavor is even better the second day. My mother-in-law gave me this recipe, and it's frequently requested by my husband and our two sons.

- 1/2 cup butter, softened
- 1 cup sugar
- 1 egg
- 1 teaspoon vanilla extract
- 1-1/2 cups mashed ripe bananas (about 3 medium)
- 1-1/2 cups all-purpose flour
- 1 teaspoon baking powder
- 1 teaspoon baking soda
- 1/2 teaspoon salt
- 1/4 cup baking cocoa

1. In a mixing bowl, cream butter and sugar. Add egg and vanilla; beat until thoroughly combined. Blend in the bananas. Combine the flour, baking powder, baking soda and salt; add to creamed mixture and mix well.

2. Divide batter in half. Add cocoa to half; spread into a greased 13-in. x 9-in. x 2-in. baking pan. Spoon remaining batter on top and swirl with a knife.

3. Bake at 350° for 25 minutes or until the bars test done. Cool. **Yield:** 2-1/2 to 3 dozen.

Banana Bets

These tips will come in handy when you find your pantry overstocked with bananas:

• You and your guests will be pleasantly surprised by the way grilled bananas complement charbroiled steaks or other meat. Grill the bananas with skins on for 6 to 8 minutes, turning once after half the time.

• Overripe bananas can be saved for later use in breads, beverages, cakes and more. Simply peel and mash the bananas, adding 1 teaspoon of lemon juice for each banana. Store in an airtight container in the freezer for up to 6 months.

🎗 🎗 🎗

Chocolate Mint Brownies

(Pictured above)

Helen Baines, Elkton, Maryland

One of the best things about this recipe is the brownies get more moist if you leave them in the fridge a day or two. The problem at our house is no one can leave them alone that long!

- 1 cup all-purpose flour
- 1/2 cup butter, softened
- 1/2 teaspoon salt
- 4 eggs
- 1 teaspoon vanilla extract
- 1 can (16 ounces) chocolate syrup
- 1 cup sugar

FILLING:
- 2 cups confectioners' sugar
- 1/2 cup butter, softened
- 1 tablespoon water
- 1/2 teaspoon mint extract
- 3 drops green food coloring

TOPPING:
- 1 package (10 ounces) mint chocolate chips
- 9 tablespoons butter

1. In a large mixing bowl, combine the first seven ingredients. Beat at medium speed for 3 minutes. Pour batter into a greased 13-in. x 9-in. x 2-in. baking pan. Bake at 350° for 30 minutes (top of brownies will still appear wet). Cool completely.

2. Combine filling ingredients in a medium mixing bowl; beat until creamy. Spread over cooled brownies. Refrigerate until set.

3. For the topping, melt the chocolate chips and butter over low heat in a small saucepan. Let cool for 30 minutes or until lukewarm, stirring occasionally. Spread over filling. Chill before cutting. Store in the refrigerator. **Yield:** 5-6 dozen.

Chocolate Buttermilk Squares

(Pictured above)

Clarice Baker, Stromsburg, Nebraska

Every time I take a pan of these to a picnic, it comes back clean! At home, they disappear as fast as I can bake them.

1 cup butter
1/4 cup baking cocoa
1 cup water
2 cups sugar
2 cups all-purpose flour
1/2 teaspoon salt
1/2 cup buttermilk
1 teaspoon baking soda
2 eggs, beaten
1 teaspoon vanilla extract
3 to 4 drops red food coloring, optional

FROSTING:
1/2 cup butter
1/4 cup baking cocoa
1/4 cup buttermilk
3-3/4 confectioners' sugar
1 teaspoon vanilla extract
Dash salt
3/4 cup chopped almonds, optional

1. In a saucepan, bring butter, cocoa and water to a boil. Cool. Meanwhile, in a large mixing bowl, combine the sugar, flour and salt. Pour cocoa mixture over dry ingredients. Mix well.

2. Combine buttermilk and baking soda; add to cocoa mixture along with eggs, vanilla and food coloring if desired. Mix until well combined.

3. Pour into a greased and floured 15-in. x 10-in. x 1-in. baking pan. Bake at 350° for 20 minutes.

4. For frosting, melt butter, cocoa and buttermilk. Stir in sugar, vanilla and salt. Spread over warm bars and top with nuts if desired. **Yield:** 15 servings.

🎀🎀🎀
Fruitcake Cookies

(Pictured at right)

Hazel Staley, Gaithersburg, Maryland

This recipe's one people always ask for. They tell me it's habit-forming! I'm the kind of cook who starts with a basic recipe, then throws in "extras" to make it my own. I'm also the type who doesn't like making the same old things over and over. So it's good my husband is happy to eat just about anything I serve.

> 6 cups chopped pecans (about 1-1/2 pounds)
> 2 cups graham cracker crumbs
> 1-1/2 cups raisins
> 1-1/4 cups chopped candied cherries (about 1/2 pound)
> 1-1/4 cups chopped candied pineapple (about 1/2 pound)
> 4-1/2 cups miniature marshmallows
> 1/2 cup evaporated milk
> 1/4 cup butter
> 1-1/2 cups flaked coconut

1. In a large bowl, combine pecans, cracker crumbs, raisins, cherries and pineapple. In a large saucepan, combine marshmallows, milk and butter. Cook over low heat, stirring constantly, until melted.

2. Pour over pecan mixture and mix well. Shape into 1-in. balls and roll in the coconut, washing your hands frequently. **Yield:** 7-8 dozen.

🎀🎀🎀
Maple Butterscotch Brownies

(Pictured at right)

Grace Vonhold, Rochester, New York

Generally, I'll make a double recipe of these brownies—they go so fast no matter where I take them! I've baked them for family dinners and church suppers, and never had any left over. They're very easy to make, plus they keep and freeze well.

> 1-1/2 cups packed brown sugar
> 1/2 cup butter, melted
> 1-1/2 teaspoons maple flavoring
> 2 eggs
> 1-1/2 cups all-purpose flour
> 1 teaspoon baking powder
> 1 cup chopped walnuts
> **Confectioners' sugar, optional**

1. In a large bowl, combine brown sugar, butter and maple flavoring. Beat in the eggs, one at a time. Combine flour and baking powder; add to egg mixture. Stir in walnuts.

2. Pour into a greased 9-in. square baking pan. Bake at 350° for 30 minutes or until a toothpick comes out clean. Cool. Dust with confectioners' sugar if desired. **Yield:** 16 brownies.

2 squares (1 ounce *each*) unsweetened chocolate
1/2 cup butter
2 eggs
1 cup sugar
1/2 cup all-purpose flour
FILLING:
1-1/2 cups confectioners' sugar
1/2 cup creamy peanut butter
1/4 cup butter, softened
2 to 3 tablespoons half-and-half cream *or* milk
GLAZE:
1 square (1 ounce) semisweet baking chocolate
1 tablespoon butter

1. In a small saucepan, melt chocolate and butter over low heat; set aside. In a mixing bowl, beat eggs and sugar until light and pale colored. Add flour and melted chocolate; stir well.

2. Pour into a greased 9-in. square baking pan. Bake at 350° for 25 minutes or until a toothpick inserted near the center comes out clean. Cool.

3. For filling, beat confectioners' sugar, peanut butter and butter in a mixing bowl. Stir in cream or milk until mixture reaches desired spreading consistency. Spread over cooled brownies; cover and chill until firm.

4. For glaze, melt chocolate and butter in a saucepan, stirring until smooth. Drizzle over the filling. Chill before cutting. Store in the refrigerator. **Yield:** about 5 dozen.

Chocolate Peanut Butter Brownies

(Pictured above)

Patsy Burgin, Lebanon, Indiana

Back when my sons were away at college, I sent these brownies to them regularly. They told me that they had to hide a few from their roommates just so they could make sure there would be some left for them!

Swiss Chocolate Brownies

(Pictured at right)

Gloria Stange, Claresholm, Alberta

I bake these brownies frequently for big occasions—everyone thinks that they're quite nice.

1 cup water
1/2 cup butter
1-1/2 squares (1-1/2 ounces) unsweetened chocolate
2 cups all-purpose flour
2 cups sugar
1 teaspoon baking soda
1/2 teaspoon salt
2 eggs, lightly beaten
1/2 cup sour cream
1/2 teaspoon vanilla extract
1 cup chopped walnuts
ICING:
1/2 cup butter
1-1/2 squares (1-1/2 ounces) unsweetened chocolate
3 cups confectioners' sugar, *divided*
5 tablespoons milk
1 teaspoon vanilla extract

1. In a saucepan, bring water, butter and chocolate to a boil. Boil for 1 minute. Remove from the heat; cool.

2. In a mixing bowl, combine flour, sugar, baking soda and salt. Add chocolate mixture and mix. Add eggs, sour cream and vanilla; mix. Fold in walnuts.

3. Pour into a greased 15-in. x 10-in. x 1-in. baking pan. Bake at 350° for 20-25 minutes or until brownies test done. Cool for 10 minutes.

4. For icing, melt butter and chocolate. Place in a mixing bowl; mix in 1-1/2 cups confectioners' sugar. Add milk, vanilla and remaining sugar; beat until smooth. Spread over warm brownies. **Yield:** about 3 dozen.

Frosted Cashew Cookies

(Pictured on page 169)

Sheila Wyum, Rutland, North Dakota

It was my sister's sister-in-law who discovered this recipe. We enjoy the cookies at Christmas, but they're rich and elegant for a special coffee and can be tucked in a field lunch box besides. They were named grand champion at our county fair.

- 1/2 cup butter
- 1 cup packed brown sugar
- 1 egg
- 1/3 cup sour cream
- 1/2 teaspoon vanilla extract
- 2 cups all-purpose flour
- 3/4 teaspoon *each* baking powder, baking soda and salt
- 1-3/4 cups salted cashew halves

Fudge Puddles

(Pictured at right)

Kimarie Maassen, Avoca, Iowa

The inspiration for these cookies came one year while I was out Christmas shopping. They became an instant favorite with my husband's family.

- 1/2 cup butter, softened
- 1/2 cup creamy peanut butter
- 1/2 cup sugar
- 1/2 cup packed light brown sugar
- 1 egg
- 1/2 teaspoon vanilla extract
- 1-1/4 cups all-purpose flour
- 3/4 teaspoon baking soda
- 1/2 teaspoon salt

FUDGE FILLING:
- 1 cup (6 ounces) milk chocolate chips
- 1 cup (6 ounces) semisweet chocolate chips
- 1 can (14 ounces) sweetened condensed milk
- 1 teaspoon vanilla extract

Chopped peanuts

1. In a mixing bowl, cream butter, peanut butter and sugars; add egg and vanilla. Stir together flour, baking soda and salt; add to creamed mixture. Mix well. Chill.

2. Shape into 48 balls, 1 in. each. Place in lightly greased mini-muffin tins. Bake at 325° for 14-16 minutes or until lightly browned. Remove from oven and immedi-

BROWNED BUTTER FROSTING:
- 1/2 cup butter
- 3 tablespoons half-and-half cream
- 1/4 teaspoon vanilla extract
- 2 cups confectioners' sugar

Additional cashew halves, optional

1. In a mixing bowl, cream the butter and brown sugar. Beat in egg, sour cream and vanilla; mix well. Combine dry ingredients; add to creamed mixture and mix well. Fold in the cashews.

2. Drop by rounded teaspoonfuls onto greased baking sheets. Bake at 375° for 8-10 minutes or until lightly browned. Cool on a wire rack.

3. For the frosting, lightly brown butter in a small saucepan. Remove from the heat; add cream and vanilla. Beat in confectioners' sugar until smooth and thick. Frost cookies. Top each with a cashew half if desired. **Yield:** about 3 dozen.

ately make "wells" in the center of each by lightly pressing with a melon baller. Cool in pans for 5 minutes, then carefully remove to wire racks.

3. For filling, melt chocolate chips in a double boiler over simmering water. Stir in milk and vanilla; mix well. Using a small pitcher or pastry bag, fill each shell with filling. Sprinkle with peanuts. (Leftover filling can be stored in the refrigerator and served warm over ice cream.) **Yield:** 4 dozen.

🎀🎀🎀
Black Forest Brownies
(Pictured at right)

Toni Reeves, Medicine Hat, Alberta

Although I enjoy sweets, other recipes have failed me. But not this one! It's easy, and the ingredients are always on hand. Even people who don't like most sweets can't pass up these.

- 1-1/3 cups all-purpose flour
- 1 teaspoon baking powder
- 1/2 teaspoon salt
- 1 cup butter
- 1 cup baking cocoa
- 4 eggs, beaten
- 2 cups sugar
- 1-1/2 teaspoons vanilla extract
- 1 teaspoon almond extract
- 1 cup chopped maraschino cherries
- 1/2 cup chopped nuts

ICING:
- 1/4 cup butter, softened
- 1 teaspoon vanilla extract
- 2 cups confectioners' sugar
- 6 tablespoons baking cocoa
- 1/4 cup milk
- 1/4 cup chopped nuts

1. Combine flour, baking powder and salt; set aside. In a large saucepan, melt butter. Remove from the heat and stir in cocoa until smooth. Blend in eggs, sugar and extracts. Stir in flour mixture, cherries and nuts.

2. Pour into a greased 13-in. x 9-in. x 2-in. baking pan. Bake at 350° for 35 minutes or until a toothpick inserted near the center comes out clean.

3. For the icing, blend butter, vanilla, sugar, cocoa and milk until smooth; spread over hot brownies. Sprinkle with nuts. Cool. **Yield:** 3 dozen.

🎀🎀🎀
Frosted Banana Bars
(Pictured below)

Karen Dryak, Niobrara, Nebraska

These bars are always a hit at potlucks in the small farming community where my husband and I live. I also provide them for coffee hour after church. They don't last long.

- 1/2 cup butter, softened
- 2 cups sugar
- 3 eggs
- 1-1/2 cups mashed ripe bananas (about 3 medium)
- 1 teaspoon vanilla extract
- 2 cups all-purpose flour
- 1 teaspoon baking soda

Pinch salt

FROSTING:
- 1/2 cup butter, softened
- 1 package (8 ounces) cream cheese, softened
- 4 cups confectioners' sugar
- 2 teaspoons vanilla extract

1. In a mixing bowl, cream butter and sugar. Beat in eggs, bananas and vanilla. Combine the flour, baking soda and salt; add to creamed mixture and mix well.

2. Pour into a greased 15-in. x 10-in. x 1-in. baking pan. Bake at 350° for 25 minutes or until a toothpick inserted hear the center comes out clean. Cool.

3. For the frosting, cream butter and cream cheese in a mixing bowl. Gradually add confectioners' sugar and vanilla; beat well. Spread over bars. **Yield:** 3 dozen.

Apricot Angel Brownies

(Pictured above)

Tamara Sellman, Barrington, Illinois

To tell the truth, I'm not a "chocoholic". I enjoy fruit desserts and custards more than anything. So my brownies have neither milk nor dark chocolate—but still satisfy every sweet tooth.

  2 **bars (2 ounces *each*) white baking chocolate**
1/3 **cup butter**
1/2 **cup packed brown sugar**
  2 **eggs, beaten**
1/4 **teaspoon vanilla extract**
3/4 **cup all-purpose flour**
1/2 **teaspoon baking powder**
1/4 **teaspoon salt**
  1 **cup finely chopped dried apricots**
1/4 **cup sliced almonds**
1/4 **cup flaked coconut**

1. In a saucepan, melt chocolate and butter over low heat, stirring constantly until all of the chocolate is melted. Remove from the heat; stir in brown sugar, eggs and vanilla until blended. Set aside.

2. In a bowl, combine flour, baking powder and salt. Stir in white chocolate mixture. Combine apricots, almonds and coconut; stir half into the batter.

3. Pour into a greased 9-in. square baking pan. Sprinkle remaining apricot mixture on top. Bake at 350° for 25 minutes or until golden brown. Cool. **Yield:** about 2 dozen.

Special Strawberry Torte, p. 191

Chocolate Truffle Cheesecake, p. 192

Casserole Carrot Cake, p. 187

Cakes & Cheesecakes

Special occasions call for special desserts. Whether you're planning a backyard barbecue or Christmas dinner, you'll find a bounty of beautiful cakes, tortes and cheesecakes right here.

Chocolate Chip Cookie Dough Cheesecake, p. 188

Cranberry Cheesecake 186

Peanut Butter Cheesecake 187

Casserole Carrot Cake 187

Walnut Apple Cake 188

Chocolate Chip Cookie Dough Cheesecake 188

Caramel-Fudge Chocolate Cake 189

Orange Chiffon Cake 189

Family-Favorite Cheesecake 190

Tiny Cherry Cheesecakes 190

Cranberry-Orange Pound Cake 191

Special Strawberry Torte 191

Banana Pecan Torte 192

Chocolate Truffle Cheesecake 192

Coconut Gingerbread Cake 193

Carrot Layer Cake 193

No-Bake Cherry Cheesecake 194

Apple Danish Cheesecake 195

California Lemon Pound Cake 195

Tangy Lemon Cheesecake 196

Cranberry Upside-Down Cake 196

Peanut Butter Chocolate Cake 197

S'more Cheesecake 198

Plantation Gingerbread 199

Fresh Grapefruit Cake 199

Frozen Chocolate Cheesecake Tart 200

Apple Pear Cake 200

Tropical Cheesecake 201

Fresh Grapefruit Cake, p. 199

🎗🎗🎗
Cranberry Cheesecake
(Pictured above)

Nancy Zimmerman, Cape May Court House, New Jersey

The holidays wouldn't be complete without cranberries and eggnog. I use them both in this flavorful cheesecake.

>   1 cup sugar
>   2 tablespoons cornstarch
>   1 cup cranberry juice
> 1-1/2 cups fresh *or* frozen cranberries
> **CRUST:**
>   1 cup graham cracker crumbs (about 14 squares)
>   3 tablespoons *each* sugar and melted butter
> **FILLING:**
>   4 packages (8 ounces *each*) cream cheese, softened
>   1 cup sugar
>   3 tablespoons all-purpose flour
>   4 eggs
>   1 cup eggnog*
>   1 tablespoon vanilla extract

1. In a saucepan, combine the first four ingredients; bring to a boil. Reduce heat; cook and stir over medium heat for 2 minutes. Remove from the heat; set aside.

2. In a small bowl, combine cracker crumbs and sugar; stir in butter. Press onto the bottom of a greased 9-in. springform pan. Bake at 325° for 10 minutes. Cool on a wire rack.

3. In a mixing bowl, beat the cream cheese and sugar until smooth. Add the flour and beat well. Add the eggs; beat on low just until combined. Add the eggnog and vanilla; beat just until blended. Pour two-thirds of the filling over the crust.

4. Top with half of the cranberry mixture (cover and chill remaining cranberry mixture). Carefully spoon remaining filling on top. Bake at 325° for 60-70 minutes or until center is almost set. Cool on a wire rack for 10 minutes. Carefully run a knife around edge of pan to loosen; cool 1 hour longer. Refrigerate overnight.

5. Remove sides of pan. Spoon remaining cranberry mixture over cheesecake. **Yield:** 12 servings.

   *****Editor's Note:** This recipe was tested with commercially prepared eggnog.

Peanut Butter Cheesecake

(Pictured at right)

Lois Brooks, Newark, Delaware

The first time I served this cheesecake, my friends all went wild over it. They were surprised when I told them the crust is made of pretzels. The pairing of sweet and salty plus creamy and crunchy left everyone asking for another slice.

- 1-1/2 **cups crushed pretzels**
- 1/3 **cup butter, melted**

FILLING:
- 5 **packages (8 ounces *each*) cream cheese, softened**
- 1-1/2 **cups sugar**
- 3/4 **cup creamy peanut butter**
- 2 **teaspoons vanilla extract**
- 3 **eggs**
- 1 **cup peanut butter chips**
- 1 **cup semisweet chocolate chips**

TOPPING:
- 1 **cup (8 ounces) sour cream**
- 3 **tablespoons creamy peanut butter**
- 1/2 **cup sugar**
- 1/2 **cup finely chopped unsalted peanuts**

1. In a small bowl, combine pretzels and butter. Press onto the bottom and 1 in. up the sides of a greased 10-in. springform pan. Bake at 350° for 5 minutes. Cool on a wire rack.

2. In a mixing bowl, beat cream cheese and sugar until smooth. Add peanut butter and vanilla; mix well. Add eggs; beat on low just until combined. Stir in chips. Pour over the crust. Bake at 350° for 50-55 minutes or until center is almost set. Cool on a wire rack for 15 minutes (leave the oven on).

3. Meanwhile, in a mixing bowl, combine sour cream, peanut butter and sugar; spread over filling. Sprinkle with nuts. Return to the oven for 5 minutes. Cool on a wire rack for 10 minutes. Carefully run a knife around the edge of the pan to loosen; cool 1 hour longer. Refrigerate overnight. Remove sides of pan. **Yield:** 12-14 servings.

Casserole Carrot Cake

(Pictured on page 184)

Judie Arnold, East Peoria, Illinois

I learned to make this yummy cake in a microwave cooking class. It's nice to invite company for dinner at the last minute and have a great homemade dessert in no time.

- 1 **cup all-purpose flour**
- 1 **cup sugar**
- 1-1/4 **teaspoons ground cinnamon**
- 1 **teaspoon baking powder**
- 1 **teaspoon baking soda**
- 1/2 **teaspoon salt**
- 1/4 **teaspoon ground cloves**
- 1/4 **teaspoon ground ginger**
- 1/2 **cup vegetable oil**
- 2 **eggs**
- 1-1/2 **cups grated *or* finely chopped carrots (about 4 medium)**
- 1 **can (8 ounces) crushed pineapple, well drained**
- 3/4 **cup chopped pecans**
- 1 **can (16 ounces) cream cheese frosting**

1. In a mixing bowl, combine the first eight ingredients. Add oil; mix well. Add eggs, one at a time, beating well after each. Stir in carrots, pineapple and pecans.

2. Transfer to a greased 8-in. round microwave-safe casserole dish. Microwave, uncovered, at 70% power for 12-14 minutes, rotating a half turn once or until a moist area about 1-1/2 in. in diameter remains in the center (when touched, cake will cling to your finger while area underneath will be almost dry).

3. Cool completely on a wire rack. Invert onto a serving plate. Frost cake. Store in the refrigerator. **Yield:** 6-8 servings.

    Editor's Note: This recipe was tested in a 2-qt. round Pyrex casserole dish in an 850-watt microwave.

2 eggs
2 cups sugar
1/2 cup vegetable oil
2 teaspoons vanilla extract
2 cups all-purpose flour
2-1/2 teaspoons ground cinnamon
2 teaspoons baking soda
1 teaspoon salt
1/4 teaspoon ground nutmeg
4 cups chopped peeled tart apples
1 cup chopped walnuts

BUTTER SAUCE:

3/4 cup sugar
3 tablespoons all-purpose flour
1 cup milk
2 tablespoons butter
1 teaspoon vanilla extract

Walnut halves, optional

1. In a mixing bowl, combine eggs, sugar, oil and vanilla; mix well. Combine dry ingredients; add to the egg mixture and mix well (batter will be stiff). Stir in apples and walnuts. Spread into a greased 13-in. x 9-in. x 2-in. baking pan. Bake at 350° for 45-50 minutes or until a toothpick inserted near the center comes out clean. Cool on a wire rack.

2. For the sauce, combine sugar, flour, milk and butter in a saucepan. Bring to a boil over medium heat; boil and stir for 2 minutes. Remove from the heat; stir in vanilla. Cut cake into squares; top with warm sauce. Garnish with walnut halves if desired. **Yield:** 12-15 servings.

🎀 🎀 🎀

Walnut Apple Cake

(Pictured above)

Jacquelyn Remsberg, La Canada, California

I first tasted this delicious cake at a Halloween party and quickly asked for the recipe. It's not too sweet, and the butter sauce makes it a super dessert.

🎀 🎀 🎀

Chocolate Chip Cookie Dough Cheesecake

(Pictured on page 185)

Julie Craig, Jackson, Wisconsin

I created this recipe to combine two of my all-time favorites—cheesecake for the grown-up in me and chocolate chip cookie dough for the little girl in me.

1-3/4 cups crushed chocolate chip cookies *or*
      chocolate wafer crumbs
1/4 cup sugar
1/3 cup butter, melted

FILLING:

3 packages (8 ounces *each*) cream cheese, softened
1 cup sugar
3 eggs
1 cup (8 ounces) sour cream
1/2 teaspoon vanilla extract

COOKIE DOUGH:

1/4 cup butter, softened
1/4 cup sugar

1/4 cup packed brown sugar
1 tablespoon water
1 teaspoon vanilla extract
1/2 cup all-purpose flour
1-1/2 cups miniature semisweet chocolate chips,
      divided

1. In a small bowl, combine cookie crumbs and sugar; stir in butter. Press onto the bottom and 1 in. up the sides of a greased 9-in. springform pan; set aside.

2. In a mixing bowl, beat cream cheese and sugar until smooth. Add eggs; beat on low just until combined. Add sour cream and vanilla; beat just until blended. Pour over crust; set aside.

3. In another mixing bowl, cream butter and sugars on medium speed for 3 minutes. Add water and vanilla. Gradually add flour. Stir in 1 cup chocolate chips.

4. Drop dough by teaspoonfuls over filling, gently pushing dough below surface (dough should be completely covered by filling). Bake at 350° for 45-55 minutes or until center is almost set. Cool on a wire rack 10 minutes.

5. Carefully run a knife around edge of pan to loosen; cool 1 hour longer. Refrigerate overnight; remove sides of pan. Sprinkle with remaining chips. **Yield:** 12-14 servings.

✿✿✿ Caramel-Fudge Chocolate Cake

(Pictured at right)

Karen Stucky, Freeman, South Dakota

To satisfy the chocolate lovers in our family, I added hot fudge topping and chocolate chips to a caramel-covered dessert that's quite popular in our area. The moist cake layer is a breeze to prepare using a boxed mix. Rich toppings make it decadent.

- 1 package (18-1/4 ounces) chocolate cake mix
- 1 cup miniature semisweet chocolate chips, *divided*
- 1 jar (12-1/4 ounces) caramel ice cream topping, warmed
- 1 jar (11-3/4 ounces) hot fudge ice cream topping, warmed
- 1 carton (8 ounces) frozen whipped topping, thawed
- 1/2 cup English toffee bits *or* almond brickle chips

1. Prepare cake batter according to package directions. Stir in 3/4 cup chocolate chips. Pour into a greased 13-in. x 9-in. x 2-in. baking pan. Bake at 350° for 35–40 minutes or until a toothpick inserted near the center comes out clean.

2. Immediately poke holes in the cake with a meat fork or skewer. Spread caramel and fudge toppings over cake. Cool on a wire rack. Frost with whipped topping. Sprinkle with toffee bits and remaining chocolate chips. Store in the refrigerator. **Yield:** 12-15 servings.

✿✿✿ Orange Chiffon Cake

(Pictured above)

Marjorie Ebert, South Dayton, New York

It wasn't until a few years ago that I started entering our county fair. Since then, my moist Orange Chiffon Cake has been awarded several blue ribbons.

- 2 cups all-purpose flour
- 1-1/2 cups sugar
- 4 teaspoons baking powder
- 1 teaspoon salt
- 6 eggs, *separated*
- 3/4 cup fresh orange juice
- 1/2 cup vegetable oil
- 2 tablespoons grated orange peel
- 1/2 teaspoon cream of tartar

ORANGE GLAZE:
- 1/2 cup butter
- 2 cups confectioners' sugar
- 2 to 4 tablespoons fresh orange juice
- 1/2 teaspoon grated orange peel

1. In a large mixing bowl, combine the first four ingredients. Add egg yolks, orange juice, oil and peel; beat until smooth, about 5 minutes. In another mixing bowl, beat egg whites and cream of tartar until stiff but not dry. Fold into orange mixture.

2. Spoon into an ungreased 10-in. tube pan. Bake at 350° for 45-50 minutes or until a toothpick inserted near the center comes out clean.

3. Immediately invert pan to cool. When cool, remove cake from the pan. For glaze, melt butter in a small saucepan; add remaining ingredients. Stir until smooth. Pour over top of cake, allowing it to drizzle down sides. **Yield:** 16 servings.

2-1/2 cups graham cracker crumbs (about 40 squares)
1/3 cup sugar
1/2 teaspoon ground cinnamon
1/2 cup butter, melted

FILLING:
3 packages (8 ounces *each*) cream cheese, softened
1-1/2 cups sugar
1 teaspoon vanilla extract
4 eggs, *separated*

TOPPING:
1/2 cup sour cream
2 tablespoons sugar
1/2 teaspoon vanilla extract
1/2 cup heavy whipping cream, whipped

1. In a small bowl, combine the cracker crumbs, sugar and cinnamon; stir in butter. Press onto the bottom and 2 in. up the sides of a greased 9-in. springform pan. Bake at 350° for 5 minutes. Cool on a wire rack.

2. Reduce heat to 325°. In a mixing bowl, beat cream cheese, sugar and vanilla until smooth. Add egg yolks; beat on low just until combined. In a small mixing bowl, beat egg whites until soft peaks form; fold into cream cheese mixture. Pour over crust.

3. Bake 1 hour or until center is almost set. Cool on a wire rack for 10 minutes. Run a knife around edge of pan to loosen; cool 1 hour more. Refrigerate until completely cooled. Combine the sour cream, sugar and vanilla; fold in whipped cream. Spread over cheesecake. Refrigerate overnight. Remove sides of pan. **Yield:** 12 servings.

Family-Favorite Cheesecake

(Pictured above)

Esther Wappner, Mansfield, Ohio

This fluffy, delicate cheesecake has been a family favorite for almost 20 years. A friend gave me the recipe back when I was single. I've shared it at many gatherings over the years and have even started baking it for our friends instead of Christmas cookies.

Tiny Cherry Cheesecakes

(Pictured at right)

Janice Hertlein, Esterhazy, Saskatchewan

I prepare these cheesecakes every Christmas and for many weddings. I've received countless compliments and recipe requests.

1 cup all-purpose flour
1/3 cup sugar
1/4 cup baking cocoa
1/2 cup cold butter
2 tablespoons cold water

FILLING:
2 packages (3 ounces *each*) cream cheese, softened
1/4 cup sugar
2 tablespoons milk
1 teaspoon vanilla extract
1 egg
1 can (21 ounces) cherry *or* strawberry pie filling

1. In a small bowl, combine flour, sugar and cocoa; cut in butter until crumbly. Gradually add water, tossing with a fork until dough forms a ball. Shape into 24 balls.

2. Place in greased miniature muffin cups; press dough onto the bottom and up the sides of each cup. In a mixing bowl, beat cream cheese and sugar until smooth. Beat in milk and vanilla. Add egg; beat on low just until combined. Spoon 1 tablespoonful into each cup.

3. Bake at 325° for 15-18 minutes or until set. Cool on a wire rack for 30 minutes. Carefully remove from pans to cool completely. Top with pie filling. Store in the refrigerator. **Yield:** 2 dozen.

★★★

Cranberry-Orange Pound Cake

(Pictured at right)

Sheree Swistun, Winnipeg, Manitoba

At the Ontario resort my husband and I operate, we prepare the meals for our guests. This recipe is a keeper.

      1-1/2 cups butter, softened
      2-3/4 cups sugar
          6 eggs
          1 teaspoon vanilla extract
      2-1/2 teaspoons grated orange peel
          3 cups all-purpose flour
          1 teaspoon baking powder
      1/2 teaspoon salt
          1 cup (8 ounces) sour cream
      1-1/2 cups chopped fresh *or* frozen cranberries
VANILLA BUTTER SAUCE:
          1 cup sugar
          1 tablespoon all-purpose flour
      1/2 cup half-and-half cream
      1/2 cup butter, softened
      1/2 teaspoon vanilla extract

1. In a mixing bowl, cream butter. Gradually beat in sugar until light and fluffy, about 5-7 minutes. Add eggs, one at a time, beating well after each. Stir in vanilla and orange peel. Combine dry ingredients; add to creamed mixture alternately with sour cream. Beat on low just until blended. Fold in berries.

2. Pour into a greased and floured 10-in. fluted tube pan. Bake at 350° for 65-70 minutes or until a toothpick inserted near the center comes out clean. Cool in pan for 10 minutes; remove to a wire rack and cool completely.

3. In a small saucepan, combine sugar and flour. Stir in cream and butter; bring to a boil over medium heat, stirring constantly. Boil for 2 minutes. Remove from the heat and stir in vanilla. Serve warm over cake. **Yield:** 16 servings (1-1/2 cups sauce).

★★★

Special Strawberry Torte

(Pictured on page 184)

Alyce Kafka, Wagner, South Dakota

The reason this is such a favorite is it's a little different yet quick and easy. Plus, it looks like you really fussed.

          1 package (18-1/4 ounces) yellow cake mix
          4 eggs, *separated*
      2/3 cup plus 2 tablespoons sugar, *divided*
      1/4 cup sliced almonds
          2 cups whipped topping
          3 to 3-1/2 cups sliced fresh strawberries
Fresh mint, optional

1. In a mixing bowl, prepare cake mix according to package directions, substituting four yolks for the whole eggs. Pour the batter into two greased and floured 9-in. round cake pans.

2. In another bowl, beat egg whites until soft peaks form. Gradually add 2/3 cup sugar, 1 tablespoon at a time, beating until stiff peaks form. Carefully spread over batter; sprinkle with almonds and remaining sugar.

3. Bake at 350° for 40-45 minutes or until meringue is golden and a toothpick inserted near the center of cake comes out clean.

4. Cool 10 minutes; remove from pans to a wire rack, meringue side up, to cool completely. Place one cake with meringue side up on a serving plate. Spread with half the whipped topping and top with half of the strawberries. Cover with remaining cake, topping and berries. Garnish with mint if desired. **Yield:** 10-12 servings.

1 cup butter, softened
2-1/2 cups sugar
4 eggs
2 cups mashed ripe bananas (about 4 medium)
2 teaspoons vanilla extract
3-1/2 cups all-purpose flour
2 teaspoons baking soda
3/4 teaspoon salt
1/2 cup buttermilk
1 cup chopped pecans, toasted

FROSTING:
1 package (8 ounces) cream cheese, softened
1/2 cup butter, softened
3-1/2 cups confectioners' sugar
1 teaspoon vanilla extract
Toasted chopped pecans

🏅🏅🏅

Banana Pecan Torte

(Pictured above)

Linda Fryar, Stanton, Texas

A friend shared this recipe with me. It's been in her family for years. Now, my family loves it, too.

1. In a mixing bowl, cream butter and sugar. Add the eggs, one at a time, beating well after each. Beat in bananas and vanilla. Combine dry ingredients; add to creamed mixture alternately with buttermilk. Stir in pecans.

2. Pour into three greased and floured 9-in. round baking pans. Bake at 350° for 30-35 minutes or until a toothpick inserted near the center comes out clean. Cool in pans 10 minutes; remove to wire racks to cool completely.

3. For the frosting, beat cream cheese, butter and sugar in a small mixing bowl. Add vanilla. Spread between layers and on top of cake. Sprinkle with pecans. **Yield:** 12-16 servings.

🏅🏅🏅

Chocolate Truffle Cheesecake

(Pictured on page 184)

Mary Jones, Cumberland, Maine

If you delight in the taste of chocolate, then this is the cheese-cake for you. Every creamy bite melts in your mouth. It's so impressive yet not difficult to prepare.

1-1/2 cups chocolate wafer crumbs
2 tablespoons sugar
1/4 cup butter, melted
FILLING:
1/4 cup semisweet chocolate chips
1/4 cup heavy whipping cream
3 packages (8 ounces *each*) cream cheese, softened
1 cup sugar
1/3 cup baking cocoa
3 eggs
1 teaspoon vanilla extract
TOPPING:
1-1/2 cups semisweet chocolate chips
1/4 cup heavy whipping cream

1 teaspoon vanilla extract
Whipped cream and miniature chocolate kisses, optional

1. In a small bowl, combine cookie crumbs and sugar; stir in butter. Press onto the bottom and 1-1/2 in. up the sides of a greased 9-in. springform pan. Bake at 350° for 10 minutes. Cool on a wire rack.

2. Reduce heat to 325°. In a saucepan over low heat, melt chocolate chips; stir until smooth. Remove from the heat; add cream and mix well. Set aside.

3. In a mixing bowl, beat cream cheese and sugar until smooth. Add cocoa and beat well. Add eggs; beat on low just until combined. Stir in vanilla and reserved chocolate mixture just until blended. Pour over crust. Bake for 45-50 minutes or until center is almost set.

4. For topping, melt chocolate chips in a saucepan over low heat, stirring until smooth. Remove from the heat. Stir in cream and vanilla; mix well. Spread over filling. Refrigerate overnight.

5. Carefully run a knife around edge of pan to loosen. Remove sides of pan. Just before serving, garnish with whipped cream and miniature chocolate kisses if desired. **Yield:** 12 servings.

✿✿✿
Coconut Gingerbread Cake
(Pictured at right)

Paula Hartlett, Mineola, New York

This unusual dessert came from a little book I bought at a flea market many years ago. The broiled orange-coconut topping really dresses up a boxed gingerbread mix. When I bring it to potlucks and family get-togethers, it never lasts long!

> 1 package (14-1/2 ounces) gingerbread mix
> 1 large navel orange
> 1-1/3 cups flaked coconut
> 1/2 cup packed brown sugar
> 2 tablespoons orange juice

1. Prepare and bake cake according to package directions, using a greased 8-in. square baking pan. Grate 1 tablespoon of peel from the orange; set aside. Peel and section orange, removing white pith; dice the orange.

2. When cake tests done, remove from oven and cool slightly. Combine coconut, brown sugar, orange juice, diced orange and reserved peel; spread over warm cake. Broil 4 in. from heat 2-3 minutes or until top is lightly browned. Cool on a wire rack. **Yield:** 9 servings.

✿✿✿
Carrot Layer Cake
(Pictured above)

Linda Van Holland, Innisfail, Alberta

Most folks are bowled over by this moist, not-too-sweet cake. The rich pecan filling is an unexpected treat.

FILLING:
> 1 cup sugar
> 2 tablespoons all-purpose flour
> 1/4 teaspoon salt
> 1 cup heavy whipping cream
> 1/2 cup butter
> 1 cup chopped pecans
> 1 teaspoon vanilla extract

CAKE:
> 1-1/4 cups vegetable oil
> 2 cups sugar

> 2 cups all-purpose flour
> 2 teaspoons ground cinnamon
> 2 teaspoons baking powder
> 1 teaspoon baking soda
> 1 teaspoon salt
> 4 eggs
> 4 cups finely shredded carrots
> 1 cup raisins
> 1 cup chopped pecans

FROSTING:
> 3/4 cup butter, softened
> 2 packages (3 ounces *each*) cream cheese, softened
> 1 teaspoon vanilla extract
> 3 cups confectioners' sugar

1. In a heavy saucepan, combine sugar, flour and salt. Stir in cream; add butter. Cook and stir over medium heat until butter is melted; bring to a boil. Reduce heat. Simmer, uncovered, for 30 minutes, stirring occasionally. Stir in nuts and vanilla. Set aside to cool.

2. In a mixing bowl, beat oil and sugar for 1 minute. Combine flour, cinnamon, baking powder, baking soda and salt; add to the creamed mixture alternately with eggs. Mix well. Stir in carrots, raisins and nuts. Pour into three greased and floured 9-in. round baking pans.

3. Bake at 350° for 35-40 minutes, until a toothpick inserted near center comes out clean. Cool in pans 10 minutes. Remove to wire racks; cool completely.

4. For frosting, beat butter, cream cheese and vanilla until smooth. Gradually beat in sugar. Spread filling between cake layers. Frost sides and top of cake. Store in the refrigerator. **Yield:** 16-20 servings.

🏵 🏵 🏵

No-Bake Cherry Cheesecake

(Pictured above)

Pam Noffke, Tyler, Texas

I'm always tight on time. Using a prepared graham cracker crust and canned pie filling, I can extend a no-bake mix to make two light, fancy-looking pies in less than 15 minutes.

    1 package (11.1 ounces) no-bake cheesecake mix
  1/3 **cup butter, melted**
    2 tablespoons sugar
1-1/2 **cups cold milk**
    1 package (8 ounces) cream cheese, softened
    1 cup confectioners' sugar

    2 cups whipped topping
    1 graham cracker crust (9 inches)
    2 cans (21 ounces *each*) cherry pie filling

1. In an ungreased 9-in. pie plate, combine cheesecake crust mix, butter and sugar; mix until the crumbs are moistened. Press onto the bottom and up the sides of the plate. Refrigerate.

2. In a mixing bowl, combine cheesecake filling mix and milk; beat on medium speed for 3 minutes. In another mixing bowl, beat cream cheese and confectioners' sugar. Add to cheesecake mixture; beat well. Fold in whipped topping.

3. Spoon into chilled crust and purchased crust. Refrigerate for at least 1 hour. Top with pie filling. **Yield:** 2 pies (6-8 servings each).

🎀 🎀 🎀
Apple Danish Cheesecake

(Pictured at right)

Ann Wandler, Camrose, Alberta

As a teacher, I have sampled a multitude of staff room goodies over the years. This one is an excellent brunch item.

- 1 cup all-purpose flour
- 1/2 cup ground almonds
- 1/4 cup sugar
- 1/2 cup cold butter
- 1/4 teaspoon almond extract

FILLING:
- 1 package (8 ounces) cream cheese, softened
- 1/4 cup sugar
- 1/4 teaspoon cream of tartar
- 1 egg

TOPPING:
- 1/3 cup packed brown sugar
- 1 tablespoon all-purpose flour
- 1 teaspoon ground cinnamon
- 4 cups thinly sliced peeled tart apples
- 1/3 cup slivered almonds

1. In a small bowl, combine flour, almonds and sugar; cut in butter until crumbly. Add extract. Shape dough into a ball; place between two sheets of waxed paper.

2. Roll out into a 10-in. circle. Transfer to a greased 9-in. springform pan; gently press dough against bottom and up sides of pan. Refrigerate for 30 minutes.

3. In a mixing bowl, beat cream cheese, sugar and cream of tartar until smooth. Add egg; beat on low just until combined. Pour over crust. In a bowl, combine brown sugar, flour and cinnamon. Add apples and stir until coated. Spoon over the filling. Sprinkle with almonds.

4. Bake at 350° for 40-45 minutes or until golden brown. Cool on a wire rack for 10 minutes. Carefully run a knife around edge of pan to loosen; cool 1 hour longer. Refrigerate overnight. Remove sides of pan. **Yield:** 8-10 servings.

· ·

🎀 🎀 🎀
California Lemon Pound Cake

(Pictured above)

Richard Killeaney, Spring Valley, California

Citrus trees grow abundantly in California, and I'm always looking for new recipes that use the fruit from the orange and lemon trees in my yard. This is one of my favorites!

- 1 cup butter
- 1/2 cup shortening
- 3 cups sugar
- 5 eggs
- 3 cups all-purpose flour
- 1 teaspoon salt
- 1/2 teaspoon baking powder
- 1 cup milk
- 1 tablespoon lemon extract
- 1 tablespoon grated lemon peel

GLAZE:
- 1/4 cup butter, softened
- 1 to 1-1/4 cups confectioners' sugar
- 2 tablespoons lemon juice
- 1 teaspoon grated lemon peel

1. In a large mixing bowl, cream butter, shortening and sugar until light and fluffy. Add eggs, one at a time, beating well after each. Combine flour, salt and baking powder; gradually add to creamed mixture alternately with the milk. Mix well after each addition. Add lemon extract and peel. Mix on low until blended.

2. Pour into a greased fluted tube pan. Bake at 350° for 70 minutes or until a toothpick inserted near the center comes out clean. Turn out onto a rack to cool. For glaze, combine all ingredients and drizzle over cooled cake. **Yield:** 22 servings.

🎀 🎀 🎀
Tangy Lemon Cheesecake
(Pictured at right)

Pam Persons, Towanda, Kansas

This dessert gets added spark from a gingersnap crust and a luscious lemon sauce. The mix of sweet and tart is delightful.

 2-1/2 **cups crushed gingersnaps (about 40 cookies)**
 1/3 **cup butter, melted**
FILLING:
 3 **packages (8 ounces *each*) cream cheese, softened**
 1 **cup sugar**
 3 **eggs**
 1 **tablespoon lemon juice**
 1 **tablespoon vanilla extract**
SAUCE:
 1/2 **cup sugar**
 2 **tablespoons cornstarch**
 3/4 **cup water**
 2 **tablespoons butter**
 1/4 **cup lemon juice**
 1 **tablespoon grated lemon peel**

1. In a small bowl, combine cookie crumbs and butter; mix well. Press onto the bottom and 2 in. up the sides of a greased 9-in. springform pan; set aside.

2. In a mixing bowl, beat cream cheese and sugar until smooth. Add eggs; beat on low just until combined. Add lemon juice and vanilla; beat just until blended.

3. Pour into crust. Bake at 350° for 35-40 minutes or until center is almost set. Cool on a wire rack for 10 minutes. Carefully run a knife around the edge of pan to loosen; cool 1 hour longer.

4. In a saucepan, combine sugar and cornstarch. Stir in water until smooth; bring to a boil. Reduce heat; cook and stir over medium heat for 2 minutes or until thickened. Remove from the heat; stir in butter, lemon juice and peel.

5. Refrigerate cheesecake and sauce overnight. Serve sauce over cheesecake. **Yield:** 12 servings.

🎀 🎀 🎀
Cranberry Upside-Down Cake
(Pictured above)

Doris Heath, Bryson City, North Carolina

This recipe started out as a pineapple upside-down cake. I changed a few things because everyone at my house likes cranberries.

 1/2 **cup butter**
 2 **cups sugar, *divided***
 1 **can (16 ounces) whole-berry cranberry sauce**
 1/2 **cup coarsely chopped pecans**
 3 **eggs, *separated***
 1/3 **cup orange juice**
 1 **cup all-purpose flour**
 1 **teaspoon baking powder**
 1/4 **teaspoon salt**

1. Melt butter in a 10-in. iron skillet. Add 1 cup sugar; cook and stir 3 minutes over medium heat. Remove from heat. Spoon cranberry sauce over butter mixture; sprinkle pecans over all. Set aside.

2. In a mixing bowl, beat egg yolks until foamy. Gradually add remaining sugar; beat well. Blend in orange juice. Combine flour, baking powder and salt; add to egg mixture. Beat egg whites until stiff; fold into batter. Carefully spoon over topping in skillet.

3. Bake at 375° about 30 minutes or until cake tests done. Cool 5 minutes in skillet; invert onto large serving plate. Serve warm. **Yield:** 10 servings.

Peanut Butter Chocolate Cake

(Pictured above)

Dorcas Yoder, Weyers Cave, Virginia

In our chocolate-loving house, this cake disappears very quickly! Cream cheese and peanut butter make the frosting extra-creamy.

2 cups all-purpose flour
2 cups sugar
2/3 cup baking cocoa
2 teaspoons baking soda
1 teaspoon baking powder
1/2 teaspoon salt
2 eggs
1 cup milk
2/3 cup vegetable oil
1 teaspoon vanilla extract
1 cup brewed coffee, room temperature

PEANUT BUTTER FROSTING:
1 package (3 ounces) cream cheese, softened
1/4 cup creamy peanut butter
2 cups confectioners' sugar
2 tablespoons milk
1/2 teaspoon vanilla extract
Miniature semisweet chocolate chips, optional

1. In a mixing bowl, combine the first six ingredients. Add eggs, milk, oil and vanilla; beat for 2 minutes. Stir in coffee (batter will be thin).

2. Pour into a greased 13-in. x 9-in. x 2-in. baking pan. Bake at 350° for 35-40 minutes or until a toothpick inserted near the center comes out clean. Cool completely on a wire rack.

3. For the frosting, beat cream cheese and peanut butter in a mixing bowl until smooth. Beat in sugar, milk and vanilla. Spread over cake. Sprinkle with chocolate chips if desired. Store in the refrigerator. **Yield:** 12-16 servings.

🎀 🎀 🎀

S'more Cheesecake

(Pictured above)

Robin Andrews, Cary, North Carolina

This luscious dessert is just as wonderfully tasty as the camp-fire snack that inspired it. It's a great way to savor a beloved summer classic any time of the year.

> 2-1/4 cups graham cracker crumbs (about 36 squares)
> 1/3 cup sugar
> 1/2 cup butter, melted

FILLING:
> 2 packages (8 ounces *each*) cream cheese, softened
> 1 can (14 ounces) sweetened condensed milk
> 2 teaspoons vanilla extract
> 3 eggs
> 1 cup miniature semisweet chocolate chips
> 1 cup miniature marshmallows

TOPPING:
> 1 cup miniature marshmallows
> 1/2 cup semisweet chocolate chips
> 1 tablespoon shortening

1. In a small bowl, combine cracker crumbs and sugar; stir in the butter. Press onto the bottom and 1-3/4 in. up the sides of a greased 10-in. springform pan; set aside.

2. In a mixing bowl, beat the cream cheese, milk and vanilla until smooth. Add eggs; beat on low just until combined. Stir in chocolate chips and marshmallows. Pour over crust.

3. Bake at 325° for 40-45 minutes or until center is al-most set. Sprinkle with marshmallows. Bake 4-6 min-utes longer or until marshmallows are puffed. Mean-while, melt chocolate chips and shortening; stir until smooth. Drizzle over marshmallows. Cool on a wire rack for 10 minutes.

4. Carefully run a knife around edge of pan to loosen; cool 1 hour longer. Refrigerate overnight. Remove sides of pan. **Yield:** 12 servings.

Plantation Gingerbread

(Pictured above)

Wanda Burchell, Lynnville, Tennessee

I like to make this recipe for Christmas. The wonderful aroma of the gingerbread fills the entire house while it's baking, so everyone knows a delicious slice is coming soon.

1	cup butter, softened
1	cup sugar
3	eggs
1	cup molasses
3/4	cup hot water
2-1/2	cups all-purpose flour
1-1/2	teaspoons ground ginger
1	teaspoon baking soda
1	teaspoon ground cinnamon
1/2	teaspoon ground nutmeg
1/2	teaspoon salt
1	cup heavy whipping cream
1 to 2	tablespoons confectioners' sugar

Additional nutmeg, optional

1. In a mixing bowl, cream butter and sugar for 3 minutes. Add eggs; beat on low speed for 2 minutes. Gradually add the molasses and hot water. Combine flour, ginger, baking soda, cinnamon, nutmeg and salt; gradually add to creamed mixture. Beat on low for 1 minute.

2. Pour into a greased 13-in. x 9-in. x 2-in. baking pan. Bake at 350° for 30-35 minutes or until a toothpick inserted near the center comes out clean. Cool.

3. In a mixing bowl, beat cream and confectioners' sugar until soft peaks form. Serve with the gingerbread. Sprinkle with nutmeg if desired. **Yield:** 12-16 servings.

Fresh Grapefruit Cake

(Pictured on page 185)

Debbie Register, Youngstown, Florida

This dessert is particularly good for a backyard barbecue. It's a pleasing, unexpected use for grapefruit. My husband and son both enjoy it. Second helpings are common.

2/3	cup butter
1-3/4	cups sugar
2	eggs
3	cups cake flour
2-1/2	teaspoons baking powder
1/2	teaspoon salt
1/2	cup fresh grapefruit juice
3/4	cup milk
1	teaspoon grated grapefruit peel
1-1/2	teaspoons vanilla extract

FROSTING:

1-1/2	cups sugar
2	egg whites
1	tablespoon light corn syrup
1/8	teaspoon salt
1/3	cup fresh grapefruit juice
1	tablespoon grated grapefruit peel
2	teaspoons vanilla extract

1. In a large mixing bowl, cream butter. Gradually add sugar; beat well. Add eggs, one at a time, beating well after each addition. Sift together flour, baking powder and salt; add to creamed mixture alternately with grapefruit juice, beginning and ending with flour mixture. Gradually add milk. Stir in peel and vanilla; mix well.

2. Pour batter into 2 greased and floured 9-in. round baking pans. Bake at 350° for about 30 minutes or until a toothpick inserted near the center comes out clean. Cool in pans 10 minutes; remove to a wire rack to cool completely.

3. For frosting, combine first five ingredients in the top of a double boiler. Beat at low speed with a portable electric mixer for 30 seconds. Place over boiling water; beat constantly at high speed 7 minutes or until stiff peaks form. Remove from the heat; add grapefruit peel and vanilla; beat 1-2 minutes or until frosting is thick enough to spread. Spread between layers and frost entire cake. **Yield:** 12-16 servings.

2-1/4 cups crushed chocolate cream-filled sandwich cookies (about 22 cookies)
1/3 cup butter, melted
FILLING:
2 packages (8 ounces *each*) cream cheese, softened
1/3 cup confectioners' sugar
1/3 cup heavy whipping cream
1 teaspoon vanilla extract
3 cups vanilla chips, melted and cooled
1/2 cup miniature semisweet chocolate chips
Chocolate curls, optional

Frozen Chocolate Cheesecake Tart

(Pictured above)

Heather Bennett, Dunbar, West Virginia

When I made this irresistible cheesecake for dinner, my husband said it was the best dessert he'd eaten in his whole life.

1. In a small bowl, combine cookie crumbs and butter. Press onto the bottom and up the sides of a greased 9-in. fluted tart pan with a removable bottom. Cover; place in freezer, being careful not to push up on the removable pan bottom. Freeze for at least 1 hour.

2. In a mixing bowl, beat cream cheese and sugar until smooth. Add cream, vanilla and melted vanilla chips; beat for 3 minutes. Stir in chocolate chips; pour over crust. Cover and freeze for 8 hours or overnight.

3. Uncover and refrigerate 3-4 hours before serving. Garnish with chocolate curls if desired. Refrigerate leftovers. **Yield:** 12 servings.

Apple Pear Cake

(Pictured below)

Mary Ann Lees, Centreville, Alabama

When my sister Catherine made an apple cake for me, I asked her for the recipe. I made it a short time later and added some pears to the recipe, since we have pear trees on our acreage. The cake was very moist and tasted so good. Now every time I make it, people want my recipe.

2 cups shredded peeled apples
2 cups shredded peeled pears
2 cups sugar
1-1/4 cups vegetable oil
1 cup raisins
1 cup chopped pecans
2 eggs, beaten
1 teaspoon vanilla extract
3 cups all-purpose flour
2 teaspoons *each* baking soda and ground cinnamon
1/2 teaspoon *each* ground nutmeg and salt
CREAM CHEESE FROSTING:
1 package (3 ounces) cream cheese, softened
1/4 cup butter, softened
3 cups confectioners' sugar
2 tablespoons milk
1/2 teaspoon vanilla extract

1. In a large bowl, combine the first eight ingredients. Combine dry ingredients; stir into the fruit mixture.

2. Pour into a greased 13-in. x 9-in. x 2-in. baking pan. Bake at 325° for 1 hour or until a toothpick inserted near the center comes out clean. Cool on a wire rack.

3. For frosting, beat cream cheese and butter in a mixing bowl until fluffy. Add sugar, milk and vanilla; mix well. Spread over cooled cake. Store in the refrigerator. **Yield:** 12-15 servings.

🎗️ 🎗️ 🎗️

Tropical Cheesecake

(Pictured above)

Shawntel Kemp, Pickens, Oklahoma

I don't bake many sweet items, but I like to put together this cheesecake for parties. The colorful fruit topping is refreshing, and the coconut gives each slice a delicious tropical taste.

 1 cup flaked coconut
 1/4 cup chopped almonds
 2 tablespoons butter, melted

FILLING:
 2 packages (8 ounces *each*) cream cheese, softened
 1 cup sugar
 3 tablespoons cornstarch
 3 eggs
 1 cup (8 ounces) sour cream
 3 tablespoons lemon juice
 2 teaspoons vanilla extract
 1/4 teaspoon almond extract

TOPPING:
 1/3 cup apricot preserves
 1/2 cup pineapple tidbits
 2 to 4 kiwifruit, peeled, sliced and halved
 1/4 to 3/4 cup flaked coconut, toasted

1. In a small bowl, combine coconut and almonds; stir in butter. Press onto the bottom of a greased 9-in. springform pan. Bake at 350° for 10 minutes. Cool on a wire rack.

2. In a mixing bowl, beat cream cheese and sugar until smooth. Add cornstarch and beat well. Add eggs; beat on low just until combined. Add sour cream, lemon juice and extracts; beat just until blended. Pour over crust.

3. Bake at 350° for 45-50 minutes or until center is almost set. Cool on a wire rack for 1 hour. Refrigerate overnight. Remove sides of pan.

4. In a small saucepan, heat preserves, stirring to break up any apricot pieces. Arrange pineapple and kiwi on top of cheesecake. Brush preserves over fruit and on sides of cheesecake. Press coconut onto the sides of the cheesecake. Chill until serving. **Yield:** 10-12 servings.

Maple Peanut Delights, p. 204

Strawberry Banana Trifle, p. 209

Cherry Cheese Pizza, p. 210

202 *Contest Winning Recipes*

Just Desserts

When you want a sweet treat that's a little out of the ordinary, turn to this satisfying chapter. You'll find trifles and truffles, pies and pizza, cobblers and kuchen.

Sunshine Sherbet, p. 207

Maple Peanut Delights 204
Grapefruit Meringue Pie.....................204
Chocolate Praline Ice Cream Topping..205
Rhubarb Elderberry Crisp 205
Peanut Butter Pie................................206
Caramel Fried Ice Cream....................206
Sunshine Sherbet 207
Cinnamon Peanut Brittle 207
Fresh Blueberry Pie 208
Snappy Pumpkin Dessert.....................208
Strawberry Banana Trifle 209
Chocolate Dessert Wraps.....................209
Coffee Shop Fudge.............................210
Cherry Cheese Pizza...........................210
Raspberry Truffles...............................211
Buttery Almond Crunch.....................211
Pear Crisp...212
Magic Pumpkin Buckle.......................212
Frosted Brownie Pizza.........................213
Date Pudding Cobbler 213
Gingered Apricot-Apple Crumble........214
Nutty Chocolate Marshmallow Puffs....214
Fondant-Filled Candies.......................215
Strawberry Peach Melba.....................215
Apple Meringue Pie............................216
Rhubarb Granola Crisp.......................217

Anise Hard Candy..............................217
Macaroon Apple Cobbler 218
Toasted Coconut Truffles 218
Pulled Molasses Taffy 219
Cashew Caramel Fudge......................219
Chocolate Pecan Caramels 220
ABC Slump 220
Almond Plum Kuchen 221
Berry Apple Crumble..........................222
Holiday Pecan Logs............................223
Cherry Nut Crisp................................223
Maple Pecan Pie 224
Fried Sweet Potato Pies.......................224
Applescotch Crisp...............................225
Pumpkin Trifle...................................225
Cream Cheese Rhubarb Pie................226
Caramel Apricot Grunt.......................226
English Toffee Bars 227

Pear Crisp, p. 212

Maple Peanut Delights
(Pictured on page 202)

Katie Stutzman, Goshen, Indiana

This wonderful candy recipe makes a big batch—enough to fill several Christmas gift boxes and still have treats left for my husband, Albert, and our grandchildren. One of our daughters-in-law shared the recipe a few years ago.

    1   package (8 ounces) cream cheese, softened
    1/2 cup butter, softened
    6   cups confectioners' sugar
    1   teaspoon maple flavoring
    2   pounds dark chocolate candy coating
    1   cup chopped peanuts

1. In a mixing bowl, beat cream cheese, butter, confectioners' sugar and flavoring until smooth. Cover and refrigerate for 1 hour. Shape into 1-in. balls.

2. In a microwave or heavy saucepan, melt candy coating, stirring often. Dip balls in coating; sprinkle with peanuts. Place on waxed paper-lined baking sheets. Refrigerate. **Yield:** about 8 dozen.

Grapefruit Meringue Pie
(Pictured above)

Barbara Soliday, Winter Haven, Florida

There's a grapefruit tree in our backyard, so I like to use fresh grapefruit juice when I make this refreshing pie. I just love the unique citrus flavor of this dessert.

    1-1/3 cups sugar
      1/3 cup cornstarch
        2 cups pink grapefruit juice
      3/4 cup water
        3 egg yolks, lightly beaten
        2 tablespoons butter
      1/2 teaspoon lemon extract
        1 pastry shell (9 inches), baked
    MERINGUE:
        3 egg whites
      1/4 teaspoon cream of tartar
        6 tablespoons sugar

1. In a saucepan, combine sugar and cornstarch. Gradually add grapefruit juice and water. Cook and stir over medium-high heat until thickened and bubbly, about 2 minutes. Reduce heat; cook and stir 2 minutes longer.

2. Gradually stir 1/2 cup into egg yolks; return all to the pan. Bring to a gentle boil; cook and stir for 2 minutes. Remove from the heat; stir in butter and extract. Pour hot filling into pastry shell.

3. In a mixing bowl, beat the egg whites and cream of tartar on medium speed until foamy. Gradually beat in sugar, 1 tablespoon at a time, on high just until stiff peaks form and sugar is dissolved. Spread meringue evenly over hot filling, sealing edges to crust.

4. Bake at 350° for 12-15 minutes or until the meringue is golden brown. Cool on a wire rack for 1 hour. Refrigerate for at least 3 hours before serving. Store in the refrigerator. **Yield:** 6-8 servings.

🎀🎀🎀
Chocolate Praline
Ice Cream Topping

(Pictured at right)

Angie Zalewski, Dripping Springs, Texas

Friends tell me they look forward to ice cream socials just to have this topping.

    1 cup heavy whipping cream
  2/3 cup packed brown sugar
  2/3 cup butter
    1 cup (6 ounces) semisweet chocolate chips
    1 cup chopped pecans
Ice cream

1. In a saucepan over medium heat, bring cream, brown sugar and butter to a boil, stirring constantly. Reduce heat; simmer for 2 minutes, stirring occasionally.

2. Remove from the heat; stir in the chocolate chips until melted and smooth. Stir in pecans. Serve warm over ice cream. Store in the refrigerator. **Yield:** 3 cups.

🎀🎀🎀
Rhubarb Elderberry Crisp

(Pictured at right)

Carolyn Scouten, Wyalusing, Pennsylvania

Rhubarb and elderberries are quite abundant around these parts, so I combined the two in this wonderful crisp. It's been well received by our friends.

      1 cup all-purpose flour
    3/4 cup quick-cooking oats
  1-1/2 cups sugar, *divided*
      1 teaspoon ground cinnamon
    1/2 cup cold butter
      3 cups diced rhubarb
      2 cups elderberries *or* blackberries
      2 tablespoons cornstarch
      1 cup water
      1 teaspoon vanilla extract

1. In a bowl, combine the flour, oats, 1/2 cup sugar and cinnamon; cut in butter until mixture resembles coarse crumbs. Set aside half for topping. Press remaining crumb mixture into an ungreased 11-in. x 7-in. x 2-in. baking dish. Top with rhubarb and berries.

2. In a small saucepan, combine cornstarch and remaining sugar. Gradually stir in water; bring to a boil.

Reduce heat; cook and stir for 1-2 minutes or until thickened. Remove from the heat; stir in vanilla. Pour over the fruit. Sprinkle with the reserved crumb mixture.

3. Bake at 350° for 50-55 minutes or until golden brown. Serve warm or cold. **Yield:** 10 servings.

Peanut Butter Pie

(Pictured at left)

Gloria Pittman, Shelby, North Carolina

This creamy pie is always a treat at our house. I haven't met anyone who doesn't like it.

- 1/3 cup creamy peanut butter
- 1 package (3 ounces) cream cheese, softened
- 2 tablespoons butter, softened
- 1 cup confectioners' sugar
- 1/4 cup milk
- 1 carton (8 ounces) frozen whipped topping, thawed
- 1 chocolate crumb crust (9 inches)
- 2 tablespoons chopped peanuts, optional

Chocolate curls, optional

1. In a mixing bowl, beat peanut butter, cream cheese and butter until smooth. Add sugar and milk; fold in whipped topping. Pour into the crust.

2. Cover and freeze for at least 4 hours. Remove from the freezer just before serving. Garnish with peanuts and chocolate curls if desired. **Yield:** 6 servings.

Caramel Fried Ice Cream

(Pictured at right)

Darlene Markel, Sublimity, Oregon

For birthday parties or outdoor barbecues, this is a hit. I've substituted strawberry or Neapolitan for the vanilla ice cream.

- 1 quart vanilla ice cream
- 1/4 cup heavy whipping cream
- 2 teaspoons vanilla extract
- 2 cups flaked coconut, finely chopped
- 2 cups finely crushed cornflakes
- 1/2 teaspoon ground cinnamon

CARAMEL SAUCE:
- 1 cup sugar
- 1/2 cup butter
- 1/2 cup evaporated milk

Oil for deep-fat frying

1. Using a 1/2-cup ice cream scoop, place eight scoops of ice cream on a baking sheet. Cover and freeze for 2 hours or until firm.

2. In a bowl, combine whipping cream and vanilla. In another bowl, combine coconut, cornflakes and cinnamon. Remove ice cream from freezer; wearing plastic gloves, shape the ice cream into balls. Dip balls into cream mixture, then roll in coconut mixture, making sure to coat entire surface. Place coated balls on a baking sheet. Cover and freeze at least 3 hours or until firm.

3. For caramel sauce, heat sugar in a heavy saucepan over medium heat until partially melted and golden, stirring occasionally. Add butter. Gradually add milk, stirring constantly. Cook and stir for 8 minutes or until sauce is thick and golden; keep warm.

4. Heat oil in an electric skillet or deep-fat fryer to 375°. Fry ice cream balls until golden, about 30 seconds. Drain on paper towels. Serve immediately with caramel sauce. **Yield:** 8 servings.

✿✿✿
Sunshine Sherbet
(Pictured on page 203)

Barbara Looney, Fort Knox, Kentucky

My mother and I created this recipe. Warm, humid evenings in Georgia, where I grew up, were all the inspiration we needed! It's always welcomed by family and friends.

        2 **cups sugar**
    1-1/2 **cups water**
        2 **cups milk**
        2 **cups heavy whipping cream**
    1-1/2 **cups orange juice**
        1 **can (12 ounces) evaporated milk**
      1/3 **cup lemon juice**
        2 **teaspoons grated orange peel**
        8 **drops red food coloring, optional**
      1/2 **teaspoon yellow food coloring, optional**

1. In a saucepan over medium heat, bring sugar and water to a boil; boil for 5 minutes. Cool completely. Add remaining ingredients; mix well.

2. Pour mixture into the cylinder of an ice cream freezer; freeze according to manufacturer's directions. Remove from freezer 10 minutes before serving. **Yield:** about 2 quarts.

✿✿✿
Cinnamon Peanut Brittle
(Pictured at right)

Grace Miller, Mansfield, Ohio

I made this sweet and crunchy candy for Christmas and sent some with my husband to work. His co-workers liked it so much they asked for more. It has a lovely glossy appearance.

        1 **cup sugar**
      1/2 **cup light corn syrup**
        2 **cups salted peanuts**
        1 **teaspoon butter**
      1/2 **teaspoon ground cinnamon**
        1 **teaspoon baking soda**
        1 **teaspoon vanilla extract**

1. In a 2-qt. microwave-safe bowl, combine sugar and corn syrup. Heat, uncovered, on high for 4 minutes; stir. Heat 3 minutes longer. Stir in the peanuts, butter and cinnamon.

2. Microwave, uncovered, on high for 30-60 seconds or until mixture turns a light amber color (mixture will be very hot). Quickly stir in baking soda and vanilla until light and foamy. Immediately pour onto a greased baking sheet and spread with a metal spatula.

3. Refrigerate for 20 minutes or until firm; break into small pieces. Store in an airtight container. **Yield:** 1-1/4 pounds.

Editor's Note: This recipe was tested in an 850-watt microwave.

🎀🎀🎀
Fresh Blueberry Pie

(Pictured at right)

Linda Kernan, Mason, Michigan

I've been making this dessert for 30 years. It represents our state well because Michigan is the leader in blueberry production.

- 3/4 cup sugar
- 3 tablespoons cornstarch
- 1/8 teaspoon salt
- 1/4 cup cold water
- 5 cups fresh blueberries, *divided*
- 1 tablespoon butter
- 1 tablespoon lemon juice
- 1 pastry shell (9 inches), baked

1. In a saucepan over medium heat, combine sugar, cornstarch, salt and water until smooth. Add 3 cups blueberries. Bring to a boil; cook and stir 2 minutes or until thickened and bubbly. Remove from heat.

2. Add butter, lemon juice and remaining berries; stir until butter is melted. Cool. Pour into the pastry shell. Refrigerate until serving. **Yield:** 6-8 servings.

🎀🎀🎀
Snappy Pumpkin Dessert

(Pictured below)

Nilah Fischer, Morton, Illinois

Our town has a pumpkin-canning factory, so we're known as the "Pumpkin Capital of the World". New pumpkin recipes are always welcomed by our family. This one's a favorite.

- 2-1/2 cups finely crushed gingersnaps (about 40 cookies)
- 1/2 cup butter, melted
- 1 package (8 ounces) cream cheese, softened
- 1/2 cup confectioners' sugar
- 2 tablespoons milk

TOPPING:

- 3 cups cold milk
- 2 packages (3.4 ounces *each*) instant vanilla pudding mix
- 1 can (15 ounces) solid-pack pumpkin
- 2-1/2 teaspoons pumpkin pie spice
- 2 cups whipped topping

Additional whipped topping, optional

1. Combine gingersnap crumbs and butter; press into an ungreased 13-in. x 9-in. x 2-in. baking pan. Bake at 325° for 10 minutes. Cool.

2. In a mixing bowl, beat the cream cheese, confectioners' sugar and milk until fluffy. Spread over the crust. In another mixing bowl, beat milk and pudding mix for 1 minute. Add pumpkin and pie spice; beat until well blended. Fold in whipped topping.

3. Spread over the cream cheese layer. Refrigerate for at least 3 hours. Cut into squares; garnish with whipped topping if desired. **Yield:** 12-15 servings.

Strawberry Banana Trifle

(Pictured on page 202)

Kim Waterhouse, Randolph, Maine

No matter where I take this dessert, the bowl gets emptied in minutes. It's fun to make because everyone oohs and aahs over how pretty it is.

        1 cup sugar
      1/4 cup cornstarch
        3 tablespoons strawberry gelatin powder
        1 cup cold water
        1 pint fresh strawberries, sliced
  1-3/4 cups cold milk
        1 package (3.4 ounces) instant vanilla pudding
            mix
        3 medium firm bananas, sliced
        1 tablespoon lemon juice
        6 cups cubed angel food cake
        2 cups heavy whipping cream, whipped
Additional strawberries *or* banana slices, optional

1. In a saucepan, combine the sugar, cornstarch and gelatin; stir in water until smooth. Bring to a boil; cook and stir for 2 minutes or until thickened. Remove from the heat. Stir in strawberries; set aside.

2. In a mixing bowl, combine milk and pudding mix. Beat on low speed for 2 minutes; set aside. Toss bananas with lemon juice; drain and set aside.

3. Place half of the cake cubes in a trifle bowl or 3-qt. serving bowl. Layer with half of the pudding, bananas, strawberry sauce and whipped cream. Repeat layers.

4. Cover and refrigerate for at least 2 hours. Garnish with additional fruit if desired. **Yield:** 14 servings.

Chocolate Dessert Wraps

(Pictured at right)

Laurie Gwaltney, Indianapolis, Indiana

I came up with this chocolate and peanut butter treat when I needed a unique, fast dessert for a special dinner. The filled tortillas take just minutes on the grill and get a chewy consistency from marshmallows.

      1/2 cup creamy peanut butter*
        4 flour tortillas (8 inches)
        1 cup miniature marshmallows
      1/2 cup miniature semisweet chocolate chips
Vanilla ice cream
Chocolate shavings, optional

1. Spread 2 tablespoons of peanut butter on each tortilla. Sprinkle 1/4 cup marshmallows and 2 tablespoons chocolate chips on half of each tortilla. Roll up, beginning with the topping side. Wrap each tortilla in heavy-duty foil; seal tightly.

2. Grill, covered, over low heat for 5-10 minutes or until heated through. Unwrap tortillas and place on dessert

plates. Serve with ice cream. Garnish with chocolate shavings if desired. **Yield:** 4 servings.

   ***Editor's Note:** Crunchy peanut butter is not recommended for this recipe.

This recipe is one that my son, Jackson, and I worked on together. After several efforts, we decided this version was a winner. It is smooth, creamy and has an irresistible crunch from pecans. The coffee and cinnamon provide subtle flavor.

- 1 cup chopped pecans
- 3 cups (18 ounces) semisweet chocolate chips
- 1 can (14 ounces) sweetened condensed milk
- 2 tablespoons strong brewed coffee, room temperature
- 1 teaspoon ground cinnamon
- 1/8 teaspoon salt
- 1 teaspoon vanilla extract

1. Line an 8-in. square pan with foil and butter the foil; set aside. Place pecans in a microwave-safe pie plate. Microwave, uncovered, on high for 4 minutes, stirring after each minute; set aside.

2. In a 2-qt. microwave-safe bowl, combine chocolate chips, milk, coffee, cinnamon and salt. Microwave, uncovered, on high for 1-1/2 minutes. Stir until smooth. Stir in vanilla and pecans. Immediately spread into the prepared pan.

3. Cover and refrigerate until firm, about 2 hours. Remove from pan; cut into 1-in. squares. Cover and store at room temperature (70°-80°). **Yield:** 2 pounds.

Editor's Note: This recipe was tested in an 850-watt microwave.

🎀 🎀 🎀

Coffee Shop Fudge

(Pictured above)

Beth Osborne Skinner, Bristol, Tennessee

🎀 🎀 🎀

Cherry Cheese Pizza

(Pictured on page 202)

Elaine Darbyshire, Golden, British Columbia

This dessert pizza is a great way to use cherries—my family likes it better than cherry pie. Each bite just melts in your mouth. People who sample it rave about it.

- 1 cup all-purpose flour
- 1/8 teaspoon baking powder
- 1/4 cup cold butter
- 2 tablespoons shortening
- 3 to 4 tablespoons water
- 1 package (8 ounces) cream cheese, softened
- 1/2 cup sugar
- 2 eggs
- 1 teaspoon vanilla extract
- 1/3 cup chopped pecans *or* almonds

TOPPING:
- 2-1/2 cups fresh *or* frozen pitted tart cherries *or* 1 can (15 or 16 ounces) pitted tart cherries
- 1/3 cup sugar
- 2 tablespoons cornstarch
- 1 tablespoon butter
- 1/8 teaspoon almond extract
- 1/8 teaspoon red food coloring
- Whipped cream and fresh mint, optional

1. In a bowl, combine flour and baking powder; cut in butter and shortening until mixture resembles coarse crumbs. Gradually add water, tossing with a fork until dough forms a ball.

2. Roll out into a 14-in. circle. Place on an ungreased 12-in. pizza pan. Flute edges to form a rim; prick bottom of crust. Bake at 350° for 15 minutes.

3. In a mixing bowl, beat cream cheese and sugar until smooth. Beat in eggs and vanilla. Stir in nuts. Spread over crust. Bake 10 minutes longer. Cool. Drain cherries, reserving 1/3 cup juice. Set cherries and juice aside.

4. In a saucepan, combine sugar and cornstarch; stir in reserved juice until smooth. Add cherries. Cook and stir over medium heat until mixture comes to a boil. Cook and stir 2 minutes longer. Remove from the heat; stir in butter, extract and food coloring. Cool to room temperature; spread over cream cheese layer. Garnish with whipped cream and mint if desired. **Yield:** 10-12 slices.

🎀🎀🎀
Raspberry Truffles

(Pictured at right)

Helen Vail, Glenside, Pennsylvania

Christmas is my very favorite time of year. I make many cookies, cakes and candies—including this easy but elegant recipe—to give to relatives and friends. The aroma of the chocolate and raspberry is heavenly when you're making these.

> 1 tablespoon butter
> 2 tablespoons heavy whipping cream
> 1-1/3 cups semisweet chocolate chips
> 7-1/2 teaspoons seedless raspberry jam
> 6 ounces white *or* dark chocolate candy coating
> 2 tablespoons shortening

1. In a heavy saucepan, combine butter, cream and chocolate chips. Cook over low heat for 4-5 minutes or until chocolate is melted. Remove from the heat; stir in jam until combined.

2. Transfer to a freezer container. Cover; freeze 20 minutes. Drop by teaspoonfuls onto a foil-lined baking sheet. Freeze 15 minutes. Roll into balls; freeze until firm.

3. In a microwave or heavy saucepan, melt candy coating and shortening, stirring often. Cool slightly; spoon over balls. Place on a wire rack over waxed paper. Let stand for 15 minutes or until firm. Store in an airtight container in the refrigerator. **Yield:** 4 dozen.

🎀🎀🎀
Buttery Almond Crunch

(Pictured at left)

Mildred Clothier, Oregon, Illinois

This delectable candy is crisp but not as hard as peanut brittle. Some people say it reminds them of the toffee center of a well-known candy bar.

> 1 tablespoon plus 1/2 cup butter, softened, *divided*
> 1/2 cup sugar
> 1 tablespoon light corn syrup
> 1 cup sliced almonds

1. Line an 8-in. square pan with foil; butter the foil with 1/2 tablespoon butter. Set aside.

2. Spread the sides of a heavy saucepan with 1/2 tablespoon butter. Add 1/2 cup of butter, sugar and corn syrup. Bring to a boil over medium-high heat, stirring constantly. Cook and stir until mixture is golden brown, about 3 minutes. Stir in almonds. Quickly pour into prepared pan.

3. Refrigerate until firm. Invert pan and remove foil. Break candy into pieces. **Yield:** 10 ounces.

⚜ ⚜ ⚜
Pear Crisp
(Pictured on page 203)

Joanne Korevaar, Burgessville, Ontario

Since he's a livestock truck driver, my husband often starts work around 2 or 3 a.m. A piece of this crisp will keep him going till breakfast.

8 medium ripe pears, peeled and thinly sliced
1/4 cup orange juice
1/2 cup sugar
1 teaspoon ground cinnamon
1/4 teaspoon ground allspice
1/4 teaspoon ground ginger

TOPPING:
1 cup all-purpose flour
1 cup old-fashioned oats
1/2 cup packed brown sugar
1/2 teaspoon baking powder
1/2 cup cold butter
Fresh mint and additional pear slices, optional

1. Toss pears with orange juice; place in a greased 13-in. x 9-in. x 2-in. baking dish. Combine the sugar, cinnamon, allspice and ginger; sprinkle over the pears.

2. In a bowl, combine the flour, oats, brown sugar and baking powder; cut in the butter until crumbly. Sprinkle over pears.

3. Bake at 350° for 35-40 minutes or until topping is golden and fruit is tender. Serve warm. Garnish with mint and additional pears if desired. **Yield:** 12 servings.

⚜ ⚜ ⚜
Magic Pumpkin Buckle
(Pictured above)

Darlene Markel, Stayton, Oregon

Probably my family's favorite pumpkin dessert, this is something I've been making since our two daughters—now in their 20s—were small. The crust mixture, which is actually poured in first, rises to the top during baking to form a rich topping. You don't get a soggy bottom crust like you sometimes do with a pie.

1/2 cup butter, melted
1 cup all-purpose flour
1 cup sugar
4 teaspoons baking powder
1/2 teaspoon salt
1 cup milk
1 teaspoon vanilla extract
FILLING:
3 cups canned pumpkin
1 cup evaporated milk
2 eggs
1 cup sugar
1/2 cup packed brown sugar
1 tablespoon all-purpose flour
1 teaspoon ground cinnamon
1/2 teaspoon salt
1/4 teaspoon *each* ground ginger, cloves and
      nutmeg
TOPPING:
1 tablespoon butter
2 tablespoons sugar

1. Pour butter into a 13-in. x 9-in. x 2-in. baking dish; set aside. In a bowl, combine the flour, sugar, baking powder and salt. Stir in milk and vanilla until smooth. Pour into the prepared pan.

2. In a mixing bowl, beat the pumpkin, milk and eggs. Combine the remaining filling ingredients; add to pumpkin mixture. Pour over crust mixture (do not stir). Dot with butter and sprinkle with sugar.

3. Bake at 350° for 55-60 minutes or until a knife inserted near the center comes out clean and the top is golden brown. **Yield:** 12 servings.

1/2 cup butter
2 squares (1 ounce *each*) unsweetened chocolate
1 cup sugar
3/4 cup all-purpose flour
2 eggs, beaten

FROSTING:
1 cup confectioners' sugar
1/3 cup creamy peanut butter
1-1/2 teaspoons vanilla extract
2 to 4 tablespoons milk

TOPPINGS:
3/4 cup plain M&M's
1/2 cup flaked coconut, toasted
1/2 cup chopped pecans, toasted

1. In a saucepan over low heat, melt butter, chocolate and sugar. Remove from the heat; stir in flour until smooth. Add eggs and beat until smooth. Spread onto a greased 12-in. pizza pan.

2. Bake at 350° for 15 minutes or until a toothpick inserted near the center comes out clean. Cool completely.

3. For frosting, in a mixing bowl, beat sugar, peanut butter, vanilla and enough milk to achieve desired spreading consistency. Spread over brownie crust. Top with M&M's, coconut and pecans. **Yield:** 8-10 servings.

Frosted Brownie Pizza

(Pictured above)

Paula Riehl, Boise, Idaho

It's impossible to eat just one piece of this pizza with a chocolaty crust, creamy peanut butter frosting and sweet toppings.

Date Pudding Cobbler

(Pictured at right)

Carolyn Miller, Guys Mills, Pennsylvania

There were eight children in my family when I was a girl, and all of us enjoyed this cobbler. I now serve it for everyday and special occasions alike.

1 cup all-purpose flour
1-1/2 cups packed brown sugar, *divided*
2 teaspoons baking powder
1 tablespoon cold butter
1/2 cup milk
3/4 cup chopped dates
3/4 cup chopped walnuts
1 cup water
Whipped cream and ground cinnamon, optional

1. In a bowl, combine flour, 1/2 cup brown sugar and baking powder. Cut in butter until crumbly. Gradually add milk, dates and walnuts.

2. In a saucepan, combine water and remaining brown sugar; bring to a boil. Remove from the heat; add the date mixture and mix well.

3. Transfer to a greased 8-in. square baking pan. Bake at 350° for 30 minutes or until golden brown. If desired, top each serving with a dollop of whipped cream and sprinkling of cinnamon. **Yield:** 9 servings.

Gingered Apricot-Apple Crumble

(Pictured above)

Sylvia Rice, Didsbury, Alberta

Hot or cold, plain or topped with ice cream or whipped topping, this crumble is tasty. For variety, leave out the apricots and make a traditional apple crisp.

    1 cup orange juice *or* apricot nectar
  3/4 cup finely chopped dried apricots
  1/3 cup honey
  1/4 cup maple syrup
    2 tablespoons lemon juice
    8 cups sliced peeled tart apples (about 8 large)
    3 tablespoons all-purpose flour
    1 teaspoon ground cinnamon
  1/2 teaspoon ground ginger *or* 1 teaspoon minced fresh gingerroot
  1/2 teaspoon ground cardamom

TOPPING:
  3/4 cup all-purpose flour
  1/2 cup quick-cooking oats
  1/2 cup chopped pecans, optional
  1/4 cup vegetable oil
  1/4 cup maple syrup

1. In a bowl, combine the first five ingredients; set aside. Arrange apples in an ungreased 13-in. x 9-in. x 2-in. baking dish. Combine flour, cinnamon, ginger and cardamom; stir into apricot mixture. Spoon over apples.

2. Combine topping ingredients; sprinkle over fruit. Bake at 350° for 50-60 minutes or until topping is golden brown and fruit is tender. **Yield:** 12 servings.

Nutty Chocolate Marshmallow Puffs

(Pictured at right)

Pat Ball, Abilene, Texas

We like to do things big here in Texas, so don't expect a dainty little barely-a-bite truffle from this surprising recipe. Folks are delighted to discover a big fluffy marshmallow inside the chocolate and nut coating.

    2 cups milk chocolate chips
    1 can (14 ounces) sweetened condensed milk
    1 jar (7 ounces) marshmallow creme
  40 large marshmallows
    4 cups coarsely chopped pecans (about 1 pound)

1. In a microwave or heavy saucepan, heat chocolate chips, milk and marshmallow creme just until melted; stir until smooth (mixture will be thick).

2. With tongs, immediately dip marshmallows, one at a time, in chocolate mixture. Shake off excess chocolate; quickly roll in pecans. Place on waxed paper-lined baking sheets. (Reheat chocolate mixture if necessary for easier coating.)

3. Refrigerate until firm. Store in the refrigerator in an airtight container. **Yield:** 40 candies.

Fondant-Filled Candies

(Pictured at right)

Debbi Loney, Central City, Kentucky

Here's an easy way to make two festive and unique candies from one recipe! Half of the creamy fondant is flavored with mint for the centers of peppermint patties. Then you mix a little maraschino cherry juice with the rest of the fondant and use it to "wrap" cherries before dipping them in chocolate.

> 2/3 cup sweetened condensed milk
> 1 tablespoon light corn syrup
> 4-1/2 to 5 cups confectioners' sugar
> 2 to 4 drops peppermint oil*
> 2-1/2 pounds dark chocolate candy coating, *divided*
> 1 jar (16 ounces) maraschino cherries

1. In a mixing bowl, combine milk and corn syrup. Gradually beat in confectioners' sugar (mixture will be stiff). Divide into two portions. For peppermint patties, add the peppermint oil to one portion. Shape 1/2 teaspoonfuls into balls and flatten.

2. In a microwave or heavy saucepan, melt 1 pound of candy coating, stirring often. With a slotted spoon, dip peppermint disks in coating; place on waxed paper to harden. Refrigerate in an airtight container.

3. For chocolate-covered cherries, drain cherries, reserving 3 tablespoons of juice; set cherries aside. Combine juice with remaining fondant. Add additional confectioners' sugar if necessary to form a stiff mixture.

4. Roll into 1-in. balls; flatten into 2-in. circles. Wrap each circle around a cherry and carefully shape into a ball. Place on waxed paper-lined baking sheets. Cover loosely. Melt remaining candy coating; dip cherries in coating. Place on waxed paper to harden.

5. Refrigerate in an airtight container for 1-2 weeks for candy to ripen and center to soften. **Yield:** 4-1/2 dozen.

*Editor's Note: Peppermint oil can be found in some pharmacies or at kitchen and cake decorating supply stores.

Strawberry Peach Melba

(Pictured at right)

Marion Karlin, Waterloo, Iowa

I get oohs and aahs when setting out this cool, fruity dessert. It combines my three all-time favorites—peaches, strawberries and ice cream. It's so simple I can assemble it for company after we all finish the main course.

> 3 cups fresh *or* frozen whole strawberries
> 1 cup confectioners' sugar
> 1/4 cup water
> 1 teaspoon lemon juice
> 2 teaspoons cornstarch
> 1 tablespoon cold water
> 1 teaspoon vanilla extract
> 4 slices *or* scoops vanilla ice cream
> 1 can (15 ounces) sliced peaches, drained

Whipped topping

1. In a saucepan, mash strawberries; add sugar, water and lemon juice. Cook and stir until mixture comes to a boil. Combine cornstarch and cold water until smooth; stir into strawberry mixture. Cook and stir for 2 minutes or until thickened and bubbly.

2. Remove from heat; stir in vanilla. Strain to remove pulp. Place pan in an ice-water bath to cool, stirring occasionally. Serve strawberry sauce over ice cream; top with peaches and whipped topping. **Yield:** 4 servings.

🎀🎀🎀

Apple Meringue Pie

(Pictured above)

Virginia Kraus, Pocahontas, Illinois

I received this recipe from my mother-in-law, and it's one of my husband's favorites. It's a nice variation on traditional apple pie.

    7 cups thinly sliced peeled tart apples
    2 tablespoons lemon juice
  2/3 cup sugar
    2 tablespoons all-purpose flour
  1/3 cup milk
    2 egg yolks, beaten
    1 teaspoon grated lemon peel
Pastry for single-crust pie (9 inches)
    1 tablespoon butter, cubed
MERINGUE:

    3 egg whites
  1/4 teaspoon cream of tartar
    6 tablespoons sugar

1. In a large bowl, toss apples with lemon juice. In a small bowl, whisk sugar, flour, milk, egg yolks and lemon peel until smooth. Pour over apples and toss to coat.

2. Line a 9-in. pie plate with pastry; trim to 1/2 in. beyond edge of pie plate and flute edges. Pour filling into crust; dot with butter. Cover edges loosely with foil. Bake at 400° for 20 minutes. Remove foil; bake 25-30 minutes longer or until apples are tender. Reduce heat to 350°.

3. In a mixing bowl, beat the egg whites and cream of tartar on medium speed until foamy. Gradually beat in sugar, 1 tablespoon at a time, on high just until stiff peaks form and sugar is dissolved. Spread evenly over hot filling, sealing edges to crust.

4. Bake 15 minutes or until golden. Cool on a wire rack. Store in the refrigerator. **Yield:** 6-8 servings.

When my husband and I moved to our house in town, the rhubarb patch had to come along! This is a hit whether I serve it warm with ice cream or cold.

4 cups chopped fresh *or* frozen rhubarb, thawed and drained
1-1/4 cups all-purpose flour, *divided*
1/4 cup sugar
1/2 cup strawberry jam
1-1/2 cups granola cereal
1/2 cup packed brown sugar
1/2 cup chopped pecans
1/2 teaspoon ground cinnamon
1/2 teaspoon ground ginger
1/2 cup cold butter
Ice cream, optional

1. In a bowl, combine the rhubarb, 1/4 cup flour and the sugar; stir in jam and set aside. In another bowl, combine the granola, brown sugar, pecans, cinnamon, ginger and remaining flour. Cut in butter until the mixture resembles coarse crumbs.

2. Press 2 cups of the granola mixture into a greased 8-in. square baking dish; spread rhubarb mixture over the crust. Sprinkle with remaining granola mixture. Bake at 375° for 30-40 minutes or until filling is bubbly and topping is golden brown. Serve warm with ice cream if desired. **Yield:** 9 servings.

🏵 🏵 🏵

Rhubarb Granola Crisp

(Pictured above)

Arlene Beitz, Cambridge, Ontario

🏵 🏵 🏵

Anise Hard Candy

(Pictured below)

Jobyna Carpenter, Poulsbo, Washington

Making this old-fashioned candy has become an annual Christmas project. The recipe is from a friend.

1-1/2 teaspoons butter, softened
3/4 cup water
2/3 cup light corn syrup
2 cups sugar
1 teaspoon anise extract
Red food coloring
2 to 3 tablespoons confectioners' sugar

1. Coat an 8-in. square baking pan with the butter; set aside. In a large heavy saucepan, combine water, corn syrup and sugar. Bring to a boil over medium heat, stirring occasionally. Cover and cook for 3 minutes to dissolve any sugar crystals.

2. Uncover; cook over medium-high heat, without stirring, until a candy thermometer reads 300° (hard-crack stage). Remove from heat; stir in extract and food coloring (keep face away from mixture; odor is strong). Pour into prepared pan. Using a sharp knife, score into 3/4-in. squares. Cool.

3. Separate into squares, using a sharp knife if necessary. Place confectioners' sugar in a baking pan; add candy and roll until coated. Brush off excess sugar with a pastry brush. Store at room temperature in an airtight container. **Yield:** about 1 pound (about 8 dozen).

Editor's Note: We recommend that you test your candy thermometer before each use by bringing water to a boil; the thermometer should read 212°. Adjust recipe temperature up or down based on your test.

🎀🎀🎀
Macaroon Apple Cobbler

(Pictured at right)

Phyllis Hinck, Lake City, Minnesota

Especially when I'm just serving a dessert, I like to prepare this. I usually make it with fresh apples.

    4 cups thinly sliced peeled tart apples
  1/3 cup sugar
  1/2 teaspoon ground cinnamon
  1/2 cup flaked coconut
  1/4 cup chopped pecans
TOPPING:
  1/2 cup butter, softened
  1/2 cup sugar
    1 egg
  1/2 teaspoon vanilla extract
  3/4 cup all-purpose flour
  1/4 teaspoon baking powder

1. Place the apples in an ungreased 9-in. pie plate. Combine sugar and cinnamon; sprinkle over apples. Top with coconut and pecans; set aside.

2. In a mixing bowl, cream butter and sugar. Add egg and vanilla; mix well. Combine flour and baking powder; add to the creamed mixture until blended. Carefully spread over apples.

3. Bake at 350° for 25-30 minutes or until top is golden brown and fruit is tender. Serve warm. **Yield:** 6-8 servings.

🎀🎀🎀
Toasted Coconut Truffles

(Pictured below)

Beth Nagel, West Lafayette, Indiana

"Ooh" and "Mmmm" are common comments when folks taste these delectable bites. Toasted coconut in the coating makes the truffles especially tempting. I always include them in my Christmas packages and gift containers.

    4 cups (24 ounces) semisweet chocolate chips
    1 package (8 ounces) cream cheese, softened
      and cubed
  3/4 cup sweetened condensed milk
    3 teaspoons vanilla extract
    2 teaspoons water
    1 pound white candy coating
    2 tablespoons flaked coconut, finely chopped
      and toasted

1. In a microwave or heavy saucepan, melt chocolate chips. Add the cream cheese, milk, vanilla and water; beat with a hand mixer until blended. Cover and refrigerate until easy to handle, about 1-1/2 hours.

2. Shape into 1-in. balls and place on waxed paper-lined baking sheets. Loosely cover and refrigerate for 1-2 hours or until firm.

3. In a microwave or heavy saucepan, melt candy coating, stirring often. Dip balls in coating; place on waxed paper-lined baking sheets. Sprinkle with coconut. Refrigerate until firm, about 15 minutes. Store in the refrigerator in an airtight container. **Yield:** 5-1/2 dozen.

Pulled Molasses Taffy

(Pictured at right)

Betty Woodman, Wolfe Island, Ontario

French-Canadian children traditionally make this soft, chewy taffy on November 25, the feast day of St. Catherine.

- **5 teaspoons butter, softened, *divided***
- **1/4 cup water**
- **1-1/4 cups packed brown sugar**
- **2 tablespoons cider vinegar**
- **1/4 teaspoon salt**
- **1/3 cup molasses**

1. Butter a 15-in. x 10-in. x 1-in. pan with 3 teaspoons butter; set aside. In a heavy saucepan, combine water, brown sugar, vinegar and salt. Bring to a boil over medium heat. Cook and stir until a candy thermometer reads 245° (firm-ball stage), stirring occasionally. Add molasses and remaining butter. Cook, uncovered, until thermometer reads 260° (hard-ball stage), stirring occasionally.

2. Remove from heat; pour into prepared pan. Cool for 5 minutes or until cool enough to handle. With buttered fingers, quickly pull half of the candy until firm but pliable. Pull and shape into a 1/2-in. rope. Cut into 1-1/4-in. pieces. Repeat with remaining taffy.

3. Wrap pieces individually in foil or waxed paper; twist ends. Store in airtight containers in the refrigerator. Remove from the refrigerator 30 minutes before serving. **Yield:** 14-1/2 dozen.

Editor's Note: For easier candy making, enlist family members to help twist and pull the taffy with you. We recommend that you test your candy thermometer before each use by bringing water to a boil; the thermometer should read 212°. Adjust your recipe temperature up or down based on your test.

Cashew Caramel Fudge

(Pictured below)

Cathy Grubelnik, Raton, New Mexico

A pretty plate of this yummy confection makes a great present! Cashews and caramel are such a delicious combination. I especially enjoy making this fudge for a holiday treat.

- **2 teaspoons plus 1/2 cup butter, softened, *divided***
- **1 can (5 ounces) evaporated milk**
- **2-1/2 cups sugar**
- **2 cups (12 ounces) semisweet chocolate chips**
- **1 jar (7 ounces) marshmallow creme**
- **24 caramels,* quartered**
- **3/4 cup salted cashew halves**
- **1 teaspoon vanilla extract**

1. Line a 9-in. square baking pan with foil; butter the foil with 2 teaspoons butter. Set aside.

2. In a large heavy saucepan, combine milk, sugar and remaining butter. Cook and stir over medium heat until sugar is dissolved. Bring to a rapid boil; boil for 5 minutes, stirring constantly.

3. Remove from the heat; stir in chocolate chips and marshmallow creme until melted. Fold in caramels, cashews and vanilla; mix well. Pour into prepared pan. Cool. Remove from pan and cut into 1-in. squares. Store at room temperature. **Yield:** about 3 pounds.

*Editor's Note: This recipe was tested with Hershey caramels.

I haven't missed a year making this candy for the holidays since 1964! It is made like a pan of upside-down bars.

- 1 tablespoon plus 1 cup butter, softened, *divided*
- 1-1/2 cups coarsely chopped pecans, toasted
- 1 cup (6 ounces) semisweet chocolate chips
- 2 cups packed brown sugar
- 1 cup light corn syrup
- 1/4 cup water
- 1 can (14 ounces) sweetened condensed milk
- 2 teaspoons vanilla extract

1. Line a 13-in. x 9-in. x 2-in. baking pan with foil; butter the foil with 1 tablespoon butter. Sprinkle with pecans and chocolate chips; set aside.

2. In a heavy saucepan over medium heat, melt remaining butter. Add brown sugar, corn syrup and water. Cook and stir until mixture comes to a boil. Stir in milk. Cook, stirring constantly, until a candy thermometer reads 248° (firm-ball stage). Remove from heat and stir in vanilla. Pour into prepared pan (do not scrape saucepan). Cool completely before cutting. **Yield:** about 2-1/2 pounds (about 6-3/4 dozen).

Editor's Note: We recommend that you test your candy thermometer before each use by bringing water to a boil; the thermometer should read 212°. Adjust your recipe temperature up or down based on your test.

Chocolate Pecan Caramels

(Pictured above)

June Humphrey, Strongsville, Ohio

ABC Slump

(Pictured at right)

Becky Burch, Marceline, Missouri

The "ABC" in this recipe's name comes from the apple, blueberries and cranberries it uses. The other part refers to the way the dumplings "slump" during cooking on the stove.

- 1 cup chopped peeled tart apple
- 1 cup fresh *or* frozen blueberries
- 3/4 cup fresh *or* frozen cranberries
- 1 cup water
- 2/3 cup sugar

DUMPLINGS:

- 3/4 cup all-purpose flour
- 1/4 cup sugar
- 1 teaspoon baking powder
- 1/4 teaspoon ground cinnamon
- 1/8 teaspoon ground nutmeg
- 3 tablespoons cold butter
- 1/3 cup milk

Half-and-half cream

1. In a 3-qt. saucepan, combine fruit, water and sugar; bring to a boil. Reduce heat. Cover; simmer 5 minutes.

2. Meanwhile, in a bowl, combine the flour, sugar, baking powder, cinnamon and nutmeg; cut in butter until mixture resembles coarse crumbs. Add milk; stir just until moistened.

3. Drop into six mounds onto simmering fruit. Cover and simmer for about 10 minutes or until a toothpick inserted into a dumpling comes out clean (do not lift the cover while simmering). Serve warm with cream. **Yield:** 6 servings.

🎀🎀🎀

Almond Plum Kuchen

(Pictured above)

Norma Enders, Edmonton, Alberta

You'll find this dessert both easy and tasty. Everyone comments on how the orange and plum flavors go together so well. We like it best when it is served warm with ice cream.

1-1/2 cups all-purpose flour
  3/4 cup packed brown sugar
  1/2 cup ground almonds
    1 tablespoon grated orange peel
  3/4 cup cold butter
FILLING:
    3 eggs
  3/4 cup sugar
  1/2 cup all-purpose flour
  1/2 cup ground almonds

    1 tablespoon grated orange peel
  1/2 teaspoon baking powder
    7 to 8 cups quartered fresh plums
TOPPING:
  1/4 cup sugar
  1/4 cup all-purpose flour
  1/4 cup butter, softened
  1/2 cup sliced almonds

1. In a bowl, combine the first four ingredients; cut in butter until the mixture resembles coarse crumbs. Press into a greased 13-in. x 9-in. x 2-in. baking dish. Bake at 375° for 15 minutes.

2. Meanwhile, in a mixing bowl, beat eggs and sugar until thick and lemon-colored, about 5 minutes. Stir in flour, almonds, orange peel and baking powder.

3. Arrange plums over crust; pour egg mixture over plums. Combine the first three topping ingredients; sprinkle over filling. Top with almonds. Bake for 40-45 minutes or until golden brown. **Yield:** 12 servings.

🎀 🎀 🎀

Berry Apple Crumble

(Pictured above)

Ginger Isham, Williston, Vermont

You can serve this crumble as a snack, and it's also great for a breakfast gathering or church supper. It is good hot or cold.

8 to 10 tart apples, peeled and sliced
2 tablespoons cornstarch
1 can (12 ounces) frozen apple juice concentrate, thawed
2 tablespoons butter
1 teaspoon ground cinnamon
1 teaspoon lemon juice
1 cup fresh *or* frozen blackberries
1 cup fresh *or* frozen raspberries

TOPPING:
2 cups quick-cooking oats
1/2 cup all-purpose flour
1/2 cup chopped walnuts
1/3 cup vegetable oil
1/3 cup maple syrup

1. Place the apples in a greased 13-in. x 9-in. x 2-in. baking dish; set aside.

2. In a saucepan, combine cornstarch and apple juice. Bring to a boil; cook and stir for 2 minutes or until thickened. Add butter, cinnamon and lemon juice. Pour over the apples. Sprinkle with berries.

3. In a bowl, combine the oats, flour and walnuts; add oil and syrup. Sprinkle over berries. Bake at 350° for 40-45 minutes or until filling is bubbly and topping is golden brown. **Yield:** 10-12 servings.

Holiday Pecan Logs

(Pictured at right)

Maxine Ruhl, Fort Scott, Kansas

For 50 years, I've turned to this beloved recipe to make candy to give away at Christmas.

- 2 teaspoons plus 1/2 cup butter, softened, *divided*
- 3-3/4 cups confectioners' sugar
- 1/2 cup instant nonfat dry milk powder
- 1/2 cup sugar
- 1/2 cup light corn syrup
- 1 teaspoon vanilla extract
- 1 package (14 ounces) caramels*
- 1 tablespoon milk *or* half-and-half cream
- 2 cups chopped pecans

1. Butter an 8-in. square pan with 2 teaspoons butter; set aside. Combine confectioners' sugar and milk powder; set aside.

2. In a heavy saucepan, combine 1/2 cup butter, sugar and corn syrup; cook and stir until sugar is dissolved and mixture comes to a boil. Stir in confectioners' sugar mixture, about a third at a time, until blended. Remove from the heat; stir in vanilla. Continue stirring until the

mixture mounds slightly when dropped from a spoon.

3. Spread into prepared pan. Cool. Cut candy into four strips; cut each strip in half. Shape each into a log; wrap in waxed paper and twist ends. Freeze or refrigerate until firm.

4. In a microwave or heavy saucepan, melt caramels with milk, stirring often. Roll logs in caramel mixture, then in pecans. Wrap in waxed paper. Store at room temperature in airtight containers. Cut into slices with a serrated knife. **Yield:** about 3-1/4 pounds.

*Editor's Note: This recipe was tested with Hershey caramels.

Cherry Nut Crisp

(Pictured below)

Melissa Radulovich, Byers, Colorado

I used my favorite cherry pie recipe to create this one after my fiance asked me to make a treat for his rugby team.

- 2 cans (14-1/2 ounces *each*) pitted tart cherries
- 1 cup sugar
- 1/4 cup quick-cooking tapioca
- 1 teaspoon almond extract
- 1/8 teaspoon salt
- 4 to 5 drops red food coloring, optional

CRUST:
- 1 cup all-purpose flour
- 1/3 cup sugar
- 1/4 teaspoon salt
- 1/8 teaspoon baking powder
- 6 tablespoons butter, melted

TOPPING:
- 1/2 cup all-purpose flour
- 1/2 cup packed brown sugar
- 1/2 cup chopped pecans
- 1/3 cup quick-cooking oats
- 6 tablespoons cold butter

1. Drain cherries, reserving 3/4 cup juice (discard remaining juice or save for another use). In a bowl, combine the cherries, sugar, tapioca, extract, salt, food coloring if desired and reserved juice; set aside for 15 minutes, stirring occasionally.

2. Meanwhile, combine crust ingredients. Press onto the bottom and 1 in. up the sides of a greased 9-in. square baking dish; set aside.

3. In another bowl, combine the first four topping ingredients; cut in butter until mixture resembles coarse crumbs. Stir the cherry mixture; pour into crust. Sprinkle with topping.

4. Bake at 400° for 10 minutes. Reduce heat to 375°; bake 30-35 minutes longer or until filling is bubbly and topping is golden brown. **Yield:** 9 servings.

✿✿✿
Maple Pecan Pie
(Pictured at right)

Mildred Wescom, Belvidere, Vermont

Our Vermont maple syrup can't be beat, and this is one of my favorite pies. It's also quick and easy to make.

    3 eggs
1/2 cup sugar
    1 cup maple syrup
    3 tablespoons butter, melted
1/2 teaspoon vanilla extract
1/4 teaspoon salt
    1 cup pecan halves
    1 unbaked pastry shell (9 inches)

1. In a bowl, whisk eggs and sugar until smooth. Add syrup, butter, vanilla, salt and pecans. Pour into pie shell.

2. Bake at 375° for 40-45 minutes or until a knife inserted near the center comes out clean. **Yield:** 8 servings.

✿✿✿
Fried Sweet Potato Pies
(Pictured above)

Marilyn Moseley, Toccoa, Georgia

My dad grew sweet potatoes, so they have graced our table for as long as I can recall. These, though, resulted from an experiment at a church bake sale when we had excess pastry. People couldn't get enough!

4-1/2 cups self-rising flour*
    3 tablespoons sugar
1/2 cup shortening
    2 eggs
    1 cup milk

FILLING:
    3 cups mashed sweet potatoes
    2 cups sugar
    3 eggs, lightly beaten
    1 can (5 ounces) evaporated milk
1/4 cup butter, melted
    3 tablespoons all-purpose flour
    1 teaspoon vanilla extract
Oil for frying
Confectioners' sugar, optional

1. In a bowl, combine flour and sugar; cut in shortening until mixture resembles coarse crumbs. Combine eggs and milk; add to crumb mixture, tossing with a fork until a ball forms. Cover and chill several hours.

2. In a large bowl, combine the seven filling ingredients; stir until smooth. Divide the dough into 25 portions. On a floured surface, roll each portion into a 5-in. circle. Spoon 2 tablespoons of filling on half of each circle. Moisten edges with water; fold dough over filling and press edges with a fork to seal. Prick tops with a fork 4-5 times.

3. In an electric skillet, heat 1/2 in. of oil to 375°. Fry pies, a few at a time, for 1 minute on each side or until golden brown. Drain on paper towels. Dust with confectioners' sugar if desired. Store in the refrigerator. **Yield:** 25 pies.

    *Editor's Note: As a substitute for each cup of self-rising flour, place 1-1/2 teaspoons baking powder and 1/2 teaspoon salt in a measuring cup. Add all-purpose flour to equal 1 cup. For 1/2 cup of self-rising flour, place 3/4 teaspoon baking powder and 1/4 teaspoon salt in a measuring cup; add flour to equal 1/2 cup.

Applescotch Crisp

(Pictured at right)

Elaine Nicholl, Nottingham, Pennsylvania

Just as soon as the first crop of apples is off the trees, I fix this crisp. It's popular at potlucks, and it's a nice snack. In fact, I'm reluctant to make it in the evening—I'm afraid someone will sneak down to the refrigerator at midnight and claim it!

- **4 cups sliced peeled tart apples**
- **1/2 cup packed brown sugar**
- **2/3 cup plus 1 tablespoon all-purpose flour,** *divided*
- **1/2 cup water**
- **1/4 cup milk**
- **1/2 cup quick-cooking oats**
- **1 package (3-1/2 ounces) cook-and-serve butterscotch pudding mix**
- **1/4 cup sugar**
- **1 teaspoon ground cinnamon**
- **1/2 teaspoon salt**
- **1/2 cup cold butter**

Ice cream, optional

1. Place apples in an ungreased 11-in. x 7-in. x 2-in. baking dish. In a bowl, whisk brown sugar, 1 tablespoon

flour, water and milk. Pour over apples. In another bowl, combine oats, pudding mix, sugar, cinnamon, salt and remaining flour. Cut in butter until mixture resembles coarse crumbs. Sprinkle over apples.

2. Bake at 350° for 45-50 minutes or until topping is golden brown and fruit is tender. Serve with ice cream if desired. **Yield:** 8 servings.

Pumpkin Trifle

(Pictured at right)

Melody Hurlbut, St. Agatha, Ontario

This trifle is convenient. It tastes like a traditional pumpkin pie, even though you don't have to make a crust or bake it.

- **2 to 3 cups crumbled unfrosted spice cake, muffins** *or* **gingerbread**
- **1 can (15 ounces) solid-pack pumpkin**
- **1 teaspoon ground cinnamon**
- **1/4 teaspoon ground nutmeg**
- **1/4 teaspoon ground ginger**
- **1/4 teaspoon ground allspice**
- **2-1/2 cups cold milk**
- **4 packages (3.4 ounces** *each***) instant butterscotch pudding mix**
- **2 cups heavy whipping cream**

Maraschino cherries, optional

1. Set aside 1/4 cup of cake crumbs for top. Divide remaining crumbs into four portions; sprinkle one portion in bottom of a trifle bowl or 3-qt. serving bowl.

2. In a large mixing bowl, combine pumpkin, spices, milk and pudding mixes; mix until smooth. Spoon half

into the serving bowl. Sprinkle with a second portion of cake crumbs.

3. Whip cream until stiff; spoon half into bowl. Sprinkle with a third portion of crumbs. Top with the remaining pumpkin mixture, then last portion of crumbs and remaining whipped cream. Sprinkle the reserved crumbs on top, around the edge of the bowl. Place cherries in the center if desired. Cover and chill at least 2 hours before serving. **Yield:** 12-15 servings.

✿ ✿ ✿
Cream Cheese Rhubarb Pie

(Pictured above)

Beverly Huhn, Orwell, Ohio

Whenever my mom and I have a "rhubarb attack", we make this pie! Thank goodness for springtime treats.

> 1/4 cup cornstarch
> 1 cup sugar

Pinch salt

> 1/2 cup water
> 3 cups sliced fresh *or* frozen rhubarb
> (1/2-inch pieces)
> 1 unbaked pie shell (9 inches)

TOPPING:

> 1 package (8 ounces) cream cheese, softened
> 2 eggs
> 1/2 cup sugar

Whipped cream and sliced almonds

1. In a saucepan, combine cornstarch, sugar and salt. Add water; stir until well mixed. Add rhubarb. Cook, stirring often, until mixture boils and thickens. Pour into the pie shell; bake at 425° for 10 minutes.

2. Meanwhile, for topping, beat cream cheese, eggs and sugar until smooth. Pour over pie. Return to oven; reduce heat to 325°. Bake for 35 minutes or until set. Cool. Chill several hours or overnight. Garnish with whipped cream and sliced almonds. **Yield:** 8 servings.

- -

✿ ✿ ✿
Caramel Apricot Grunt

(Pictured at right)

Shari Dore, Brantford, Ontario

This recipe is one we enjoyed at my grandmother's house for years. It's perfect for dessert or church socials.

> 2 cans (15-1/4 ounces *each*) apricot halves,
> undrained
> 2 teaspoons quick-cooking tapioca
> 1/3 cup packed brown sugar
> 1 tablespoon *each* butter and lemon juice

DUMPLINGS:

> 1-1/2 cups all-purpose flour
> 1/2 cup sugar
> 2 teaspoons baking powder
> 2 tablespoons cold butter
> 1/2 cup milk

TOPPING:

> 1/4 cup packed brown sugar
> 2 tablespoons water

Half-and-half cream, optional

1. In a saucepan, combine apricots and tapioca; let stand for 15 minutes. Add next three ingredients. Cook; stir until mixture comes to a full boil. Reduce heat to low; keep warm.

2. For dumplings, combine flour, sugar and baking powder in a bowl; cut in butter until crumbly. Add milk; mix just until combined. Pour warm fruit mixture into an ungreased 2-qt. baking dish (mixture will be very thick). Drop the batter into six mounds onto fruit mixture.

3. Cover and bake at 425° for 15 minutes or until a toothpick inserted into a dumpling comes out clean (do not lift the cover while baking). In a saucepan, bring brown sugar and water to a boil; cook until sugar is dissolved. Spoon over dumplings; bake, uncovered, 5 minutes longer. Serve with cream if desired. **Yield:** 6 servings.

English Toffee Bars

(Pictured above)

Dianne Brooks, Augusta, Kansas

My mother and I get together every year around Christmas-time to make this delicious chocolate-coated toffee, using a recipe she got years ago in a cooking class. It's a tradition I plan to continue with my daughters and grandchildren. Our families and friends wait with mouths watering for their packages.

    1 tablespoon plus 1-3/4 cups butter, softened,
        divided
    2 cups sugar
    1 tablespoon light corn syrup
    1 cup chopped pecans
  1/4 teaspoon salt
    1 pound milk chocolate candy coating

1. Butter a 15-in. x 10-in. x 1-in. baking pan with 1 tablespoon butter; set aside. In a heavy 3-qt. saucepan, melt remaining butter. Add sugar and corn syrup; cook and stir over medium heat until a candy thermometer reads 295° (soft-crack stage). Remove from heat; stir in pecans and salt.

2. Quickly pour into prepared pan. Let stand for 5 minutes. Using a sharp knife, score into squares; cut along scored lines. Let stand at room temperature until cool.

3. Separate into squares, using a sharp knife if necessary. In a microwave or heavy saucepan, melt candy coating, stirring often. Dip squares, one at a time, in coating. Place on waxed paper until set. **Yield:** 2-1/4 pounds.

   Editor's Note: We recommend that you test your candy thermometer before each use by bringing water to a boil; the thermometer should read 212°. Adjust your recipe temperature up or down based on your test.

General Recipe Index

This handy index lists every recipe by food category, major ingredient and/or cooking method, so you can easily locate recipes to suit your needs.

APPETIZERS & SNACKS
Cold Appetizers
 Colorful Crab Appetizer Pizza, 8
 Mexican Deviled Eggs, 16
Dips
 Beefy Taco Dip, 19
 Corn and Bacon Dip, 11
 Fiesta Appetizer, 21
 Hot Kielbasa Dip, 13
 White Bean Dip, 15
Hot Appetizers
 Bacon Cheeseburger Balls, 8
 Breaded Cauliflower, 17
 Fried Onion Rings, 18
 Ground Beef Snack Quiches, 12
 Mozzarella Sticks, 14
 Mushroom Bacon Bites, 12
 Orange-Pecan Hot Wings, 16
 Sweet-Hot Sausage Meatballs, 9
 Sweet-Sour Chicken Dippers, 20
 Taco Meatball Ring, 10
 Taco Tater Skins, 13
 Toasted Zucchini Snacks, 9
Snacks
 Apple Salsa with Cinnamon Chips, 19
Spreads
 Asparagus Appetizer Spread, 10
 Bacon-Broccoli Cheese Ball, 17
 Creamy Crab Cheesecake, 21
 Four-Cheese Pate, 15
 Three-in-One Cheese Ball, 18

APPLES
ABC Slump, 220
Apple-a-Day Casserole, 149
Apple Beef Stew, 122
Apple Danish Cheesecake, 195
Apple-Ham Grilled Cheese, 42
Apple Meringue Pie, 216
Apple Pear Cake, 200
Apple Salsa with Cinnamon Chips, 19
Applescotch Crisp, 225
Berry Apple Crumble, 222
Blackberry Apple Jelly, 136
Chicken with Apple Cream Sauce, 103
Gingered Apricot-Apple Crumble, 214
Macaroon Apple Cobbler, 218
Pork and Apple Supper, 124
Scalloped Apples, 139
Sweet Potatoes with Apples, 141
Walnut Apple Cake, 188

APRICOTS
Apricot Angel Brownies, 183
Caramel Apricot Grunt, 226
Gingered Apricot-Apple Crumble, 214

ARTICHOKES
Artichoke Heart Salad, 26
Artichoke Spinach Casserole, 140
Spinach Artichoke Pie, 134

ASPARAGUS
Asparagus Appetizer Spread, 10
Creamy Asparagus Chowder, 51
Sesame Beef and Asparagus Salad, 27

BACON & CANADIAN BACON
Bacon-Broccoli Cheese Ball, 17
Bacon Cheeseburger Balls, 8
Bacon Cheeseburger Pizza, 86
Bacon Potato Pancakes, 73
Bacon Swiss Bread, 158
Baked Potato Soup, 46
Best-Ever Potato Soup, 63
Broccoli Cauliflower Salad, 37
Broccoli Orange Salad, 29
Cheddar-Mushroom Stuffed Potatoes, 133
Corn and Bacon Dip, 11
Lettuce with Hot Bacon Dressing, 35
Mushroom Bacon Bites, 12
Pleasing Potato Pizza, 90
Taco Tater Skins, 13
Two-Meat Pizza with Wheat Crust, 116

BANANAS
Aloha Quick Bread, 160
Banana Pecan Torte, 192
Black-Bottom Banana Bars, 176
Frosted Banana Bars, 182
Fudgy Banana Muffins, 77
Strawberry Banana Trifle, 209

BARS & BROWNIES
Bars
 Black-Bottom Banana Bars, 176
 Caramel-Chocolate Oat Squares, 174
 Chocolate Buttermilk Squares, 178
 Frosted Banana Bars, 182
Brownies
 Apricot Angel Brownies, 183
 Best Cake Brownies, 175
 Black Forest Brownies, 182
 Chocolate Cream Cheese Brownies, 171
 Chocolate Crunch Brownies, 173
 Chocolate Mint Brownies, 177
 Chocolate Peanut Butter Brownies, 180
 Cinnamon Brownies, 172
 Frosted Brownie Pizza, 213
 German Chocolate Brownies, 175
 Maple Butterscotch Brownies, 179
 Raspberry Truffle Brownies, 171
 Swiss Chocolate Brownies, 180

BEANS & LENTILS
Festive Green Bean Casserole, 133
Green Bean Potato Salad, 31
Lentil Barley Soup, 59
Three Bean Casserole, 144
Three-Bean Soup, 46
Warm Bean and Chard Salad, 26
Western-Style Beef 'n' Beans, 117
White Bean Dip, 15

BEEF (also see Ground Beef)
Main Dishes
    Apple Beef Stew, 122
    Marinated Flank Steak, 101
    Pot Roast with Cranberry Sauce, 91
    Salsa Beef Skillet, 107
    Stew with Confetti Dumplings, 108
    Tangy Beef Brisket, 113
    Tenderloin with Creamy Garlic Sauce, 121
    Western-Style Beef 'n' Beans, 117
    Zucchini Con Carne, 102
Salad
    Sesame Beef and Asparagus Salad, 27
Sandwiches
    Barbecued Beef Sandwiches, 54
Soup
    Hungarian Goulash Soup, 50

BEVERAGES
Breakfast Wassail, 69
Cappuccino Mix, 72
Morning Orange Drink, 71

BISCUITS & SCONES
Flaky Dill Biscuits, 166
Poppy Seed Lemon Scones, 159
Tex-Mex Biscuits, 160

BLACKBERRIES
Berry Apple Crumble, 222
Blackberry Apple Jelly, 136
Rhubarb Elderberry Crisp, 205

BLUEBERRIES
ABC Slump, 220
Fresh Blueberry Pie, 208

BREADS (also see Biscuits & Scones; Corn Bread & Cornmeal; Muffins; Pancakes; Rolls & Buns; Yeast Bread)
Aloha Quick Bread, 160
Bacon Swiss Bread, 158
Citrus Streusel Quick Bread, 163
Gingerbread Loaf, 165
Italian Cheese Bread, 157
Savory Chicken Vegetable Strudel, 155
Savory Italian Rounds, 158
Strawberries 'n' Cream Bread, 162
Tomato Pizza Bread, 167
Triple-Chocolate Quick Bread, 156

BREAKFAST & BRUNCH
Apple Nut Muffins, 74
Bacon Potato Pancakes, 73
Breakfast Wassail, 69
Burst o' Lemon Muffins, 74
Cappuccino Mix, 72
Cappuccino Muffins, 76
Caramel Pecan Rolls, 67
Cherry Almond Muffins, 69
Chocolate Cookie Muffins, 66
Cinnamon Rolls in a Snap, 68
Cocoa Macaroon Muffins, 75
Crustless Swiss Quiche, 77
Dijon Ham Muffins, 70
Egg and Corn Quesadilla, 68
Fudgy Banana Muffins, 77
Hash Brown Egg Dish, 75
Mashed Potato Cinnamon Rolls, 73
Morning Maple Muffins, 72
Morning Orange Drink, 71
Orange-Raisin Sticky Muffins, 70

Spiced Pear Muffins, 78
Sticky Bun Coffee Ring, 79
Sunrise Mini Pizzas, 78
Sweet Raspberry Muffins, 66

BROCCOLI
Bacon-Broccoli Cheese Ball, 17
Broccoli Cauliflower Salad, 37
Broccoli Corn Bread, 165
Broccoli Fish Bundles, 92
Broccoli Ham Stroganoff, 98
Broccoli Orange Salad, 29
Picante Broccoli Chicken Salad, 28
Wild Rice Floret Bake, 143

BUNS (see Rolls & Buns)

BUTTERSCOTCH
Applescotch Crisp, 225
Maple Butterscotch Brownies, 179

CABBAGE & SAUERKRAUT
Cajun Cabbage, 118
Calico Chowchow, 141
Classic Cabbage Rolls, 82
Grape and Cabbage Salad, 34
Red Cabbage Casserole, 151
Reuben Meatballs, 95
Tasty Reuben Soup, 60

CAKES & TORTES (also see Cheesecakes)
Apple Pear Cake, 200
Banana Pecan Torte, 192
California Lemon Pound Cake, 195
Caramel-Fudge Chocolate Cake, 189
Carrot Layer Cake, 193
Casserole Carrot Cake, 187
Coconut Gingerbread Cake, 193
Cranberry-Orange Pound Cake, 191
Cranberry Upside-Down Cake, 196
Fresh Grapefruit Cake, 199
Orange Chiffon Cake, 189
Peanut Butter Chocolate Cake, 197
Plantation Gingerbread, 199
Special Strawberry Torte, 191
Walnut Apple Cake, 188

CANDIES
Anise Hard Candy, 217
Buttery Almond Crunch, 211
Cashew Caramel Fudge, 219
Chocolate Pecan Caramels, 220
Cinnamon Peanut Brittle, 207
Coffee Shop Fudge, 210
English Toffee Bars, 227
Fondant-Filled Candies, 215
Holiday Pecan Logs, 223
Maple Peanut Delights, 204
Nutty Chocolate Marshmallow Puffs, 214
Pulled Molasses Taffy, 219
Raspberry Truffles, 211
Toasted Coconut Truffles, 218

CARAMEL
Caramel Apricot Grunt, 226
Caramel-Chocolate Oat Squares, 174
Caramel Fried Ice Cream, 206
Caramel-Fudge Chocolate Cake, 189
Caramel Pecan Rolls, 67
Chocolate Pecan Caramels, 220

CARROTS
Carrot Layer Cake, 193
Casserole Carrot Cake, 187
Creamy Carrot Casserole, 138

CASSEROLES
Main Dishes
Au Gratin Sausage Skillet, 99
Broccoli Ham Stroganoff, 98
Cajun Cabbage, 118
Chicken 'n' Chips, 100
Chicken Stroganoff, 110
Chicken Wild Rice Casserole, 120
Creamy Chicken and Rice, 104
Firecracker Casserole, 99
Four-Cheese Chicken Fettuccine, 101
French Country Casserole, 96
Great Pork Chop Bake, 112
Ham and Sweet Potato Cups, 105
Mashed Potato Beef Casserole, 115
Meatball Hash Brown Bake, 91
Meatball Sub Casserole, 129
Meaty Mac 'n' Cheese, 109
Microwave Tuna Casserole, 92
Pizza Tot Casserole, 116
Pork and Apple Supper, 124
Sloppy Joe Under a Bun, 110
Southwestern Veggie Bake, 123
Spinach Beef Biscuit Bake, 94
Western-Style Beef 'n' Beans, 117
Side Dishes
Apple-a-Day Casserole, 149
Artichoke Spinach Casserole, 140
Cheesy Corn Spoon Bread, 136
Church Supper Potatoes, 149
Colorful Oven Vegetables, 137
Company Mac and Cheese, 144
Creamy Carrot Casserole, 138
End-of-Summer Vegetable Bake, 151
Festive Green Bean Casserole, 133
Golden Mashed Potatoes, 150
Microwave Mac 'n' Cheese, 142
Mushroom Corn Casserole, 137
Picante Biscuit Bake, 138
Red Cabbage Casserole, 151
Spinach Artichoke Pie, 134
Squash Stuffing Casserole, 146
Sweet Potatoes with Apples, 141
Swiss Potato Squares, 147
Three Bean Casserole, 144

CAULIFLOWER
Breaded Cauliflower, 17
Broccoli Cauliflower Salad, 37
Cream of Cauliflower Soup, 45
Savory Cauliflower Pie, 146
Wild Rice Floret Bake, 143

CHEESE
Appetizers & Snacks
Bacon-Broccoli Cheese Ball, 17
Bacon Cheeseburger Balls, 8
Creamy Crab Cheesecake, 21
Four-Cheese Pate, 15
Mozzarella Sticks, 14
Three-in-One Cheese Ball, 18
Breads
Bacon Swiss Bread, 158
Chive-Cheese Corn Bread, 161
Italian Cheese Bread, 157

Savory Italian Rounds, 158
Tex-Mex Biscuits, 160
Three-Cheese Twists, 164
Desserts
Apple Danish Cheesecake, 195
Cherry Cheese Pizza, 210
Chocolate Chip Cookie Dough Cheesecake, 188
Chocolate Cream Cheese Brownies, 171
Chocolate Truffle Cheesecake, 192
Cranberry Cheesecake, 186
Cream Cheese Rhubarb Pie, 226
Family-Favorite Cheesecake, 190
Frozen Chocolate Cheesecake Tart, 200
No-Bake Cherry Cheesecake, 194
Peanut Butter Cheesecake, 187
S'more Cheesecake, 198
Tangy Lemon Cheesecake, 196
Tiny Cherry Cheesecakes, 190
Tropical Cheesecake, 201
Main Dishes
Au Gratin Sausage Skillet, 99
Bacon Cheeseburger Pizza, 86
Chili Nacho Supper, 123
Crustless Swiss Quiche, 77
Li'l Cheddar Meat Loaves, 129
Meaty Mac 'n' Cheese, 109
Quick Chicken Cordon Bleu, 106
Shrimp Monterey, 84
Sandwiches
Apple-Ham Grilled Cheese, 42
Ham and Cheese Calzones, 48
Sides Dishes
Cheddar-Mushroom Stuffed Potatoes, 133
Cheesy Corn Spoon Bread, 136
Company Mac and Cheese, 144
Grilled Three-Cheese Potatoes, 135
Microwave Mac 'n' Cheese, 142
Swiss Potato Squares, 147
Vegetables Mornay, 132
Soups
Chunky Cheese Soup, 61
Creamy Swiss Onion Soup, 52
Spicy Cheeseburger Soup, 59

CHEESECAKES
Apple Danish Cheesecake, 195
Chocolate Chip Cookie Dough Cheesecake, 188
Chocolate Truffle Cheesecake, 192
Cranberry Cheesecake, 186
Creamy Crab Cheesecake, 21
Family-Favorite Cheesecake, 190
Frozen Chocolate Cheesecake Tart, 200
No-Bake Cherry Cheesecake, 194
Peanut Butter Cheesecake, 187
S'more Cheesecake, 198
Tangy Lemon Cheesecake, 196
Tiny Cherry Cheesecakes, 190
Tropical Cheesecake, 201

CHERRIES
Black Forest Brownies, 182
Cherry Almond Muffins, 69
Cherry Almond Preserves, 139
Cherry Cheese Pizza, 210
Cherry Nut Crisp, 223
Fondant-Filled Candies, 215
No-Bake Cherry Cheesecake, 194
Tiny Cherry Cheesecakes, 190

CHICKEN

Appetizers & Snacks
  Orange-Pecan Hot Wings, 16
  Sweet-Sour Chicken Dippers, 20

Bread
  Savory Chicken Vegetable Strudel, 155

Main Dishes
  Chicken 'n' Chips, 100
  Chicken Corn Fritters, 89
  Chicken Fajita Pizza, 96
  Chicken Stroganoff, 110
  Chicken Wild Rice Casserole, 120
  Chicken with Apple Cream Sauce, 103
  Chicken with Pineapple Sauce, 115
  Crab-Stuffed Chicken Breasts, 126
  Creamy Chicken and Rice, 104
  Four-Cheese Chicken Fettuccine, 101
  Mom's Chicken 'n' Buttermilk Dumplings, 87
  Old-Fashioned Chicken Potpie, 109
  Oven-Fried Chicken, 112
  Quick Chicken Cordon Bleu, 106
  Sesame Chicken with Mustard Sauce, 120
  Southern Chicken Roll-Ups, 108
  Summertime Chicken Tacos, 85

Salads
  Crunchy Chicken Salad, 30
  Grilled Chicken Pasta Salad, 34
  Hot Chicken Salad, 38
  Lemony Chicken Fruit Salad, 27
  Picante Broccoli Chicken Salad, 28

Soups
  Chicken Tomato Soup, 47
  Comforting Chicken Noodle Soup, 49
  Lentil Barley Soup, 59
  Southern Chicken Rice Soup, 58
  Spicy White Chili, 60

CHILI
Baked Chili, 50
Garden Harvest Chili, 43
Spicy White Chili, 60
Zesty Colorado Chili, 53

CHOCOLATE

Bars & Brownies
  Apricot Angel Brownies, 183
  Best Cake Brownies, 175
  Black-Bottom Banana Bars, 176
  Black Forest Brownies, 182
  Caramel-Chocolate Oat Squares, 174
  Chocolate Buttermilk Squares, 178
  Chocolate Cream Cheese Brownies, 171
  Chocolate Mint Brownies, 177
  Chocolate Peanut Butter Brownies, 180
  Cinnamon Brownies, 172
  Frosted Brownie Pizza, 213
  German Chocolate Brownies, 175
  Raspberry Truffle Brownies, 171
  Swiss Chocolate Brownies, 180

Breads
  Chocolate Cookie Muffins, 66
  Chocolate Crunch Brownies, 173
  Cocoa Macaroon Muffins, 75
  Fudgy Banana Muffins, 77
  Triple-Chocolate Quick Bread, 156

Cakes & Cheesecakes
  Caramel-Fudge Chocolate Cake, 189
  Chocolate Chip Cookie Dough Cheesecake, 188
  Chocolate Truffle Cheesecake, 192
  Frozen Chocolate Cheesecake Tart, 200

  Peanut Butter Chocolate Cake, 197
  S'more Cheesecake, 198
  Tiny Cherry Cheesecakes, 190

Candies
  Cashew Caramel Fudge, 219
  Chocolate Pecan Caramels, 220
  Coffee Shop Fudge, 210
  English Toffee Bars, 227
  Fondant-Filled Candies, 215
  Maple Peanut Delights, 204
  Nutty Chocolate Marshmallow Puffs, 214
  Raspberry Truffles, 211

Cookies
  Fudge Puddles, 181
  White Chocolate Cookies, 176

Desserts
  Chocolate Praline Ice Cream Topping, 205
  Chocolate Dessert Wraps, 209

CHOWDER
Chunky Seafood Chowder, 54
Corn and Sausage Chowder, 44
Creamy Asparagus Chowder, 51
Halibut Chowder, 43
Northwest Salmon Chowder, 56

CHUTNEY
Cranberry Chutney, 145

CINNAMON
Apple Salsa with Cinnamon Chips, 19
Cinnamon Brownies, 172
Cinnamon Peanut Brittle, 207
Cinnamon-Raisin Soft Pretzels, 161
Cinnamon Rolls in a Snap, 68
Mashed Potato Cinnamon Rolls, 73
Spiced Pear Muffins, 78

COBBLERS & CRISPS
ABC Slump, 220
Applescotch Crisp, 225
Berry Apple Crumble, 222
Caramel Apricot Grunt, 226
Cherry Nut Crisp, 223
Date Pudding Cobbler, 213
Gingered Apricot-Apple Crumble, 214
Macaroon Apple Cobbler, 218
Pear Crisp, 212
Rhubarb Elderberry Crisp, 205
Rhubarb Granola Crisp, 217

COCONUT
Aloha Quick Bread, 160
Apricot Angel Brownies, 183
Caramel Fried Ice Cream, 206
Cocoa Macaroon Muffins, 75
Coconut Gingerbread Cake, 193
Fruitcake Cookies, 179
German Chocolate Brownies, 175
Macaroon Apple Cobbler, 218
Toasted Coconut Truffles, 218
Tropical Cheesecake, 201

COFFEE
Cappuccino Mix, 72
Cappuccino Muffins, 76
Coffee Shop Fudge, 210

COLESLAW
Grape and Cabbage Salad, 34

CONDIMENTS (see Chutney; Jams & Jellies; Relish; Salads & Dressings; Salsa)

COOKIES (also see Bars & Brownies)
Frosted Cashew Cookies, 181
Fruitcake Cookies, 179
Fudge Puddles, 181
Molasses Spice Cutouts, 170
Rainbow Cookies, 172
Shortbread Squares, 173
Vanilla-Butter Sugar Cookies, 174
White Chocolate Cookies, 176

CORN
Chicken Corn Fritters, 89
Chili Corn Bread Salad, 32
Colorful Corn Salad, 25
Corn and Bacon Dip, 11
Corn and Sausage Chowder, 44
Corn Stuffing Balls, 134
Corn Tortilla Pizzas, 95
Corny Tomato Dumpling Soup, 57
Egg and Corn Quesadilla, 68
Mushroom Corn Casserole, 137
Salsa Corn Cakes, 132
Texas Two-Step Corn Medley, 143

CORN BREAD & CORNMEAL
Baked Chili, 50
Broccoli Corn Bread, 165
Chili Corn Bread Salad, 32
Chive-Cheese Corn Bread, 161
Green Chili Corn Muffins, 163
Salsa Corn Cakes, 132

CRANBERRIES
ABC Slump, 220
Cranberry Cheesecake, 186
Cranberry Chutney, 145
Cranberry-Orange Pound Cake, 191
Cranberry Upside-Down Cake, 196
Creamy Cranberry Salad, 35
Pot Roast with Cranberry Sauce, 91

DATES (see Raisins & Dates)

DEEP-FRYER RECIPES
Chicken Corn Fritters, 89
Fried Onion Rings, 18
Sweet-Sour Chicken Dippers, 20

DESSERTS (also see specific kinds)
Almond Plum Kuchen, 221
Cherry Cheese Pizza, 210
Chocolate Dessert Wraps, 209
Frosted Brownie Pizza, 213
Magic Pumpkin Buckle, 212
Pumpkin Trifle, 225
Snappy Pumpkin Dessert, 208
Strawberry Banana Trifle, 209

DILL
Flaky Dill Biscuits, 166
Tomato Dill Bisque, 61

DIPS (also see Salsa)
Beefy Taco Dip, 19
Corn and Bacon Dip, 11
Fiesta Appetizer, 21
Hot Kielbasa Dip, 13
White Bean Dip, 15

DRESSING (see Stuffing)

DUCK
Stuffed Duckling, 89

DUMPLINGS
Corny Tomato Dumpling Soup, 57
Mom's Chicken 'n' Buttermilk Dumplings, 87
Stew with Confetti Dumplings, 108

EGGS (also see Quiche)
Egg and Corn Quesadilla, 68
Hash Brown Egg Dish, 75
Mexican Deviled Eggs, 16
Sunrise Mini Pizzas, 78

FISH & SEAFOOD
Appetizers & Snacks
  Colorful Crab Appetizer Pizza, 8
  Creamy Crab Cheesecake, 21
Main Dishes
  Broccoli Fish Bundles, 92
  Crab-Stuffed Chicken Breasts, 126
  Gingered Honey Salmon, 88
  Lemon-Batter Fish, 127
  Marinated Catfish Fillets, 93
  Maryland Crab Cakes, 90
  Microwave Tuna Casserole, 92
  Saucy Skillet Fish, 84
  Shrimp Monterey, 84
Salad
  Eastern Shore Seafood Salad, 30
Side Dish
  Crabby Potatoes, 142
Soups
  Chunky Seafood Chowder, 54
  Halibut Chowder, 43
  Northwest Salmon Chowder, 56

FRUIT (also see specific kinds)
Desserts
  Fruitcake Cookies, 179
  Rhubarb Elderberry Crisp, 205
  Tropical Cheesecake, 201
Salads
  Layered Fresh Fruit Salad, 39
  Lemony Chicken Fruit Salad, 27

GARLIC
Garlic Beef Enchiladas, 102
Herbed Garlic Potatoes, 150
Tenderloin with Creamy Garlic Sauce, 121

GINGER
Coconut Gingerbread Cake, 193
Gingerbread Loaf, 165
Gingered Apricot-Apple Crumble, 214
Gingered Honey Salmon, 88
Plantation Gingerbread, 199
Snappy Pumpkin Dessert, 208

GRAPEFRUIT
Fresh Grapefruit Cake, 199
Grapefruit Meringue Pie, 204

GRAPES
Grape and Cabbage Salad, 34

GRILLED & BROILED
Appetizer
  Mushroom Bacon Bites, 12

Dessert
    Chocolate Dessert Wraps, 209
Main Dishes
    Cool-Kitchen Meat Loaf, 97
    Gingered Honey Salmon, 88
    Glazed Country Ribs, 128
    Marinated Catfish Fillets, 93
    Marinated Flank Steak, 101
    Meatball Shish Kabobs, 114
    Peanutty Pork Kabobs, 94
    Summertime Chicken Tacos, 85
    Surprise Meatball Skewers, 86
Salad
    Grilled Chicken Pasta Salad, 34
Sandwiches
    Cola Burgers, 52
    Garden Turkey Burgers, 47
Side Dishes
    Grilled Potato Fans, 147
    Grilled Three-Cheese Potatoes, 135

GROUND BEEF
Appetizers & Snacks
    Bacon Cheeseburger Balls, 8
    Beefy Taco Dip, 19
    Ground Beef Snack Quiches, 12
    Taco Meatball Ring, 10
Main Dishes
    Bacon Cheeseburger Pizza, 86
    Beef Stroganoff Meatballs, 125
    Blue Plate Beef Patties, 124
    Cajun Cabbage, 118
    Chili Nacho Supper, 123
    Classic Cabbage Rolls, 82
    Colorful Stuffed Peppers, 113
    Cool-Kitchen Meat Loaf, 97
    Corn Tortilla Pizzas, 95
    Fiesta Meatballs, 100
    Firecracker Casserole, 99
    Garlic Beef Enchiladas, 102
    Li'l Cheddar Meat Loaves, 129
    Mashed Potato Beef Casserole, 115
    Meatball Hash Brown Bake, 91
    Meatball Shish Kabobs, 114
    Meatball Sub Casserole, 129
    Meatballs with Cream Sauce, 107
    Meaty Mac 'n' Cheese, 109
    Mushroom Salisbury Steak, 104
    Pizza Tot Casserole, 116
    Reuben Meatballs, 95
    Skillet Bow Tie Lasagna, 85
    Sloppy Joe Under a Bun, 110
    Spaghetti 'n' Meatballs, 119
    Spinach Beef Biscuit Bake, 94
    Surprise Meatball Skewers, 86
    Tasty Meat Pie, 118
Sandwiches
    Cola Burgers, 52
    Meatball Lover's Sandwich, 62
    Super Sloppy Joes, 55
Side Dish
    Three Bean Casserole, 144
Soups
    Baked Chili, 50
    Hearty Hamburger Soup, 45
    Meatball Mushroom Soup, 56
    Pronto Taco Soup, 63
    Spicy Cheeseburger Soup, 59
    Zesty Colorado Chili, 53
    Zesty Macaroni Soup, 49

HAM
Apple-Ham Grilled Cheese, 42
Broccoli Ham Stroganoff, 98
Chunky Cheese Soup, 61
Dijon Ham Muffins, 70
Glazed Ham Balls, 83
Ham and Cheese Calzones, 48
Ham and Sweet Potato Cups, 105
Quick Chicken Cordon Bleu, 106
Swiss Potato Squares, 147

HONEY
Gingered Honey Salmon, 88

ICE CREAM & TOPPINGS
Caramel Fried Ice Cream, 206
Chocolate Praline Ice Cream Topping, 205
Strawberry Peach Melba, 215
Sunshine Sherbet, 207

JAMS & JELLIES
Blackberry Apple Jelly, 136
Cherry Almond Preserves, 139

KABOBS
Meatball Shish Kabobs, 114
Peanutty Pork Kabobs, 94
Surprise Meatball Skewers, 86

LAMB
Irish Lamb Stew, 97

LEMON
Burst o' Lemon Muffins, 74
California Lemon Pound Cake, 195
Citrus Streusel Quick Bread, 163
Lemon-Batter Fish, 127
Lemony Chicken Fruit Salad, 27
Poppy Seed Lemon Scones, 159
Sunshine Sherbet, 207
Tangy Lemon Cheesecake, 196

MAPLE
Maple Butterscotch Brownies, 179
Maple Peanut Delights, 204
Maple Pecan Pie, 224
Morning Maple Muffins, 72

MARSHMALLOW
Chocolate Crunch Brownies, 173
Chocolate Dessert Wraps, 209
Nutty Chocolate Marshmallow Puffs, 214
S'more Cheesecake, 198

MEAT LOAVES & PATTIES
Blue Plate Beef Patties, 124
Cool-Kitchen Meat Loaf, 97
Li'l Cheddar Meat Loaves, 129
Mushroom Salisbury Steak, 104

MEAT PIES
Old-Fashioned Chicken Potpie, 109
Tasty Meat Pie, 118
Turkey Dressing Pie, 111

MEATBALLS
Bacon Cheeseburger Balls, 8
Beef Stroganoff Meatballs, 125
Fiesta Meatballs, 100
Glazed Ham Balls, 83

MEATBALLS *(continued)*
Meatball Hash Brown Bake, 91
Meatball Lover's Sandwich, 62
Meatball Mushroom Soup, 56
Meatball Shish Kabobs, 114
Meatballs with Cream Sauce, 107
Reuben Meatballs, 95
Spaghetti 'n' Meatballs, 119
Spinach Turkey Meatballs, 88
Surprise Meatball Skewers, 86
Sweet-Hot Sausage Meatballs, 9
Taco Meatball Ring, 10

MELON
Chilled Cantaloupe Soup, 44

MERINGUE
Apple Meringue Pie, 216
Grapefruit Meringue Pie, 204

MICROWAVE RECIPES
Appetizer
Hot Kielbasa Dip, 13
Desserts
Caramel-Chocolate Oat Squares, 174
Casserole Carrot Cake, 187
Cinnamon Peanut Brittle, 207
Coffee Shop Fudge, 210
Main Dishes
Broccoli Ham Stroganoff, 98
Colorful Stuffed Peppers, 113
Hash Brown Egg Dish, 75
Microwave Tuna Casserole, 92
Mushroom Salisbury Steak, 104
Quick Chicken Cordon Bleu, 106
Side Dishes
Cheddar-Mushroom Stuffed Potatoes, 133
Microwave Mac 'n' Cheese, 142
Scalloped Apples, 139

MINT
Chocolate Mint Brownies, 177
Fondant-Filled Candies, 215

MIXES
Cappuccino Mix, 72

MUFFINS
Apple Nut Muffins, 74
Burst o' Lemon Muffins, 74
Cappuccino Muffins, 76
Cherry Almond Muffins, 69
Chocolate Cookie Muffins, 66
Cocoa Macaroon Muffins, 75
Dijon Ham Muffins, 70
Fudgy Banana Muffins, 77
Green Chili Corn Muffins, 163
Morning Maple Muffins, 72
Orange-Raisin Sticky Muffins, 70
Spiced Pear Muffins, 78
Sweet Onion Muffins, 156
Sweet Raspberry Muffins, 66

MUSHROOMS
Blue Plate Beef Patties, 124
Cheddar-Mushroom Stuffed Potatoes, 133
Meatball Mushroom Soup, 56
Mushroom Bacon Bites, 12
Mushroom Corn Casserole, 137
Mushroom Salisbury Steak, 104
Pork Chops with Mushroom Gravy, 83

MUSTARD
Dijon Ham Muffins, 70
Sesame Chicken with Mustard Sauce, 120
Warm Mustard Potato Salad, 39

NUTS *(also see Peanut Butter)*
Appetizer
Orange-Pecan Hot Wings, 16
Breads
Apple Nut Muffins, 74
Caramel Pecan Rolls, 67
Cherry Almond Muffins, 69
Citrus Streusel Quick Bread, 163
Candies
Buttery Almond Crunch, 211
Cashew Caramel Fudge, 219
Chocolate Pecan Caramels, 220
Chocolate Praline Ice Cream Topping, 205
Cinnamon Peanut Brittle, 207
Coffee Shop Fudge, 210
Holiday Pecan Logs, 223
Maple Peanut Delights, 204
Nutty Chocolate Marshmallow Puffs, 214
Desserts
Almond Plum Kuchen, 221
Apricot Angel Brownies, 183
Banana Pecan Torte, 192
Black Forest Brownies, 182
Cherry Nut Crisp, 223
Frosted Cashew Cookies, 181
Fruitcake Cookies, 179
Fudge Puddles, 181
German Chocolate Brownies, 175
Maple Pecan Pie, 224
Tropical Cheesecake, 201
Walnut Apple Cake, 188
White Chocolate Cookies, 176
Main Dish
Peanutty Pork Kabobs, 94

OATS
Caramel-Chocolate Oat Squares, 174

ONIONS
Creamy Swiss Onion Soup, 52
Fried Onion Rings, 18
Onion Sandwich Rolls, 166
Sweet Onion Muffins, 156

ORANGE
Broccoli Orange Salad, 29
Citrus Streusel Quick Bread, 163
Coconut Gingerbread Cake, 193
Cranberry-Orange Pound Cake, 191
Morning Orange Drink, 71
Orange Chiffon Cake, 189
Orange-Pecan Hot Wings, 16
Orange-Raisin Sticky Muffins, 70
Sunshine Sherbet, 207

OVEN ENTREES *(also see Casseroles; Meat Loaves & Patties; Meat Pies; Meatballs; Pizzas; Microwave Recipes)*
Beef & Ground Beef
Garlic Beef Enchiladas, 102
Pot Roast with Cranberry Sauce, 91
Tangy Beef Brisket, 113
Tenderloin with Creamy Garlic Sauce, 121
Chicken
Chicken with Pineapple Sauce, 115
Crab-Stuffed Chicken Breasts, 126

Oven-Fried Chicken, 112
Sesame Chicken with Mustard Sauce, 120
Fish & Seafood
Broccoli Fish Bundles, 92
Shrimp Monterey, 84
Fowl
Stuffed Duckling, 89

PANCAKES
Bacon Potato Pancakes, 73
Salsa Corn Cakes, 132

PASTA & NOODLES
Main Dishes
Beef Stroganoff Meatballs, 125
Broccoli Ham Stroganoff, 98
Chicken Stroganoff, 110
Four-Cheese Chicken Fettuccine, 101
Meaty Mac 'n' Cheese, 109
Microwave Tuna Casserole, 92
No-Fuss Pork Chops, 117
Skillet Bow Tie Lasagna, 85
Spaghetti 'n' Meatballs, 119
Salads
Grilled Chicken Pasta Salad, 34
Spicy Ravioli Salad, 31
Side Dishes
Company Mac and Cheese, 144
Microwave Mac 'n' Cheese, 142
Soups
Comforting Chicken Noodle Soup, 49
Zesty Macaroni Soup, 49

PEACHES
Strawberry Peach Melba, 215

PEANUT BUTTER
Chocolate Crunch Brownies, 173
Chocolate Dessert Wraps, 209
Chocolate Peanut Butter Brownies, 180
Fudge Puddles, 181
Peanut Butter Cheesecake, 187
Peanut Butter Chocolate Cake, 197
Peanut Butter Pie, 206

PEARS
Apple Pear Cake, 200
Pear Crisp, 212
Spiced Pear Muffins, 78

PEPPERONI
Deep-Dish Sausage Pizza, 93
Pepperoni Pan Pizza, 127
Pizza with Stuffed Crust, 105

PEPPERS & CHILIES
Bell Peppers
Colorful Stuffed Peppers, 113
Festive Green Bean Casserole, 133
Peanutty Pork Kabobs, 94
Stuffed Sweet Pepper Soup, 42
Green Chilies
Chili Corn Bread Salad, 32
Chili Nacho Supper, 123
Green Chili Corn Muffins, 163
Green Chili Pork Stew, 121
Tex-Mex Biscuits, 160

PIES
Apple Meringue Pie, 216
Cream Cheese Rhubarb Pie, 226

Fresh Blueberry Pie, 208
Fried Sweet Potato Pies, 224
Grapefruit Meringue Pie, 204
Maple Pecan Pie, 224
Peanut Butter Pie, 206

PINEAPPLE
Aloha Quick Bread, 160
Chicken with Pineapple Sauce, 115

PIZZAS
Bacon Cheeseburger Pizza, 86
Chicken Fajita Pizza, 96
Colorful Crab Appetizer Pizza, 8
Corn Tortilla Pizzas, 95
Deep-Dish Sausage Pizza, 93
Pepperoni Pan Pizza, 127
Pizza with Stuffed Crust, 105
Pleasing Potato Pizza, 90
Roasted Veggie Pizza, 82
Sunrise Mini Pizzas, 78
Two-Meat Pizza with Wheat Crust, 116

PLUMS
Almond Plum Kuchen, 221

PORK (*also see Bacon & Canadian Bacon; Ham; Sausage*)
Main Dishes
Glazed Country Ribs, 128
Great Pork Chop Bake, 112
Green Chili Pork Stew, 121
No-Fuss Pork Chops, 117
Peanutty Pork Kabobs, 94
Pork and Apple Supper, 124
Pork Chops with Mushroom Gravy, 83
Soups
Stir-Fried Pork Soup, 55
Zesty Colorado Chili, 53

POTATOES (*also see Sweet Potatoes*)
Appetizer
Taco Tater Skins, 13
Breads
Golden Potato Rolls, 154
Mashed Potato Cinnamon Rolls, 73
Main Dishes
Au Gratin Sausage Skillet, 99
Hash Brown Egg Dish, 75
Mashed Potato Beef Casserole, 115
Meatball Hash Brown Bake, 91
Pizza Tot Casserole, 116
Pleasing Potato Pizza, 90
Salads
Baked German Potato Salad, 37
Deluxe German Potato Salad, 24
Green Bean Potato Salad, 31
Idaho Potato Salad, 29
Warm Mustard Potato Salad, 39
Side Dishes
Bacon Potato Pancakes, 73
Cheddar-Mushroom Stuffed Potatoes, 133
Church Supper Potatoes, 149
Crabby Potatoes, 142
Golden Mashed Potatoes, 150
Grilled Potato Fans, 147
Grilled Three-Cheese Potatoes, 135
Herbed Garlic Potatoes, 150
Swiss Potato Squares, 147

POTATOES *(continued)*
Soups
Baked Potato Soup, 46
Best-Ever Potato Soup, 63
Sausage Potato Soup, 48

PUMPKIN
Magic Pumpkin Buckle, 212
Pumpkin Trifle, 225
Snappy Pumpkin Dessert, 208

QUICHE
Crustless Swiss Quiche, 77
Ground Beef Snack Quiches, 12

RAISINS & DATES
Cinnamon-Raisin Soft Pretzels, 161
Date Pudding Cobbler, 213
Orange-Raisin Sticky Muffins, 70

RASPBERRIES
Berry Apple Crumble, 222
Raspberry Truffle Brownies, 171
Raspberry Truffles, 211
Sweet Raspberry Muffins, 66

RELISH
Calico Chowchow, 141

RHUBARB
Cream Cheese Rhubarb Pie, 226
Rhubarb Elderberry Crisp, 205
Rhubarb Granola Crisp, 217

RICE & WILD RICE
Cajun Cabbage, 118
Chicken Wild Rice Casserole, 120
Creamy Chicken and Rice, 104
Meatball Shish Kabobs, 114
Southern Chicken Rice Soup, 58
Three-Rice Pilaf, 145
Wild Rice Floret Bake, 143
Wild Rice Soup, 58

ROLLS & BUNS
Caramel Pecan Rolls, 67
Caraway Cloverleaf Rolls, 157
Cinnamon-Raisin Soft Pretzels, 161
Cinnamon Rolls in a Snap, 68
Golden Potato Rolls, 154
Mashed Potato Cinnamon Rolls, 73
Onion Sandwich Rolls, 166
Poppy Seed Rolls, 162
Sticky Bun Coffee Ring, 79
Three-Cheese Twists, 164

SALADS & DRESSINGS *(also see Coleslaw)*
Bean Salad
Warm Bean and Chard Salad, 26
Fruit Salads
Creamy Cranberry Salad, 35
Layered Fresh Fruit Salad, 39
Gelatin Salad
Summertime Strawberry Gelatin Salad, 36
Green Salad
Lettuce with Hot Bacon Dressing, 35
Main-Dish Salads
Chili Corn Bread Salad, 32
Crunchy Chicken Salad, 30
Eastern Shore Seafood Salad, 30

Grilled Chicken Pasta Salad, 34
Hot Chicken Salad, 38
Lemony Chicken Fruit Salad, 27
Picante Broccoli Chicken Salad, 28
Sesame Beef and Asparagus Salad, 27
Spicy Ravioli Salad, 31
Potato Salads
Baked German Potato Salad, 37
Deluxe German Potato Salad, 24
Green Bean Potato Salad, 31
Idaho Potato Salad, 29
Warm Mustard Potato Salad, 39
Vegetable Salads
Artichoke Heart Salad, 26
Broccoli Cauliflower Salad, 37
Broccoli Orange Salad, 29
Colorful Corn Salad, 25
Creamy Sliced Tomatoes, 38
Creamy Summer Vegetable Salad, 33
Grape and Cabbage Salad, 34
Southern Sweet Potato Salad, 33
Zippy Radish Salad, 25

SALSA
Apple Salsa with Cinnamon Chips, 19

SANDWICHES
Apple-Ham Grilled Cheese, 42
Barbecued Beef Sandwiches, 54
Cola Burgers, 52
Garden Turkey Burgers, 47
Ham and Cheese Calzones, 48
Meatball Lover's Sandwich, 62
Super Sloppy Joes, 55

SAUSAGE *(also see Pepperoni)*
Appetizers & Snacks
Hot Kielbasa Dip, 13
Sweet-Hot Sausage Meatballs, 9
Main Dishes
Au Gratin Sausage Skillet, 99
Classic Cabbage Rolls, 82
Creamy Sausage Stew, 87
Deep-Dish Sausage Pizza, 93
French Country Casserole, 96
Two-Meat Pizza with Wheat Crust, 116
Soups
Corn and Sausage Chowder, 44
Sausage Potato Soup, 48
Tasty Reuben Soup, 60
Zesty Colorado Chili, 53

SEAFOOD *(see Fish & Seafood)*

SIDE DISHES *(also see Casseroles)*
Fruit
Scalloped Apples, 139
Sweet Potatoes with Apples, 141
Miscellaneous
Cheesy Corn Spoon Bread, 136
Corn Stuffing Balls, 134
Picante Biscuit Bake, 138
Salsa Corn Cakes, 132
Pasta
Company Mac and Cheese, 144
Microwave Mac 'n' Cheese, 142
Potatoes
Cheddar-Mushroom Stuffed Potatoes, 133
Crabby Potatoes, 142
Grilled Potato Fans, 147

Grilled Three-Cheese Potatoes, 135
Herbed Garlic Potatoes, 150
Rice
Three-Rice Pilaf, 145
Vegetables
Colorful Oven Vegetables, 137
Grandma's Sweet-Sour Veggies, 148
Root Vegetable Medley, 140
Savory Cauliflower Pie, 146
Texas Two-Step Corn Medley, 143
Vegetables Mornay, 132

SKILLET & STOVETOP SUPPERS
Beef & Ground Beef
Apple Beef Stew, 122
Beef Stroganoff Meatballs, 125
Blue Plate Beef Patties, 124
Classic Cabbage Rolls, 82
Salsa Beef Skillet, 107
Skillet Bow Tie Lasagna, 85
Spaghetti 'n' Meatballs, 119
Stew with Confetti Dumplings, 108
Zucchini Con Carne, 102
Chicken
Chicken with Apple Cream Sauce, 103
Mom's Chicken 'n' Buttermilk Dumplings, 87
Southern Chicken Roll-Ups, 108
Fish & Seafood
Lemon-Batter Fish, 127
Maryland Crab Cakes, 90
Saucy Skillet Fish, 84
Lamb
Irish Lamb Stew, 97
Pork & Sausage
Au Gratin Sausage Skillet, 99
Green Chili Pork Stew, 121
No-Fuss Pork Chops, 117
Pork and Apple Supper, 124
Pork Chops with Mushroom Gravy, 83

SOUPS *(also see Chili; Chowder)*
Baked Potato Soup, 46
Best-Ever Potato Soup, 63
Chicken Tomato Soup, 47
Chilled Cantaloupe Soup, 44
Chunky Cheese Soup, 61
Comforting Chicken Noodle Soup, 49
Cream of Cauliflower Soup, 45
Creamy Swiss Onion Soup, 52
Hearty Hamburger Soup, 45
Hungarian Goulash Soup, 50
Lentil Barley Soup, 59
Meatball Mushroom Soup, 56
Pronto Taco Soup, 63
Sausage Potato Soup, 48
Southern Chicken Rice Soup, 58
Spicy Cheeseburger Soup, 59
Stir-Fried Pork Soup, 55
Stuffed Sweet Pepper Soup, 42
Tasty Reuben Soup, 60
Three-Bean Soup, 46
Tomato Dill Bisque, 61
Wild Rice Soup, 58
Zesty Macaroni Soup, 49

SPINACH
Artichoke Spinach Casserole, 140
Church Supper Potatoes, 149
Spinach Artichoke Pie, 134

Spinach Beef Biscuit Bake, 94
Spinach Turkey Meatballs, 88

SPREADS
Asparagus Appetizer Spread, 10
Bacon-Broccoli Cheese Ball, 17
Four-Cheese Pate, 15
Three-in-One Cheese Ball, 18

SQUASH *(see Zucchini & Squash)*

STEWS
Apple Beef Stew, 122
Creamy Sausage Stew, 87
Green Chili Pork Stew, 121
Irish Lamb Stew, 97
Stew with Confetti Dumplings, 108

STRAWBERRIES
Rhubarb Granola Crisp, 217
Special Strawberry Torte, 191
Strawberries 'n' Cream Bread, 162
Strawberry Banana Trifle, 209
Strawberry Peach Melba, 215
Summertime Strawberry Gelatin Salad, 36

STUFFING
Corn Stuffing Balls, 134

SWEET POTATOES
Fried Sweet Potato Pies, 224
Ham and Sweet Potato Cups, 105
Southern Sweet Potato Salad, 33
Sweet Potatoes with Apples, 141

TOMATOES
Chicken Tomato Soup, 47
Corny Tomato Dumpling Soup, 57
Creamy Sliced Tomatoes, 38
Tomato Dill Bisque, 61
Tomato Pizza Bread, 167

TURKEY
Garden Turkey Burgers, 47
Spinach Turkey Meatballs, 88
Turkey Dressing Pie, 111

VEGETABLES *(also see specific kinds)*
Colorful Oven Vegetables, 137
Creamy Summer Vegetable Salad, 33
End-of-Summer Vegetable Bake, 151
Garden Harvest Chili, 43
Garden Turkey Burgers, 47
Grandma's Sweet-Sour Veggies, 148
Meatball Shish Kabobs, 114
Roasted Veggie Pizza, 82
Root Vegetable Medley, 140
Savory Chicken Vegetable Strudel, 155
Southwestern Veggie Bake, 123
Surprise Meatball Skewers, 86
Vegetables Mornay, 132

YEAST BREAD *(also see Rolls & Buns)*
Sesame Wheat Braids, 155

ZUCCHINI & SQUASH
Fiesta Meatballs, 100
Squash Stuffing Casserole, 146
Toasted Zucchini Snacks, 9
Zucchini Con Carne, 102

Alphabetical Recipe Index

Refer to this index for a complete alphabetical listing of all the recipes in this book.

A

ABC Slump, 220
Almond Plum Kuchen, 221
Aloha Quick Bread, 160
Anise Hard Candy, 217
Apple-a-Day Casserole, 149
Apple Beef Stew, 122
Apple Danish Cheesecake, 195
Apple-Ham Grilled Cheese, 42
Apple Meringue Pie, 216
Apple Nut Muffins, 74
Apple Pear Cake, 200
Apple Salsa with Cinnamon Chips, 19
Applescotch Crisp, 225
Apricot Angel Brownies, 183
Artichoke Heart Salad, 26
Artichoke Spinach Casserole, 140
Asparagus Appetizer Spread, 10
Au Gratin Sausage Skillet, 99

B

Bacon-Broccoli Cheese Ball, 17
Bacon Cheeseburger Balls, 8
Bacon Cheeseburger Pizza, 86
Bacon Potato Pancakes, 73
Bacon Swiss Bread, 158
Baked Chili, 50
Baked German Potato Salad, 37
Baked Potato Soup, 46
Banana Pecan Torte, 192
Barbecued Beef Sandwiches, 54
Beef Stroganoff Meatballs, 125
Beefy Taco Dip, 19
Berry Apple Crumble, 222
Best Cake Brownies, 175
Best-Ever Potato Soup, 63
Black-Bottom Banana Bars, 176
Black Forest Brownies, 182
Blackberry Apple Jelly, 136
Blue Plate Beef Patties, 124
Breaded Cauliflower, 17
Breakfast Wassail, 69
Broccoli Cauliflower Salad, 37
Broccoli Corn Bread, 165
Broccoli Fish Bundles, 92
Broccoli Ham Stroganoff, 98
Broccoli Orange Salad, 29
Burst o' Lemon Muffins, 74
Buttery Almond Crunch, 211

C

Cajun Cabbage, 118
Calico Chowchow, 141
California Lemon Pound Cake, 195
Cappuccino Mix, 72
Cappuccino Muffins, 76
Caramel Apricot Grunt, 226
Caramel-Chocolate Oat Squares, 174
Caramel Fried Ice Cream, 206

Caramel-Fudge Chocolate Cake, 189
Caramel Pecan Rolls, 67
Caraway Cloverleaf Rolls, 157
Carrot Layer Cake, 193
Cashew Caramel Fudge, 219
Casserole Carrot Cake, 187
Cheddar-Mushroom Stuffed Potatoes, 133
Cheesy Corn Spoon Bread, 136
Cherry Almond Muffins, 69
Cherry Almond Preserves, 139
Cherry Cheese Pizza, 210
Cherry Nut Crisp, 223
Chicken 'n' Chips, 100
Chicken Corn Fritters, 89
Chicken Fajita Pizza, 96
Chicken Stroganoff, 110
Chicken Tomato Soup, 47
Chicken Wild Rice Casserole, 120
Chicken with Apple Cream Sauce, 103
Chicken with Pineapple Sauce, 115
Chili Corn Bread Salad, 32
Chili Nacho Supper, 123
Chilled Cantaloupe Soup, 44
Chive-Cheese Corn Bread, 161
Chocolate Buttermilk Squares, 178
Chocolate Chip Cookie Dough Cheesecake, 188
Chocolate Cookie Muffins, 66
Chocolate Cream Cheese Brownies, 171
Chocolate Crunch Brownies, 173
Chocolate Dessert Wraps, 209
Chocolate Mint Brownies, 177
Chocolate Peanut Butter Brownies, 180
Chocolate Pecan Caramels, 220
Chocolate Praline Ice Cream Topping, 205
Chocolate Truffle Cheesecake, 192
Chunky Cheese Soup, 61
Chunky Seafood Chowder, 54
Church Supper Potatoes, 149
Cinnamon Brownies, 172
Cinnamon Peanut Brittle, 207
Cinnamon-Raisin Soft Pretzels, 161
Cinnamon Rolls in a Snap, 68
Citrus Streusel Quick Bread, 163
Classic Cabbage Rolls, 82
Cocoa Macaroon Muffins, 75
Coconut Gingerbread Cake, 193
Coffee Shop Fudge, 210
Cola Burgers, 52
Colorful Corn Salad, 25
Colorful Crab Appetizer Pizza, 8
Colorful Oven Vegetables, 137
Colorful Stuffed Peppers, 113
Comforting Chicken Noodle Soup, 49
Company Mac and Cheese, 144
Cool-Kitchen Meat Loaf, 97
Corn and Bacon Dip, 11
Corn and Sausage Chowder, 44
Corn Stuffing Balls, 134
Corn Tortilla Pizzas, 95
Corny Tomato Dumpling Soup, 57
Crab-Stuffed Chicken Breasts, 126
Crabby Potatoes, 142

Cranberry Cheesecake, 186
Cranberry Chutney, 145
Cranberry-Orange Pound Cake, 191
Cranberry Upside-Down Cake, 196
Cream Cheese Rhubarb Pie, 226
Cream of Cauliflower Soup, 45
Creamy Asparagus Chowder, 51
Creamy Carrot Casserole, 138
Creamy Chicken and Rice, 104
Creamy Crab Cheesecake, 21
Creamy Cranberry Salad, 35
Creamy Sausage Stew, 87
Creamy Sliced Tomatoes, 38
Creamy Summer Vegetable Salad, 33
Creamy Swiss Onion Soup, 52
Crunchy Chicken Salad, 30
Crustless Swiss Quiche, 77

D

Date Pudding Cobbler, 213
Deep-Dish Sausage Pizza, 93
Deluxe German Potato Salad, 24
Dijon Ham Muffins, 70

E

Eastern Shore Seafood Salad, 30
Egg and Corn Quesadilla, 68
End-of-Summer Vegetable Bake, 151
English Toffee Bars, 227

F

Family-Favorite Cheesecake, 190
Festive Green Bean Casserole, 133
Fiesta Appetizer, 21
Fiesta Meatballs, 100
Firecracker Casserole, 99
Flaky Dill Biscuits, 166
Fondant-Filled Candies, 215
Four-Cheese Chicken Fettuccine, 101
Four-Cheese Pate, 15
French Country Casserole, 96
Fresh Blueberry Pie, 208
Fresh Grapefruit Cake, 199
Fried Onion Rings, 18
Fried Sweet Potato Pies, 224
Frosted Banana Bars, 182
Frosted Brownie Pizza, 213
Frosted Cashew Cookies, 181
Frozen Chocolate Cheesecake Tart, 200
Fruitcake Cookies, 179
Fudge Puddles, 181
Fudgy Banana Muffins, 77

G

Garden Harvest Chili, 43
Garden Turkey Burgers, 47
Garlic Beef Enchiladas, 102
German Chocolate Brownies, 175
Gingerbread Loaf, 165
Gingered Apricot-Apple Crumble, 214
Gingered Honey Salmon, 88
Glazed Country Ribs, 128
Glazed Ham Balls, 83
Golden Mashed Potatoes, 150
Golden Potato Rolls, 154
Grandma's Sweet-Sour Veggies, 148
Grape and Cabbage Salad, 34
Grapefruit Meringue Pie, 204
Great Pork Chop Bake, 112

Green Bean Potato Salad, 31
Green Chili Corn Muffins, 163
Green Chili Pork Stew, 121
Grilled Chicken Pasta Salad, 34
Grilled Potato Fans, 147
Grilled Three-Cheese Potatoes, 135
Ground Beef Snack Quiches, 12

H

Halibut Chowder, 43
Ham and Cheese Calzones, 48
Ham and Sweet Potato Cups, 105
Hash Brown Egg Dish, 75
Hearty Hamburger Soup, 45
Herbed Garlic Potatoes, 150
Holiday Pecan Logs, 223
Hot Chicken Salad, 38
Hot Kielbasa Dip, 13
Hungarian Goulash Soup, 50

I

Idaho Potato Salad, 29
Irish Lamb Stew, 97
Italian Cheese Bread, 157

L

Layered Fresh Fruit Salad, 39
Lemon-Batter Fish, 127
Lemony Chicken Fruit Salad, 27
Lentil Barley Soup, 59
Lettuce with Hot Bacon Dressing, 35
Li'l Cheddar Meat Loaves, 129

M

Macaroon Apple Cobbler, 218
Magic Pumpkin Buckle, 212
Maple Butterscotch Brownies, 179
Maple Peanut Delights, 204
Maple Pecan Pie, 224
Marinated Catfish Fillets, 93
Marinated Flank Steak, 101
Maryland Crab Cakes, 90
Mashed Potato Beef Casserole, 115
Mashed Potato Cinnamon Rolls, 73
Meatball Hash Brown Bake, 91
Meatball Lover's Sandwich, 62
Meatball Mushroom Soup, 56
Meatball Shish Kabobs, 114
Meatball Sub Casserole, 129
Meatballs with Cream Sauce, 107
Meaty Mac 'n' Cheese, 109
Mexican Deviled Eggs, 16
Microwave Mac 'n' Cheese, 142
Microwave Tuna Casserole, 92
Molasses Spice Cutouts, 170
Mom's Chicken 'n' Buttermilk Dumplings, 87
Morning Maple Muffins, 72
Morning Orange Drink, 71
Mozzarella Sticks, 14
Mushroom Bacon Bites, 12
Mushroom Corn Casserole, 137
Mushroom Salisbury Steak, 104

N

No-Bake Cherry Cheesecake, 194
No-Fuss Pork Chops, 117
Northwest Salmon Chowder, 56
Nutty Chocolate Marshmallow Puffs, 214

O

Old-Fashioned Chicken Potpie, 109
Onion Sandwich Rolls, 166
Orange Chiffon Cake, 189
Orange-Pecan Hot Wings, 16
Orange-Raisin Sticky Muffins, 70
Oven-Fried Chicken, 112

P

Peanut Butter Cheesecake, 187
Peanut Butter Chocolate Cake, 197
Peanut Butter Pie, 206
Peanutty Pork Kabobs, 94
Pear Crisp, 212
Pepperoni Pan Pizza, 127
Picante Biscuit Bake, 138
Picante Broccoli Chicken Salad, 28
Pizza Tot Casserole, 116
Pizza with Stuffed Crust, 105
Plantation Gingerbread, 199
Pleasing Potato Pizza, 90
Poppy Seed Lemon Scones, 159
Poppy Seed Rolls, 162
Pork and Apple Supper, 124
Pork Chops with Mushroom Gravy, 83
Pot Roast with Cranberry Sauce, 91
Pronto Taco Soup, 63
Pulled Molasses Taffy, 219
Pumpkin Trifle, 225

Q

Quick Chicken Cordon Bleu, 106

R

Rainbow Cookies, 172
Raspberry Truffle Brownies, 171
Raspberry Truffles, 211
Red Cabbage Casserole, 151
Reuben Meatballs, 95
Rhubarb Elderberry Crisp, 205
Rhubarb Granola Crisp, 217
Roasted Veggie Pizza, 82
Root Vegetable Medley, 140

S

Salsa Beef Skillet, 107
Salsa Corn Cakes, 132
Saucy Skillet Fish, 84
Sausage Potato Soup, 48
Savory Cauliflower Pie, 146
Savory Chicken Vegetable Strudel, 155
Savory Italian Rounds, 158
Scalloped Apples, 139
Sesame Beef and Asparagus Salad, 27
Sesame Chicken with Mustard Sauce, 120
Sesame Wheat Braids, 155
Shortbread Squares, 173
Shrimp Monterey, 84
Skillet Bow Tie Lasagna, 85
Sloppy Joe Under a Bun, 110
S'more Cheesecake, 198
Snappy Pumpkin Dessert, 208
Southern Chicken Rice Soup, 58
Southern Chicken Roll-Ups, 108
Southern Sweet Potato Salad, 33
Southwestern Veggie Bake, 123
Spaghetti 'n' Meatballs, 119
Special Strawberry Torte, 191
Spiced Pear Muffins, 78
Spicy Cheeseburger Soup, 59

Spicy Ravioli Salad, 31
Spicy White Chili, 60
Spinach Artichoke Pie, 134
Spinach Beef Biscuit Bake, 94
Spinach Turkey Meatballs, 88
Squash Stuffing Casserole, 146
Stew with Confetti Dumplings, 108
Sticky Bun Coffee Ring, 79
Stir-Fried Pork Soup, 55
Strawberries 'n' Cream Bread, 162
Strawberry Banana Trifle, 209
Strawberry Peach Melba, 215
Stuffed Duckling, 89
Stuffed Sweet Pepper Soup, 42
Summertime Chicken Tacos, 85
Summertime Strawberry Gelatin Salad, 36
Sunrise Mini Pizzas, 78
Sunshine Sherbet, 207
Super Sloppy Joes, 55
Surprise Meatball Skewers, 86
Sweet-Hot Sausage Meatballs, 9
Sweet Onion Muffins, 156
Sweet Potatoes with Apples, 141
Sweet Raspberry Muffins, 66
Sweet-Sour Chicken Dippers, 20
Swiss Chocolate Brownies, 180
Swiss Potato Squares, 147

T

Taco Meatball Ring, 10
Taco Tater Skins, 13
Tangy Beef Brisket, 113
Tangy Lemon Cheesecake, 196
Tasty Meat Pie, 118
Tasty Reuben Soup, 60
Tenderloin with Creamy Garlic Sauce, 121
Tex-Mex Biscuits, 160
Texas Two-Step Corn Medley, 143
Three Bean Casserole, 144
Three-Bean Soup, 46
Three-Cheese Twists, 164
Three-in-One Cheese Ball, 18
Three-Rice Pilaf, 145
Tiny Cherry Cheesecakes, 190
Toasted Coconut Truffles, 218
Toasted Zucchini Snacks, 9
Tomato Dill Bisque, 61
Tomato Pizza Bread, 167
Triple-Chocolate Quick Bread, 156
Tropical Cheesecake, 201
Turkey Dressing Pie, 111
Two-Meat Pizza with Wheat Crust, 116

V

Vanilla-Butter Sugar Cookies, 174
Vegetables Mornay, 132

W

Walnut Apple Cake, 188
Warm Bean and Chard Salad, 26
Warm Mustard Potato Salad, 39
Western-Style Beef 'n' Beans, 117
White Bean Dip, 15
White Chocolate Cookies, 176
Wild Rice Floret Bake, 143
Wild Rice Soup, 58

Z

Zesty Colorado Chili, 53
Zesty Macaroni Soup, 49
Zippy Radish Salad, 25
Zucchini Con Carne, 102